History of Egypt, Chaldea, Syria, Babylonia and Assyria

by Gaston Maspero and
A. H. Sayce
Volume 9

Translated by M. L. McCLURE, Member of the Committee of the Egypt Exploration Fund

ISBN: 978-1-63923-899-6

All Rights reserved. No part of this book maybe reproduced without written permission from the publishers, except by a reviewer who may quote brief passages in a review to be printed in a newspaper or magazine.

Printed: March 2023

Published and Distributed By:
Lushena Books
607 Country Club Drive, Unit E
Bensenville, IL 60106
www.lushenabks.com

ISBN: 978-1-63923-899-6

CONTENTS

CHAPTER I.

THE IRANIAN CONQUEST

	PAGE
The Iranian Religions — Cyrus in Lydia and at Babylon; Cambyses in Egypt — Darius and the Organisation of the Empire	3

CHAPTER II.

THE LAST DAYS OF THE OLD EASTERN WORLD

The Median Wars — The Last Native Dynasties of Egypt — The Eastern World on the Eve of the Macedonian Conquest	199

LIST OF ILLUSTRATIONS

	PAGE
An Egyptian Wedding Party	*Frontispiece*
The ruins of Persepolis, as seen from the North	3
Hypostyle of Hall of Xerxes: Detail of Entablature	12
The Ahura-Mazdâ of the Bas-reliefs of Persepolis	12
An Iranian genius in form of a winged bull	13
Ahura-Mazdâ bestowing the tokens of royalty on an Iranian King	14
Mylitta-Anâhita	18
One of the bad Genii, subject to Angrô-Mainyus	22
The king struggling against an evil genius	23
The two Iranian altars at Nakhsh-î-Rustem	31
The two Iranian altars of Murgâb	32
The sacred fire burning on the altar	33
A royal hunting-party in Iran	39
Remains of the palace of Ecbatana	42
The Tumulus of Alyattes and the entrance to the passage	50
One of the Lydian ornaments in the Louvre	51
Mould for jewellery of Lydian origin	52
A Lydian funerary couch	53
Coin with lion's head	55
Coin bearing head of Mouflon goat	56
Money of Crœsus	56
View of the site and ruins of Ephesus	59
Crœsus on his Pyre	75
A Persian King fighting with Greeks	78
The present site of Miletus	80
A Lycian city upon its inaccessible rock	83
An Osiris stretched full length on the ground	111
The two Goddesses of the law, Ani adoring Osiris; the Trial of the Conscience; Thoth and Feather of the Law	112
Amasis in adoration before the bull Apis	113

vii

THE IRANIAN CONQUEST

THE IRANIAN RELIGIONS—CYRUS IN LYDIA AND AT BABYLON; CAMBYSES IN EGYPT—DARIUS AND THE ORGANISATION OF THE EMPIRE.

The constitution of the Median empire borrowed from the ancient peoples of the Euphrates: its religion only is peculiar to itself—Legends concerning Zoroaster, his laws; the Avesta and its history—Elements contained in it of primitive religion—The supreme god Ahura-mazdâ and his Amêsha-spentas: the Yazatas, the Fravashis—Angrô-mainyus and his agents, the Daîvas, the Pairîkas, their struggle with Ahura-mazdâ—The duties of man here below, funerals, his fate after death—Worship and temples: fire-altars, sacrifices, the Magi.

Cyrus and the legends concerning his origin: his revolt against Astyages and the fall of the Median empire—The early years of the reign of Nabonidus: revolutions in Tyre, the taking of Harrân—The end of the reign of Alyattes, Lydian art and its earliest coinage—Crœsus, his relations with continental Greece, his conquests, his alliances with Babylon and Egypt—The war between Lydia and Persia: the defeat of the Lydians, the taking of Sardes, the death of Crœsus and subsequent legends relating to it—The submission of the cities of the Asiatic littoral.

VOL. IX.   B

Cyrus in Bactriana and in the eastern regions of the Iranian table-land—The impression produced on the Chaldæan by his victories; the Jewish exiles, Ezekiel and his dreams of restoration, the new temple, the prophecies against Babylon; general discontent with Nabonidus—The attack of Cyrus and the battle of Zalzallat, the taking of Babylon and the fall of Nabonidus: the end of the Chaldæan empire and the deliverance of the Jews.

Egypt under Amasis: building works, support given to the Greeks; Naukratis, its temples, its constitution, and its prosperity—Preparations for defence and the unpopularity of Amasis with the native Egyptians—The death of Cyrus and legends relating to it: his palace at Pasargadæ and his tomb—Cambyses and Smerdis—The legendary causes of the war with Egypt—Psammetichus III., the battle of Pelusium; Egypt reduced to a Persian province.

Cambyses' plans for conquest; the abortive expeditions to the Oasis of Ammon and Carthage—The kingdom of Ethiopia, its kings, its customs: the Persians fail to reach Napata, the madness of Cambyses—The fraud of Gaumâta, the death of Cambyses and the reign of the pseudo-Smerdis, the accession of Darius—The revolution in Susiana, Chaldæa, and Media: Nebuchadrezzar III. and the fall of Babylon, the death of Orœtes, the defeat of Khshatrita, restoration of peace throughout Asia, Egyptian affairs and the re-establishment of the royal power.

The organisation of the country and its division into satrapies: the satrap, the military commander, the royal secretary; couriers, main roads, the Eyes and Ears of the king—The financial system and the provincial taxes: the daric—Advantages and drawbacks of the system of division into satrapies; the royal guard and the military organisation of the empire—The conquest of the Hapta-Hindu and the prospect of war with Greece.

THE RUINS OF PERSEPOLIS, AS SEEN FROM THE NORTH.[1]

CHAPTER I

THE IRANIAN CONQUEST

The Iranian religions—Cyrus in Lydia and at Babylon: Cambyses in Egypt—Darius and the organisation of the empire.

THE Median empire is the least known of all those which held sway for a time over the destinies of a portion of Western Asia. The reason of this is not to be ascribed to the shortness of its duration: the Chaldæan empire of Nebuchadrezzar lasted for a period quite as brief, and yet the main outlines of its

[1] Drawn by Boudier, from the engraving in Coste and Flandin. The vignette, drawn by Faucher-Gudin, from a statuette in terra-cotta, found in Southern Russia, represents a young Scythian.

history can be established with some certainty in spite of large blanks and much obscurity. Whereas at Babylon, moreover, original documents abound, enabling us to put together, feature by feature, the picture of its ancient civilisation and of the chronology of its kings, we possèss no contemporary monuments of Ecbatana to furnish direct information as to its history. To form any idea of the Median kings or their people, we are reduced to haphazard notices gleaned from the chroniclers of other lands, retailing a few isolated facts, anecdotes, legends, and conjectures, and, as these materials reach us through the medium of the Babylonians or the Greeks of the fifth or sixth century B.C., the picture which we endeavour to compose from them is always imperfect or out of perspective. We seemingly catch glimpses of ostentatious luxury, of a political and military organisation, and a method of government analogous to that which prevailed at later periods among the Persians, but more imperfect, ruder, and nearer to barbarism—a Persia, in fact, in the rudimentary stage, with its ruling spirit and essential characteristics as yet undeveloped. The machinery of state had doubtless been adopted almost in its entirety from the political organisations which obtained in the kingdoms of Assyria, Elam, and Chaldæa, with which sovereignties the founders of the Median empire had held in turns relations as vassals, enemies, and allies; but once we penetrate this veneer of Mesopotamian civilisation and reach the inner life of the people, we find in the religion they profess—mingled with some borrowed traits—a world of unfamiliar myths and dogmas of native origin.

The main outlines of this religion were already fixed when the Medes rose in rebellion against Assur-bani-pal; and the very name of *Confessor*—Fravartîsh—applied to the chief of that day, proves that it was the faith of the royal family. It was a religion common to all the Iranians, the Persians as well as the Medes, and legend honoured as its first lawgiver and expounder an ancient prophet named Zarathustra, known to us as Zoroaster.[1] Most classical writers relegated Zoroaster to some remote age of antiquity—thus he is variously said to have lived six thousand years before the death of Plato,[2] five thousand before the Trojan war,[3] one thousand before Moses, and six hundred before Xerxes' campaign against Athens; while some few only affirmed that he had lived at a comparatively recent period, and made him out a disciple of the philosopher Pythagoras, who flourished about the middle of the fifth century B.C. According to the most ancient national traditions, he was born in the Aryanem-vaêjô, or, in other words, in the region between the Araxes and the Kur, to the west of the Caspian Sea. Later

---

[1] The name Zarathustra has been interpreted in a score of different ways. The Greeks sometimes attributed to it the meaning "worshipper of the stars," probably by reason of the similarity in sound of the termination "-astres" of Zoroaster with the word "astron." Among modern writers, H. Rawlinson derived it from the Assyrian Ziru-Ishtar, "the seed of Ishtar," but the etymology now most generally accepted is that of Burnouf, according to which it would signify "the man with gold-coloured camels," the "possessor of tawny camels." The ordinary Greek form Zoroaster seems to be derived from some name quite distinct from Zarathustra.

[2] This was, as Pliny records, the opinion of Eudoxus; not Eudoxus of Cnidus, pupil of Plato, as is usually stated, but a more obscure personage, Eudoxus of Rhodes.

[3] This was the statement of Hermodorus.

tradition asserted that his conception was attended by supernatural circumstances, and the miracles which accompanied his birth announced the advent of a saint destined to regenerate the world by the revelation of the True Law. In the belief of an Iranian, every man, every living creature now existing or henceforth to exist, not excluding the gods themselves, possesses a Frôhar, or guardian spirit, who is assigned to him at his entrance into the world, and who is thenceforth devoted entirely to watching over his material and moral well-being.[1] About the time appointed for the appearance of the prophet, his Frôhar was, by divine grace, imprisoned in the heart of a Haoma,[2] and was absorbed, along with the juice of the plant, by the priest Purushâspa,[3] during a sacrifice, a ray of heavenly glory descending at the same time into the bosom of a maiden of noble race, named Dughdôva, whom Purushâspa shortly afterwards espoused. Zoroaster was engendered from the mingling of the Frôhar with the celestial ray. The evil spirit, whose supremacy he threatened, endeavoured to destroy him as soon as he saw the light, and despatched one of his agents, named Bôuiti, from the country of the far north to oppose him; but the infant prophet immediately pronounced the formula with which the psalm for the offering of the waters opens: "The will of the Lord is the rule of good!" and proceeded to pour libations in

[1] The Fravashi (for *fravarti*, from *fra-var*, "to support, nourish"), or the *frôhar* (*feruer*), is, properly speaking, the nurse, the genius who nurtures. Many of the practices relating to the conception and cult of the Fravashis seem to me to go back to the primitive period of the Irarian religions.

[2] The haoma is an *Asclepias Sarcostema Viminalis*.

[3] The name signifies "He who has many horses."

honour of the river Darêja, on the banks of which he had been born a moment before, reciting at the same time the profession of faith which puts evil spirits to flight. Bôuiti fled aghast, but his master set to work upon some fresh device. Zoroaster allowed him, however, no time to complete his plans: he rose up, and undismayed by the malicious riddles propounded to him by his adversary, advanced against him with his hands full of stones—stones as large as a house—with which the good deity supplied him. The mere sight of him dispersed the demons, and they regained the gates of their hell in headlong flight, shrieking out, "How shall we succeed in destroying him? For he is the weapon which strikes down evil beings; he is the scourge of evil beings." His infancy and youth were spent in constant disputation with evil spirits: ever assailed, he ever came out victorious, and issued more perfect from each attack. When he was thirty years old, one of the good spirits, Vôhumanô, appeared to him, and conducted him into the presence of Ahura-mazdâ, the Supreme Being. When invited to question the deity, Zoroaster asked, "Which is the best of the creatures which are upon the earth?" The answer was, that the man whose heart is pure, he excels among his fellows. He next desired to know the names and functions of the angels, and the nature and attributes of evil. His instruction ended, he crossed a mountain of flames, and underwent a terrible ordeal of purification, during which his breast was pierced with a sword, and melted lead poured into his entrails without his suffering any pain: only after this ordeal did he receive from the hands of Ahura-mazdâ the

Book of the Law, the Avesta, and he was then sent back to his native land bearing his precious burden. At that time, Vîshtâspa, son of Aurvatâspa, was reigning over Bactria. For ten years Zoroaster had only one disciple, his cousin Maidhyoi-Mâonha, but after that he succeeded in converting, one after the other, the two sons of Hvôgva, the grand vizir Jâmâspa, who afterwards married the prophet's daughter, and Frashaoshtra, whose daughter Hvôgvi he himself espoused; the queen, Hutaosa, was the next convert, and afterwards, through her persuasions, the king Vîshtâspa himself became a disciple. The triumph of the good cause was hastened by the result of a formal disputation between the prophet and the wise men of the court: for three days they essayed to bewilder him with their captious objections and their magic arts, thirty standing on his right hand and thirty on his left, but he baffled their wiles, aided by grace from above, and having forced them to avow themselves at the end of their resources, he completed his victory by reciting the Avesta before them. The legend adds, that after rallying the majority of the people round him, he lived to a good old age, honoured of all men for his saintly life. According to some accounts, he was stricken dead by lightning,[1] while others say he was killed by a Turanian soldier, Brâtrôk-rêsh, in a war against the Hyaonas.

The question has often been asked whether Zoroaster belongs to the domain of legend or of history. The only certain thing we know concerning him is his name; all

[1] This is, under very diverse forms, the version preferred by Western historians of the post-classical period.

the rest is mythical, poetic, or religious fiction. Classical writers attributed to him the composition or editing of all the writings comprised in Persian literature: the whole consisted, they said, of two hundred thousand verses which had been expounded and analysed by Hermippus in his commentaries on the secret doctrines of the Magi. The Iranians themselves averred that he had given the world twenty-one volumes—the twenty-one *Nasks* of the Avesta,[1] which the Supreme Deity had created from the twenty-one words of the Magian profession of faith, the *Ahuna Vairya*. King Vîshtâspa is said to have caused two authentic copies of the Avesta—which contained in all ten or twelve hundred chapters[2]—to be made, one of which was consigned to the archives of the empire, the other laid up in the treasury of a fortress, either Shapîgân, Shîzîgân, Samarcand, or Persepolis.[3] Alexander is said to have

---

[1] The word *Avesta*, in Pehlevi *Apastâk*, whence come the Persian forms *âvasta, ôstâ*, is derived from the Achæmenian word *Abasta*, which signifies *law* in the inscriptions of Darius. The term Zend-Avesta, commonly used to designate the sacred book of the Persians, is incorrectly derived from the expression *Apastâk u Zen*d, which in Pehlevi designates first the law itself, and then the translation and commentary in more modern language which conduces to a *knowledge* (*Zend*) of the law. The customary application, therefore, of the name Zend to the language of the Avesta is incorrect.

[2] The Dinkart fixes the number of chapters at 1000, and the Shâh-Nâmak at 1200, written on plates of gold. According to Masudi, the book itself and the two commentaries formed 12,000 volumes, written in letters of gold, the twenty-one Nasks each contained 200 pages, and the whole of these writings had been inscribed on 12,000 cow-hides.

[3] The site of Shapîgân or Shaspîgân is unknown. J. Darmesteter suggests that it ought to be read as *Shizîgân*, which would permit of the identification of the place with Shîz, one of the ancient religious centres of Iran, whose temple was visited by the Sassanids on their accession to the throne. According to the Ardâ-Vîrâf the law was preserved at Istakhr, or

burnt the former copy: the latter, stolen by the Greeks, is reported to have been translated into their language and to have furnished them with all their scientific knowledge. One of the Arsacids, Vologesus I., caused a search to be made for all the fragments which existed either in writing or in the memory of the faithful,[1] and this collection, added to in the reign of the Sassanid king, Ardashir Bâbagan, by the high priest Tansar, and fixed in its present form under Sapor I., was recognised as the religious code of the empire in the time of Sapor II., about the fourth century of the Christian era.[2] The text is composed, as may be seen, of three distinct strata, which are by no means equally ancient;[3] one can, nevertheless, make out from it with sufficient certainty the principal features of the religion and cult of Iran, such as they were under the Achæmenids, and perhaps even under the hegemony of the Medes. It is a complicated system of religion, and presupposes a long period of development. The doctrines are subtle; the ceremonial order of worship, loaded with strict observances, is interrupted at every moment by laws prescribing minute details

Persepolis, according to the Shâh-Nâmak at Samarcand in the temple of the Fire-god.

[1] Tradition speaks simply of a King Valkash, without specifying which of the four kings named Vologesus is intended. James Darmesteter has given good reasons for believing that this Valkash is Vologesus I. (50–75 A.D.), the contemporary of Nero.

[2] This is the tradition reproduced in two versions of the Dinkart.

[3] Darmesteter declares that ancient Zoroastrianism is, in its main lines, the religion of the Median Magi, even though he assigns the latest possible date to the composition of the Avesta as now existing, and thinks he can discern in it Greek, Jewish, and Christian elements.

THE ORIGINAL CHARACTER OF AHURA-MAZDÂ   11

of ritual,[1] which were only put in practice by priests and strict devotees, and were unknown to the mass of the faithful. The primitive base of this religion is difficult to discern clearly: but we may recognise in it most of those beings or personifications of natural phenomena which were the chief objects of worship among all the ancient nations of Western Asia—the stars, Sirius, the moon, the sun, water and fire, plants, animals beneficial to mankind, such as the cow and the dog, good and evil spirits everywhere present, and beneficent or malevolent souls of mortal men, but all systematised, graduated, and reduced to sacerdotal principles, according to the prescriptions of a powerful priesthood. Families consecrated to the service of the altar had ended, as among the Hebrews, by separating themselves from the rest of the nation and forming a special tribe, that of the Magi, which was the last to enter into the composition of the nation in historic times.[1] All the Magi were not necessarily devoted to the service of religion, but all who did so devote themselves sprang from the Magian tribe; the Avesta, in its oldest form, was the sacred book of the Magi, as well as that of the priests who handed down their religious tradition under the various dynasties, native or foreign, who bore rule over Iran.

The Creator was described as "the whole circle of the

[1] Renan defined the Avesta as "the Code of a very small religious sect; it is a Talmud, a book of casuistry and strict observance. I have difficulty in believing that the great Persian empire, which, at least in religious matters, professed a certain breadth of ideas, could have had a law so strict. I think, that had the Persians possessed a sacred book of this description, the Greeks must have mentioned it."

THE IRANIAN CONQUEST

heavens," "the most steadfast among the gods," for "he clothes himself with the solid vault of the firmament as his raiment," the most beautiful, the most intelligent, he whose members are most harmoniously proportioned; his body was the light and the sovereign glory, the sun and the moon were his eyes." The theologians had gradually spiritualised the conception of this deity without absolutely

THE AHURA-MAZDÂ OF THE BAS-RELIEFS OF PERSEPOLIS.[1]

disconnecting him from the material universe. He remained under ordinary circumstances invisible to mortal eyes, and he could conceal his identity even from the highest gods, but he occasionally manifested himself in human form. He borrowed in such case from Assyria the symbol of Assur, and the sculptors depict him with the upper part of his body rising above that winged disk which is carved in a hovering attitude on the pediments of Assyrian monuments or stelæ. In later days he was

[1] Drawn by Faucher-Gudin, from Flandin and Coste.

HYPORSTYLE OF HALL OF XERXES: DETAIL OF ENTABLATURE.

portrayed under the form of a king of imposing stature and majestic mien, who revealed himself from time to time to the princes of Iran.¹ He was named Ahurô-mazdâo

AN IRANIAN GENIUS IN FORM OF A WINGED BULL.²

or Ahura-mazdâ, the omniscient lord,³ *Spentô-mainyus*, the spirit of good, *Mainyus-spenishtô*,⁴ the most beneficent of

¹ In a passage of Philo of Byblos the god is described as having the head of a falcon or an eagle, perhaps by confusion with one of the genii represented on the walls of the palaces.

² Drawn by Bondier, from a photograph.

³ *Ah*ura is derived from *Ahu* = *L*ord : *Mazd*âo can be analysed into the component parts, *maz* = *great*, and *dâo* = *he who knows*. At first the two terms were interchangeable, and even in the Gâthas the form Mazdâ Ahura is employed much more often than the form Ahura Mazdâ. In the Achæmenian inscriptions, **Auramazdâ** is only found as a single word, except in an inscription of Xerxes, where the two terms are in one passage separated and declined *Aurahya mazdâha*. The form Ormuzd, Ormazd, usually employed by Europeans, is that assumed by the name in modern Persian.

⁴ These two names are given to him more especially in connection with his antagonism to **Angrômainyus**.

spirits. Himself uncreate, he is the creator of all things, but he is assisted in the administration of the universe by legions of beings, who are all subject to him.[1] The most powerful among his ministers were originally nature-gods,

AHURA-MAZDÂ BESTOWING THE TOKENS OF ROYALTY ON AN IRANIAN KING.[2]

such as the sun, the moon, the earth, the winds, and the waters. The sunny plains of Persia and Media afforded

---

[1] Darius styles Ahura-mazdâ, *mathishta bagánám*, the greatest of the gods, and Xerxes invokes the protection of Ahura-mazdâ along with that of the gods. The classical writers also mention gods alongside of Ahura-mazdâ, as recognised not only among the Achæmenian Persians, but also among the Parthians. Darmesteter considers that the earliest Achæmenids worshipped Ahura-mazdâ alone, "placing the other gods together in a subordinate and anonymous group: May Ahura-mazdâ and the other gods protect me."

[2] Drawn by Boudier, from a photograph by Dieulafoy.

abundant witnesses of their power, as did the snow-clad peaks, the deep gorges through which rushed roaring torrents, and the mountain ranges of Ararat or Taurus, where the force of the subterranean fires was manifested by so many startling exhibitions of spontaneous conflagration.[1] The same spiritualising tendency which had already considerably modified the essential concept of Ahuramazdâ, affected also that of the inferior deities, and tended to tone down in them the grosser traits of their character. It had already placed at their head six genii of a superior order, six ever-active energies, who, after assisting their master at the creation of the universe, now presided under his guidance over the kingdoms and forces of nature.[2] These benevolent and immortal beings—*Amesha-spentas*—were, in the order of precedence, Vohu-manô (good thought), Asha-vahista (perfect holiness), Khshathra-vairya (good government), Spenta-armaiti (meek piety), Haurvatât (health), Ameretât (immortality). Each of them had a special domain assigned to him in which to display his

---

[1] All these inferior deities, heroes, and genii who presided over Persia, the royal family, and the different parts of the empire, are often mentioned in the most ancient classical authors that have come down to us.

[2] The six Amesha-spentas, with their several characteristics, are enumerated in a passage of the *De Iside*. This exposition of Persian doctrine is usually attributed to Theopompus, from which we may deduce the existence of a belief in the Amesha-spentas in the Achæmenian period. J. Darmesteter affirms, on the contrary, that "the author describes the Zoroastrianism of his own times (the second century A.D.), and quotes Theopompus for a special doctrine, that of the periods of the world's life." Although this last point is correct, the first part of Darmesteter's theory does not seem to me justified by investigation. The whole passage of Plutarch is a well-arranged composition of uniform style, which may be

energy untrammelled: Vohu-manô had charge of cattle, Asha-vahista of fire, Khshathra-vairya of metals, Spenta-armaiti of the earth, Haurvatât and Ameretât of vegetation and of water. They were represented in human form, either masculine as Vohu-manô and Asha-vahista,[1] or feminine as Spenta-armaiti, the daughter and spouse of Ahura-mazdâ, who became the mother of the first man, Gâyomaretan, and, through Gâyomaretan, ancestress of the whole human race. Sometimes Ahura-mazdâ is himself included among the Amesha-spentas, thus bringing their number up to seven; sometimes his place is taken by a certain Sraôsha (obedience to the law), the first who offered sacrifice and recited the prayers of the ritual. Subordinate to these great spirits were the Yazatas, scattered by thousands over creation, presiding over the machinery of nature and maintaining it in working order. Most of them received no special names, but many exercised wide authority, and several were accredited by the people with an influence not less than that of the greater deities themselves. Such were the regent of the stars—Tishtrya, the bull with golden horns, Sirius, the

MÂO, THE MOON-GOD.[2]

VÂTO, GOD OF THE WIND.[2]

regarded as an exposition of the system described by Theopompus, probably in the eighth of his Philippics.

[1] The image of Asha-vahista is known to us from coins of the Indo-Scythian kings of Bactriana. Vohu-manô is described as a young man.

[2] Drawn by Faucher-Gudin, from a coin of King Kanishka, published by Percy Gardner.

THE AMÊSHA-SPENTAS AND THE YAZATAS

sparkling one; Mâo, the moon-god; the wind, Vâto; the atmosphere, Vayu, the strongest of the strong, the warrior with golden armour, who gathers the storm and hurls it against the demon; Âtar, fire under its principal forms, divine fire, sacred fire, and earthly fire; Verethraghna, the author of war and giver of victory; Aurvataspa, the son of the waters, the lightning born among the clouds; and lastly, the spirit of the dawn, the watchful Mithra, "who, first of the celestial Yazatas, soars above Mount Hara,[3] before the immortal sun with his swift steeds, who, first in golden splendour, passes over the beautiful mountains and casts his glance benign on the dwellings of the Aryans."[4] Mithra was a charming youth of beautiful countenance, his head surrounded with a radiant halo. The nymph Anâhita was adored under the form of one of the incarnations of the Babylonian goddess

ATAR, THE GOD OF FIRE.[1]

AURVATASPA.[2]

MITHRA.[5]

---

[1] Drawn by Faucher-Gudin, from a coin of King Kanishka, published by Percy Gardner.

[2] Drawn by Faucher-Gudin, from coin published by Percy Gardner.

[3] Hara is Haroberezaiti, or Elburz, the mountain over which the sun rises, "around which many a star revolves, where there is neither night nor darkness, no wind of cold or heat, no sickness leading to a thousand kinds of death, nor infection caused by the Daêvas, and whose summit is never reached by the clouds."

[4] This is the Mithra whose religion became so powerful in Alexandrian and Roman times. His sphere of action is defined in the Bundehesh.

[5] Drawn by Faucher-Gudin, from a coin of King Huvishka, published by Percy Gardner.

Mylitta, a youthful and slender female, with well-developed breasts and broad hips, sometimes represented clothed in

MYLITTA-ANÂHITA.[3]

furs and sometimes nude.[1] Like the foreign goddess to whom she was assimilated, she was the dispenser of fertility and of love; the heroes of antiquity, and even Ahura-mazdâ himself, had vied with one another in their worship of her, and she had lavished her favours freely on all.[2] The less important Yazatas were hardly to be distinguished from the innumerable multitude of Fravashis. The Fravashis are the divine types of all intelligent beings. They were originally brought into being by Ahura-mazdâ as a distinct species from the human, but they had allowed themselves to be entangled in matter, and to be fettered in the bodies of men, in order to hasten the final destruction of the demons and the advent of the reign of good.[5] Once incarnate, a Fravashis devotes himself to the well-being

NANA-ANÂHITA.[4]

---

[1] The popularity of these two deities was already well established at the period we are dealing with, for Herodotus mentions Mithra and confuses him with Anâhita.

[2] Her name Ardvi-Sûra Anâhita seems to signify *the lofty and immaculate power*.

[3] Drawn by Faucher-Gudin, from Loftus.

[4] Drawn by Faucher-Gudin, from a coin of King Huvishka, published by Percy Gardner.

[5] The legend of the descent of the Fravashis to dwell among men is narrated in the Bundehesh.

of the mortal with whom he is associated; and when once more released from the flesh, he continues the struggle against evil with an energy whose efficacy is proportionate to the virtue and purity displayed in life by the mortal to whom he has been temporarily joined. The last six days of the year are dedicated to the Fravashis. They leave their heavenly abodes at this time to visit the spots which were their earthly dwelling-places, and they wander through the villages inquiring, "Who wishes to hire us? Who will offer us a sacrifice? Who will make us their own, welcome us, and receive us with plenteous offerings of food and raiment, with a prayer which bestows sanctity on him who offers it?" And if they find a man to hearken to their request, they bless him: "May his house be blessed with herds of oxen and troops of men, a swift horse and a strongly built chariot, a man who knoweth how to pray to God, a chieftain in the council who may ever offer us sacrifices with a hand filled with food and raiment, with a prayer which bestows sanctity on him who offers it!"

Ahura-mazdâ created the universe, not by the work of his hands, but by the magic of his word, and he desired to create it entirely free from defects. His creation, however, can only exist by the free play and equilibrium of opposing forces, to which he gives activity: the incompatibility of tendency displayed by these forces, and their alternations of growth and decay, inspired the Iranians with the idea that they were the result of two contradictory principles, the one beneficent and good, the other adverse to everything emanating from the former.[1] In opposition to the

[1] Spiegel, who at first considered that the Iranian dualism was derived

god of light, they necessarily formed the idea of a god of darkness, the god of the underworld, who presides over death, Angrô-mainyus. The two opposing principles reigned at first, each in his own domain, as rivals, but not as irreconcilable adversaries: they were considered as in fixed opposition to each other, and as having coexisted for ages without coming into actual conflict, separated as they were by the intervening void. As long as the principle of good was content to remain shut up inactive in his barren glory, the principle of evil slumbered unconscious in a darkness that knew no beginning; but when at last "the spirit who giveth increase"—Spentô-mainyus—determined to manifest himself, the first throes of his vivifying activity roused from inertia the spirit of destruction and of pain, Angrô-mainyus. The heaven was not yet in existence, nor the waters, nor the earth, nor ox, nor fire, nor man, nor demons, nor brute beasts, nor any living thing, when the evil spirit hurled himself upon the light to quench it for ever, but Ahuramazdâ had already called forth the ministers of his will—Amêsha-spentas, Yazatas, Fravashis—and he recited the prayer of twenty-one words in which all the elements of morality are summed up, the Ahuna-vairya: "The will of the Lord is the rule of good. Let the gifts of Vohu-manô be bestowed on the works accomplished, at this moment,

from polytheism, and was a preliminary stage in the development of monotheism, held afterwards that a rigid monotheism had preceded this dualism. The classical writers, who knew Zoroastrianism at the height of its glory, never suggested that the two principles might be derived from a superior principle, nor that they were subject to such a principle. The Iranian books themselves nowhere definitely affirm that there existed a single principle distinct from the two opposing principles.

for Mazda. He makes Ahura to reign, he who protects the poor." The effect of this prayer was irresistible: "When Ahura had pronounced the first part of the formula, Zânak Mînoî, the spirit of destruction, bowed himself with terror; at the second part he fell upon his knees; and at the third and last he felt himself powerless to hurt the creatures of Ahura-mazdâ."[1] The strife, kindled at the beginning of time between the two gods, has gone on ever since with alternations of success and defeat; each in turn has the victory for a regular period of three thousand years; but when these periods are ended, at the expiration of twelve thousand years, evil will be finally and for ever defeated. While awaiting this blessed fulness of time, as Spentô-mainyus shows himself in all that is good and beautiful, in light, virtue, and justice, so Angrô-mainyus is to be perceived in all that is hateful and ugly, in darkness, sin, and crime. Against the six Amesha-spentas he sets in array six spirits of equal power—Akem-manô, evil thought; Andra, the devouring fire, who introduces discontent and sin wherever he penetrates; Sauru, the flaming arrow of death, who inspires bloodthirsty tyrants, who incites men to theft and murder; Nâongaithya, arrogance and pride;

[1] Theopompus was already aware of this alternation of good and bad periods. According to the tradition enshrined in the first chapter of the Bundehesh, it was the result of a sort of compact agreed upon at the beginning by Ahura-mazdâ and Angrô-mainyus. Ahura-mazdâ, fearing to be overcome if he entered upon the struggle immediately, but sure of final victory if he could gain time, proposed to his adversary a truce of nine thousand years, at the expiration of which the battle should begin. As soon as the compact was made, Angrô-mainyus realised that he had been tricked into taking a false step, but it was not till after three thousand years that he decided to break the truce and open the conflict.

Tanru, thirst; and Zairi, hunger.[1] To the Yazatas he opposed the Daêvas, who never cease to torment mankind, and so through all the ranks of nature he set over against each good and useful creation a counter-creation of rival tendency. "'Like a fly he crept into' and infected 'the whole universe.' He rendered the world as dark at full noonday as in the darkest night. He covered the soil with

ONE OF THE BAD GENII, SUBJECT TO ANGRÔ-MAINYUS.[2]

vermin, with his creatures of venomous bite and poisonous sting, with serpents, scorpions, and frogs, so that there was not a space as small as a needle's point but swarmed with his vermin. He smote vegetation, and of a sudden the plants withered. . . . He attacked the flames, and mingled them with smoke and dimness. The planets, with their thousands of demons, dashed against the vault of heaven

---

[1] The last five of these spirits are enumerated in the *Vendîdad*, and the first, Akem-manô, is there replaced by Nasu, the chief spirit of evil.

[2] Drawn by Faucher-Gudin, from a photograph taken from the original bas-relief in glazed tiles in the Louvre.

and waged war on the stars, and the universe became darkened like a space which the fire blackens with its smoke." And the conflict grew ever keener over the world and over man, of whom the evil one was jealous, and whom he sought to humiliate. The children of Angrô-mainyus disguised themselves under those monstrous forms in which the imagination of the Chaldæans had clothed the allies of Mummu-Tiamât, such as lions with bulls' heads, and the wings and claws of eagles, which the Achæmenian king combats on behalf of his subjects, boldly thrusting them through with his short sword. Aêshma of the blood-stained lance, terrible in wrath, is the most trusted leader of these dread bands,[1] the chief of twenty other Daêvas of repulsive aspect — Astô-vîdhôtu, the demon of death, who would devote to destruction the estimable Fravashis;[3] Apaosha, the enemy of Tishtrya the wicked black horse,

THE KING STRUGGLING AGAINST AN EVIL GENIUS.[2]

---

[1] The name Aêshma means *anger*. He is the Asmodeus, Aêshmo-daevô, of Rabbinic legends.

[2] Drawn by Boudier, from the photograph in Marcel Dieulafoy.

[3] The name of this demon signifies *He who separates the bones*.

the bringer of drought, who interferes with the distribution of the fertilising waters; and Bûiti, who essayed to kill Zoroaster at his birth.[1] The female demons, the Druges, the Incubi (Yâtus), the Succubi (Pairîka), the Peris of our fairy tales, mingled familiarly with mankind before the time of the prophet, and contracted with them fruitful alliances, but Zoroaster broke up their ranks, and prohibited them from becoming incarnate in any form but that of beasts; their hatred, however, is still unquenched, and their power will only be effectually overthrown at the consummation of time. It is a matter of uncertainty whether the Medes already admitted the possibility of a fresh revelation, preparing the latest generations of mankind for the advent of the reign of good. The traditions enshrined in the sacred books of Iran announce the coming of three prophets, sons of Zoroaster — Ukhshyatereta, Ukhshyatnemô, and Saoshyañt[2]—who shall bring about universal salvation. Saoshyañt, assisted by fifteen men and fifteen pure women, who have already lived on earth, and are awaiting their final destiny in a magic slumber, shall offer the final sacrifice, the virtue of which shall bring about the resurrection of the dead. " The sovereign light shall accompany him and his friends, when he shall revivify

[1] The Greater Bundehesh connects the demon Bûiti with the Indian Buddha, and J. Darmesteter seems inclined to accept this interpretation. In this case we must either admit that the demon Bûiti is of relatively late origin, or that he has, in the legend of Zoroaster, taken the place of a demon whose name resembled his own closely enough to admit of the assimilation.

[2] The legend ran that they had been conceived in the waters of the lake Kañsu. The name Saoshyañt signifies *the useful one, the saviour;* Ukshyatereta, *he who makes the good increase;* Ukshyatnemô, *he who makes prayer increase.*

the world and ransom it from old age and death, from corruption and decay, and shall render it eternally living, eternally growing, and master of itself." The fatal conflict shall be protracted, but the champions of Saoshyant shall at length obtain the victory. "Before them shall bow Aêshma of the blood-stained lance and of ominous renown, and Saoshyañt shall strike down the she-demon of the unholy light, the daughter of darkness. Akem-manô strikes, but Vohu-manô shall strike him in his turn; the lying word shall strike, but the word of truth shall strike him in his turn; Haurvatât and Ameretât shall strike down hunger and thirst; Haurvatât and Ameretât shall strike down terrible hunger and terrible thirst." Angrô-mainyus himself shall be paralysed with terror, and shall be forced to confess the supremacy of good : he shall withdraw into the depths of hell, whence he shall never again issue forth, and all the reanimated beings devoted to the Mazdean law shall live an eternity of peace and contentment.

Man, therefore, incessantly distracted between the two principles, laid wait for by the Daêvas, defended by the Yazatas, must endeavour to act according to law and justice in the condition in which fate has placed him. He has been raised up here on earth to contribute as far as in him lies to the increase of life and of good, and in proportion as he works for this end or against it, is he the *ashavan*, the pure, the faithful one on earth and the blessed one in heaven, or the *anashavan*, the lawless miscreant who counteracts purity. The highest grade in the hierarchy of men belongs of right to the Mage or the *âthravan*, to the priest whose voice inspires the demons with fear, or the soldier whose club despatches the impious, but a place of honour at their side is assigned to the peasant who reclaims from the power of Angrô-mainyus the dry and sterile fields. Among the places where the earth thrives most joyously is reckoned that "where a worshipper of Ahura-mazdâ builds a house, with a chaplain, with cattle, with a wife, with sons, with a fair flock; where man grows the most corn, herbage, and fruit trees; where he spreads water on a soil without water, and drains off water where there is too much of it." He who sows corn, sows good, and promotes the Mazdean faith; "he nourishes the Mazdean religion as fifty men would do rocking a child in the cradle, five hundred women giving it suck from their breasts.[1] When the corn was created the Daêvas leaped, when it sprouted the Daêvas lost courage, when the stem set the Daêvas wept, when the ear swelled the Daêvas fled. In the house where corn is mouldering the Daêvas lodge, but when the corn sprouts, one might say that a hot iron is being turned round in their mouths." And the reason of their horror is easily divined: "Whoso eats not, has no power either to accomplish a valiant work of religion, or to labour with valour, or yet to beget children valiantly; it is by eating that the universe lives, and it dies from not eating." The faithful follower of Zoroaster owes no obligation towards the impious man or towards a stranger,[2]

[1] The original text says in a more enigmatical fashion, "he nourishes the religion of Mazdâ as a hundred feet of men and a thousand breasts of women might do."

[2] Charity is called in Parsee language, *ashô-dâd* the *gift to a pious man*, or the *gift of piety*, and the pious man, the *ashavan*, is by definition the worshipper of Ahura-mazdâ alone.

but is ever bound to render help to his coreligionist. He will give a garment to the naked, and by so doing will wound Zemaka, the demon of winter. He will never refuse food to the hungry labourer, under pain of eternal torments, and his charity will extend even to the brute beasts, provided that they belong to the species created by Ahura-mazdâ: he has duties towards them, and their complaints, heard in heaven, shall be fatal to him later on if he has provoked them. Asha-vahista will condemn to hell the cruel man who has ill-treated the ox, or allowed his flocks to suffer; and the killing of a hedgehog is no less severely punished—for does not a hedgehog devour the ants who steal the grain? The dog is in every case an especially sacred animal—the shepherd's dog, the watch-dog, the hunting-dog, even the prowling dog. It is not lawful to give any dog a blow which renders him impotent, or to slit his ears, or to cut his foot, without incurring grave responsibilities in this world and in the next; it is necessary to feed the dog well, and not to throw bones to him which are too hard, nor have his food served hot enough to burn his tongue or his throat. For the rest, the faithful Zoroastrian was bound to believe in his god, to offer to him the orthodox prayers and sacrifices, to be simple in heart, truthful, the slave of his pledged word, loyal in his very smallest acts. If he had once departed from the right way, he could only return to it by repentance and by purification, accompanied by pious deeds: to exterminate noxious animals, the creatures of Angrô-mainyus and the abode of his demons, such as the frog, the scorpion, the serpent or the ant, to clear the sterile tracts, to restore impoverished land, to construct bridges over running water, to distribute implements of husbandry to pious men, or to build them a house, to give a pure and healthy maiden in marriage to a just man,—these were so many means of expiation appointed by the prophet.[1] Marriage was strictly obligatory,[2] and seemed more praiseworthy in proportion as the kinship existing between the married pair was the closer: not only was the sister united in marriage to her brother, as in Egypt, but the father to his daughter, and the mother to her son, at least among the Magi. Polygamy was also encouraged and widely practised: the code imposed no limit on the number of wives and concubines, and custom was in favour of a man's having as many wives as his fortune permitted him to maintain. On the occasion of a death, it was forbidden to burn the corpse, to bury it, or to cast it into a river, as it would have polluted the fire, the earth, or the water—an unpardonable offence. The corpse could be disposed of in different ways. The Persians were accustomed to cover it with a thick layer of wax, and then

[1] A passage in the *Vendidad* even enumerates how many noisome beasts must be slain to accomplish one full work of expiation—"to kill 1000 serpents of those who drag themselves upon the belly, and 2000 of the other species, 1000 land frogs or 2000 water frogs, 1000 ants who steal the grain," and so on.

[2] The *Vendidad* says, "And I tell thee, O Spitama Zarathustra, the man who has a wife is above him who lives in continency;" and, as we have seen in the text, one of these forms of expiation consisted in "marrying to a worthy man a young girl who has never known a man" (*Vendidad*, 14, § 15). Herodotus of old remarked that one of the chief merits in an Iranian was to have many children: the King of Persia encouraged fecundity in his realm, and awarded a prize each year to that one of his subjects who could boast the most numerous progeny.

to bury it in the ground: the wax coating obviated the pollution which direct contact would have brought upon the soil. The Magi, and probably also strict devotees, following their example, exposed the corpse in the open air, abandoning it to the birds or beasts of prey. It was considered a great misfortune if these respected the body, for it was an almost certain indication of the wrath of Ahuramazdâ, and it was thought that the defunct had led an evil life. When the bones had been sufficiently stripped of flesh, they were collected together, and deposited either in an earthenware urn or in a stone ossuary with a cover, or in a monumental tomb either hollowed out in the heart of the mountain or in the living rock, or raised up above the level of the ground. Meanwhile the soul remained in the neighbourhood for three days, hovering near the head of the corpse, and by the recitation of prayers it experienced, according to its condition of purity or impurity, as much of joy or sadness as the whole world experiences. When the third night was past, the just soul set forth across luminous plains, refreshed by a perfumed breeze, and its good thoughts and words and deeds took shape before it "under the guise of a young maiden, radiant and strong, with well-developed bust, noble mien, and glorious face, about fifteen years of age, and as beautiful as the most beautiful;" the unrighteous soul, on the contrary, directed its course towards the north, through a tainted land, amid the squalls of a pestilential hurricane, and there encountered its past ill deeds, under the form of an ugly and wicked young woman, the ugliest and most wicked it had ever seen. The genius Rashnu Razishta, the essentially truthful, weighed its virtues or vices in an unerring balance, and acquitted or condemned it on the impartial testimony of its past life. On issuing from the judgment-hall, the soul arrived at the approach to the bridge Cinvaut, which, thrown across the abyss of hell, led to paradise. The soul, if impious, was unable to cross this bridge, but was hurled down into the abyss, where it became the slave of Angrômainyus. If pure, it crossed the bridge without difficulty by the help of the angel Sraôsha, and was welcomed by Vohu-manô, who conducted it before the throne of Ahuramazdâ, in the same way as he had led Zoroaster, and assigned to it the post which it should occupy until the day of the resurrection of the body.[1]

The religious observances enjoined on the members of the priestly caste were innumerable and minute. Ahuramazdâ and his colleagues had not, as was the fashion among the Assyrians and Egyptians, either temples or tabernacles, and though they were represented sometimes under human or animal forms, and even in some cases on bas-reliefs, yet no one ever ventured to set up in their sanctuaries those so-called animated or prophetic statues to which the majority of the nations had rendered or were rendering their solicitous homage. Altars, however, were

---

[1] All this picture of the fate of the soul is taken from the *Vendidad*, where the fate of the just is described, and in the *Yasht*, where the condition of faithful and impious souls respectively is set forth on parallel lines. The classical authors teach us nothing on this subject, and the little they actually say only proves that the Persians believed in the immortality of the soul. The main outlines of the picture here set forth go back to the times of the Achæmenids and the Medes, except the abstract conception of the goddess who leads the soul of the dead as an incarnation of his good or evil deeds.

erected on the tops of hills, in palaces, or in the centre of cities, on which fires were kindled in honour of the inferior deities or of the supreme god himself. Two altars were usually set up together, and they are thus found here and there among the ruins, as at Nakhsh-î-Rustem, the

THE TWO IRANIAN ALTARS AT NAKHSH-Î-RUSTEM.[1]

necropolis of Persepolis, where a pair of such altars exist; these are cut, each out of a single block, in a rocky mass which rises some thirteen feet above the level of the surrounding plain. They are of cubic form and squat appearance, looking like towers flanked at the four corners by supporting columns which are connected by circular

[1] Drawn by Boudier, from a heliogravure in Marcel Dieulafoy.

arches; above a narrow moulding rises a crest of somewhat triangular projections; the hearth is hollowed out on the summit of each altar.[1] At Meshed-î-Murgâb, on the site of the ancient Pasargadæ, the altars have disappeared, but the basements on which they were erected are still visible, as also the flight of eight steps by which they were approached. Those altars on which burned a perpetual fire were not left exposed to the open air: they would have run too great a risk of contracting impurities, such as dust borne by the wind, flights of birds, dew, rain, or snow. They were enclosed in slight structures, well protected by walls, and attaining in some cases considerable dimensions, or in pavilion-shaped edifices of stone adorned with columns. The sacrificial rites were of long duration, and frequent, and were rendered very complex by interminable manual acts, ceremonial gestures, and incantations. In cases where the altar was not devoted to maintaining a perpetual fire, it was kindled when necessary with small twigs previously barked and purified, and was subsequently fed with precious

THE TWO IRANIAN ALTARS OF MURGÂB.[2]

---

[1] According to Perrot and Chipiez, "it is not impossible that these altars were older than the great buildings of Persepolis, and that they were erected for the old Persian town which Darius raised to the position of capital."

[2] Drawn by Boudier, from Flandin and Coste.

woods, preferably cypress or laurel;[1] care was taken not to quicken the flame by blowing, for the human breath would have desecrated the fire by merely passing over it; death was the punishment for any one who voluntarily committed such a heinous sacrilege. The recognised offering consisted of flowers, bread, fruit, and perfumes, but these were often accompanied, as in all ancient religions, by a bloody sacrifice; the sacrifice of a horse was considered the most efficacious, but an ox, a cow, a sheep, a camel, an ass, or a stag was frequently offered: in certain circumstances, especially when it was desired to conciliate the favour of the god of the underworld, a human victim, probably as a survival of very ancient rites, was preferred.[3] The king, whose royal position made him the representative of

THE SACRED FIRE BURNING ON THE ALTAR.[2]

---

[1] Pausanias, who witnessed the cult as practised at Hierocæsaræa, remarked the curious colour of the ashes heaped upon the altar.

[2] Drawn by Faucher-Gudin, from the impression of a Persian intaglio.

[3] Most modern writers deny the authenticity of Herodotus' account, because a sacrifice of this kind is opposed to the spirit of the Magian religion, which is undoubtedly the case, as far as the latest form of the religion is concerned; but the testimony of Herodotus is so plain that the fact itself must be considered as indisputable. We may note that the passage refers to the foundation of a city; and if we remember how persistent was the custom of human sacrifice among ancient races at the foundation of buildings, we shall be led to the conclusion that the ceremony described by the Greek historian was a survival of a very ancient usage, which had not yet fallen entirely into desuetude at the Achæmenian epoch.

Ahura-mazdâ on earth, was, in fact, a high priest, and was himself able to officiate at the altar, but no one else could dispense with the mediation of the Magi. The worshippers proceeded in solemn procession to the spot where the ceremony was to take place, and there the priest, wearing the tiara on his head, recited an invocation in a slow and mysterious voice, and implored the blessings of heaven on the king and nation. He then slaughtered the victim by a blow on the head, and divided it into portions, which he gave back to the offerer without reserving any of them, for Ahura-mazdâ required nothing but the soul; in certain cases, the victim was entirely consumed by fire, but more frequently nothing but a little of the fat and some of the entrails were taken to feed and maintain the flame, and sometimes even this was omitted.[1] Sacrifices were of frequent occurrence. Without mentioning the extraordinary occasions on which a king would have a thousand bulls slain at one time,[2] the Achæmenian kings killed each day a thousand bullocks, asses, and stags: sacrifice under such circumstances was another name for butchery, the object of which was to furnish the court with a sufficient supply of pure meat. The ceremonial bore resemblance in many ways to that still employed by the modern

[1] A relic of this custom may be discerned in the expiatory sacrifice decreed in the *Vendidad:* "He shall sacrifice a thousand head of small cattle, and he shall place their entrails devoutly on the fire, with libations."

[2] The number 1000 seems to have had some ritualistic significance, for it often recurs in the penances imposed on the faithful as expiation for their sins: thus it was enjoined to slay 1000 serpents, 1000 frogs, 1000 ants who steal the grain, 1000 head of small cattle, 1000 swift horses, 1000 camels, 1000 brown oxen.

Zoroastrians of Persia and India. The officiating priest covered his mouth with the bands which fell from his mitre, to prevent the god from being polluted by his breath; he held in his hand the baresman, or sacred bunch of tamarisk, and prepared the mysterious liquor from the haoma plant.[1] He was accustomed each morning to celebrate divine service before the sacred fire, not to speak of the periodic festivals in which he shared the offices with all the members of his tribe, such as the feast of Mithra, the feast of the Fravashis,[2] the feast commemorating the rout of Angrô-mainyus,[3] the feast of the Sakæa, during which the slaves were masters of the house.[4] All the Magi were not

---

[1] The drink mentioned by the author of the *De Iside*, which was extracted from the plant Omômi, and which the Magi offered to the god of the underworld, is certainly the haoma. The rite mentioned by the Greek author, which appears to be an incantation against Ahriman, required, it seems, a potion in which the blood of a wolf was a necessary ingredient: this questionable draught was then carried to a place where the sun's rays never shone, and was there sprinkled on the ground as a libation.

[2] Menander speaks of this festival as conducted in his own times, and tells us that it was called Furdîgan; modern authorities usually admit that it goes back to the times of the Achæmenids or even beyond.

[3] Agathias says that every worshipper of Ahura-mazdâ is enjoined to kill the greatest possible number of animals created by Angrô-mainyus, and bring to the Magi the fruits of his hunting. Herodotus had already spoken of this destruction of life as one of the duties incumbent on every Persian, and this gives probability to the view of modern writers that the festival went back to the Achæmenian epoch.

[4] The festival of the Sakæa is mentioned by Ctesias. It was also a Babylonian festival, and most modern authorities conclude from this double use of the name that the festival was borrowed from the Babylonians by the Persians, but this point is not so certain as it is made out to be, and at any rate the borrowing must have taken place very early, for the festival was already well established in the Achæmenian period.

necessarily devoted to the priesthood; but those only became apt in the execution of their functions who had been dedicated to them from infancy, and who, having received the necessary instruction, were duly consecrated. These adepts were divided into several classes, of which three at least were never confounded in their functions—the sorcerers, the interpreters of dreams, and the most venerated sages—and from these three classes were chosen the ruling body of the order and its supreme head. Their rule of life was strict and austere, and was encumbered with a thousand observances indispensable to the preservation of perfect purity in their persons, their altars, their victims, and their sacrificial vessels and implements. The Magi of highest rank abstained from every form of living thing as food, and the rest only partook of meat under certain restrictions. Their dress was unpretentious, they wore no jewels, and observed strict fidelity to the marriage vow;[1] and the virtues with which they were accredited obtained for them, from very early times, unbounded influence over the minds of the common people as well as over those of the nobles: the king himself boasted of being their pupil,[2] and took no serious step in state affairs without consulting Ahura-mazdâ or the other gods by their mediation. The classical writers maintain that the Magi often cloaked monstrous vices under their apparent strictness, and it is

[1] Clement of Alexandria assures us that they were strictly celibate, but besides the fact that married Magi are mentioned several times, celibacy is still considered by Zoroastrians an inferior state to that of marriage.

[2] In the Greek period, a spurious epitaph of Darius, son of Hystaspes, was quoted, in which the king says of himself, "I was the pupil of the Magi."

possible that this was the case in later days, but even then moral depravity was probably rather the exception than the rule among them:[1] the majority of the Magi faithfully observed the rules of honest living and ceremonial purity enjoined on them in the books handed down by their ancestors.

There is reason to believe that the Magi were all-powerful among the Medes, and that the reign of Astyages was virtually the reign of the priestly caste; but all the Iranian states did not submit so patiently to their authority, and the Persians at last proved openly refractory. Their kings, lords of Susa as well as of Pasargadæ, wielded all the resources of Elam, and their military power must have equalled, if it did not already surpass, that of their suzerain lords. Their tribes, less devoted to the manner of living of the Assyrians and Chaldæans, had preserved a vigour and power of endurance which the Medes no longer possessed; and they needed but an ambitious and capable leader, to rise rapidly from the rank of subjects to that of rulers of Iran, and to become in a short time masters of Asia. Such a chief they found in Cyrus,[2] son of Cambyses; but although no more illustrious name than his occurs in the list of the founders

[1] These accusations are nearly all directed against their incestuous marriages: it seems that the classical writers took for a refinement of debauchery what really was before all things a religious practice.

[2] The original form of the name is Kûru, Kûrush, with a long *û*, which forces us to reject the proposed connection with the name of the Indian hero Kuru, in which the *u* is short. Numerous etymologies of the name Cyrus have been proposed. The Persians themselves attributed to it the sense of *the Sun*.

of mighty empires, the history of no other has suffered more disfigurement from the imagination of his own subjects or from the rancour of the nations he had conquered.[1] The Medes, who could not forgive him for having made them subject to their ancient vassals, took delight in holding him up to scorn, and not being able to deny the fact of his triumph, explained it by the adoption of tortuous and despicable methods. They would not even allow that he was of royal birth, but asserted that he was of ignoble origin, the son of a female goatherd and a certain Atradates,[2] who, belonging to the savage clan of the Mardians, lived by brigandage. Cyrus himself, according

[1] We possess two entirely different versions of the history of the origin of Cyrus, but one, that of Herodotus, has reached us intact, while that of Ctesias is only known to us in fragments from extracts made by Nicolas of Damascus, and by Photius. Spiegel and Duncker thought to recognise in the tradition followed by Ctesias one of the Persian accounts of the history of Cyrus, but Bauer refuses to admit this hypothesis, and prefers to consider it as a romance put together by the author, according to the taste of his own times, from facts partly different from those utilised by Herodotus, and partly borrowed from Herodotus himself: but it should very probably be regarded as an account of Median origin, in which the founder of the Persian empire is portrayed in the most unfavourable light. Or perhaps it may be regarded as the form of the legend current among the Pharnaspids who established themselves as satraps of Dascylium in the time of the Achæmenids, and to whom the royal house of Cappadocia traced its origin. It is almost certain that the account given by Herodotus represents a Median version of the legend, and, considering the important part played in it by Harpagus, probably that version which was current among the descendants of that nobleman. The historian Dinon, as far as we can judge from the extant fragments of his work, and from the abridgment made by Trogus Pompeius, adopted the narrative of Ctesias, mingling with it, however, some details taken from Herodotus and the romance of Xenophon, the Cyropædia.

[2] According to one of the historians consulted by Strabo, Cyrus himself, and not his father, was called Atradates.

to this account, spent his infancy and early youth in a condition not far short of slavery, employed at first in sweeping out the exterior portions of the palace, performing afterwards the same office in the private apartments, subsequently promoted to the charge of the lamps and torches, and finally admitted to the number of the royal cupbearers who filled the king's goblet at table. When he

A ROYAL HUNTING-PARTY IN IRAN.[1]

was at length enrolled in the bodyguard,[2] he won distinction by his skill in all military exercises, and having risen from rank to rank, received command of an expedition against the Cadusians. On the march he fell in with a Persian groom named Œbaras,[3] who had been cruelly scourged for

[1] Drawn by Faucher-Gudin, from the silver vase in the Museum of the Hermitage.

[2] The tradition reproduced by Dinon narrated that Cyrus had begun by serving among the Kavasses, the three hundred staff-bearers who accompanied the sovereign when he appeared in public, and that he passed next into the royal body-guard, and that once having attained this rank, he passed rapidly through all the superior grades of the military profession.

[3] This Œbaras whom Ctesias makes the accomplice of Cyrus, seems to be an antedated forestallment of the Œbaras whom the tradition followed

some misdeed, and was occupied in the transportation of manure in a boat : in obedience to an oracle the two united their fortunes, and together devised a vast scheme for liberating their compatriots from the Median yoke. How Atradates secretly prepared the revolt of the Mardians ; how Cyrus left his camp to return to the court at Ecbatana, and obtained from Astyages permission to repair to his native country under pretext of offering sacrifices, but in reality to place himself at the head of the conspirators ; how, finally, the indiscretion of a woman revealed the whole plot to a eunuch of the harem, and how he warned Astyages in the middle of his evening banquet by means of a musician or singing-girl, was frequently narrated by the Median bards in their epic poems, and hence the story spread until it reached in later times even as far as the Greeks.[1] Astyages, roused to action by the danger, abandons the pleasures of the chase in which his activity had hitherto found vent, sets out on the track of the rebel, wins a preliminary victory on the Hyrba, and kills the father of Cyrus : some days after, he again overtakes the rebels, at the entrance to the defiles leading to Pasargadæ, and for the second time fortune is on the point of declaring in his favour, when the Persian women, bringing back their husbands and sons to the conflict, urge them on to victory. The fame of their triumph having spread abroad, the

by Herodotus knows as master of the horse under Darius, and to whom that king owed his elevation to the throne.

[1] According to Ctesias, it was a singing-girl who revealed the existence of the plot to Astyages; according to Dinon, it was the bard Angarês. Windischmann has compared this name with that of the Vedic guild of singers, the Angira.

satraps and provinces successfully declared for the conqueror; Hyrcania, first, followed by the Parthians, the Sakæ, and the Bactrians: Astyages was left almost alone, save for a few faithful followers, in the palace at Ecbatana. His daughter Amytis and his son-in-law Spitamas concealed him so successfully on the top of the palace, that he escaped discovery up to the moment when Cyrus was on the point of torturing his grandchildren to force them to reveal his hiding-place: thereupon he gave himself up to his enemies, but was at length, after being subjected to harsh treatment for a time, set at liberty and entrusted with the government of a mountain tribe dwelling to the south-east of the Caspian Sea, that of the Barcanians. Later on he perished through the treachery of Œbaras, and his corpse was left unburied in the desert, but by divine interposition relays of lions were sent to guard it from the attacks of beasts of prey: Cyrus, acquainted with this miraculous circumstance, went in search of the body and gave it a magnificent burial.[1] Another legend asserted, on the contrary, that Cyrus was closely connected with the royal line of Cyaxares; this tradition was originally circulated among the great Median families who attached themselves to the Achæmenian dynasty.[2] According to this legend Astyages had no male

---

[1] The passage in Herodotus leads Marquart to believe that the murder of Astyages formed part of the primitive legend, but was possibly attributed to Cambyses, son of Cyrus, rather than to Œbaras, the companion of the conqueror's early years.

[2] This is the legend as told to Herodotus in Asia Minor, probably by the members of the family of Harpagus, which the Greek historian tried to render credible by interpreting the miraculous incidents in a rationalising manner

heirs, and the sceptre would have naturally descended from him to his daughter Mandanê and her sons. Astyages was much alarmed by a certain dream concerning his daughter: he dreamt that water gushed forth so copiously from her womb as to flood not only Ecbatana, but the whole of Asia, and the interpreters, as much terrified as himself, counselled him not to give Mandanê in marriage to a Mede. He therefore bestowed her hand on a Persian noble of the race of the Achæmenids, named Cambyses; but a second dream soon troubled the security

REMAINS OF THE PALACE OF ECBATANA.[1]

into which this union had lulled him: he saw issuing from his daughter's womb a vine whose branches overshadowed Asia, and the interpreters, being once more consulted, predicted that a grandson was about to be born to him whose ambition would cost him his crown. He therefore bade a certain nobleman of his court, named Harpagus—he whose descendants preserved this version of the story of Cyrus—to seize the infant and put it to death as soon as its mother should give it birth; but the man, touched with pity, caused the child to be exposed in the woods by one of the royal shepherds. A bitch gave suck to the tiny creature, who, however, would soon have succumbed to

[1] Drawn by Boudier, from Coste and Flandin.

the inclemency of the weather, had not the shepherd's wife, being lately delivered of a still-born son, persuaded her husband to rescue the infant, whom she nursed with the same tenderness as if he had been her own child. The dog was, as we know, a sacred animal among the Iranians: the incident of the bitch seems, then, to have been regarded by them as an indication of divine intervention, but the Greeks were shocked by the idea, and invented an explanation consonant with their own customs. They supposed that the woman had borne the name of Spakô: Spakô signifying *bitch* in the language of Media.[1] Cyrus grew to boyhood, and being accepted by Mandanê as her son, returned to the court; his grandfather consented to spare his life, but, to avenge himself on Harpagus, he caused the limbs of the nobleman's own son to be served up to him at a feast. Thenceforth Harpagus had but one idea, to overthrow the tyrant and transfer the crown to the young prince: his project succeeded, and Cyrus, having overcome Astyages, was proclaimed king by the Medes as well as by the Persians. The real history of Cyrus, as far as we can ascertain it, was less romantic. We gather that Kurush, known to us as Cyrus, succeeded his father

---

[1] Herodotus asserts that the child's foster-mother was called in Greek *Kynô*, in Median *Spakô*, which comes to the same thing, for *spaka* means *bitch* in Median. Further on he asserts that the parents of the child heard of the name of his nurse with joy, as being of good augury; "and, in order that the Persians might think that Cyrus had been preserved alive by divine agency, they spread abroad the report that Cyrus had been suckled by a *bitch*. And thus arose the fable commonly accepted." Trogus Pompeius received the original story probably through Dinon, and inserted it in his book.

Cambyses as ruler of Anshân about 559 or 558 B.C.,[1] and that he revolted against Astyages in 553 or 552 B.C.,[2] and defeated him. The Median army thereupon seizing its own leader, delivered him into the hands of the conqueror: Ecbatana was taken and sacked, and the empire fell at one blow, or, more properly speaking, underwent a transformation (550 B.C.). The transformation was, in fact, an internal revolution in which the two peoples of the same race changed places. The name of the Medes lost nothing of the prestige which it enjoyed in foreign lands, but that of the Persians was henceforth united with it, and shared its renown: like Astyages and his predecessors, Cyrus and his successors reigned equally over the two leading branches of the ancient Iranian stock, but whereas the former had been kings of the Medes and Persians, the latter became henceforth kings of the Persians and Medes.[3]

[1] The length of Cyrus' reign is fixed at thirty years by Ctesias, followed by Dinon and Trogus Pompeius, but at twenty-nine years by Herodotus, whose computation I here follow. Hitherto the beginning of his reign has been made to coincide with the fall of Astyages, which was consequently placed in 569 or 568 B.C., but the discovery of the *Annals of Nabonidus* obliges us to place the taking of Ecbatana in the sixth year of the Babylonian king, which corresponds to the year 550 B.C., and consequently to hold that Cyrus reckoned his twenty-nine years from the moment when he succeeded his father Cambyses.

[2] The inscription on the *Rassam Cylinder of Abu-Habba*, seems to make the fall of the Median king, who was suzerain of the Scythians of Harrân, coincide with the third year of Nabonidus, or the year 553-2 B.C. But it is only the date of the commencement of hostilities between Cyrus and Astyages which is here furnished, and this manner of interpreting the text agrees with the statement of the Median traditions handed down by the classical authors, that three combats took place between Astyages and Cyrus before the final victory of the Persians.

[3] This equality of the two peoples is indicated by the very terms

The change effected was so natural that their nearest neighbours, the Chaldæans, showed no signs of uneasiness at the outset. They confined themselves to the bare registration of the fact in their annals at the appointed date, without comment, and Nabonidus in no way deviated from the pious routine which it had hitherto pleased him to follow. Under a sovereign so good-natured there was little likelihood of war, at all events with external foes, but insurrections were always breaking out in different parts of his territory, and we read of difficulties in Khumê in the first year of his reign, in Hamath in his second year, and troubles in Phœnicia in the third year, which afforded an opportunity for settling the Tyrian question. Tyre had led a far from peaceful existence ever since the day when, from sheer apathy, she had accepted the supremacy of Nebuchadrezzar.[1] Baal II. had peacefully reigned there for ten years (574–564), but after his death the people had overthrown the monarchy, and various *suffetes* had followed one another rapidly—Eknibaal ruled two months, Khelbes ten months, the high priest Abbar three months, the two brothers Mutton and Gerastratus

---

employed by Darius, whom he speaks of them, in the *Great Inscription of Behistun*. He says, for example, in connection with the revolt of the false Smerdis, that "the deception prevailed greatly in the land, in Persia and Media as well as in the other provinces, and further on, that "the whole people rose, and passed over from Cambyses to him, Persia and Media as well as the other countries." In the same way he mentions "the army of Persians and Medes which was with him," and one sees that he considered Medes and Persians to be on exactly the same footing.

[1] All these events are known through the excerpt from Menander preserved to us by Josephus in his treatise *Against Apion*.

six years, all of them no doubt in the midst of endless disturbances; whereupon a certain Baalezor restored the royal dignity, but only to enjoy it for the space of one year. On his death, the inhabitants begged the Chaldæans to send them, as a successor to the crown, one of those princes whom, according to custom, Baal had not long previously given over as hostages for a guarantee of his loyalty, and Nergal-sharuzur for this purpose selected from their number Mahar-baal, who was probably a son of Ithobaal (558–557).[1] When, at the end of four years, the death of Mahar-baal left the throne vacant (554–553), the Tyrians petitioned for his brother Hirôm, and Nabonidus, who was then engaged in Syria, came south as far as Phœnicia and installed the prince.[2] This took place at the very moment when Cyrus was preparing his expedition against Astyages; and the Babylonian monarch took advantage of the agitation into which the Medes were thrown by this invasion, to carry into execution a project which he had been planning ever since his accession. Shortly after that event he had had a dream, in which Marduk,

---

[1] The fragment of Menander does not give the Babylonian king's name, but a simple chronological calculation proves him to have been Nergal-sharuzur.

[2] *Annals of Nabonidus*, where mention is made of a certain Nabu-makhdan-uzur—but the reading of the name is uncertain—who seems to be in revolt against the Chaldæans. Floigl has very ingeniously harmonised the dates of the *Annals* with those obtained from the fragment of Menander, and has thence concluded that the object of the expedition of the third year was the enthroning of Hirôm which is mentioned in the fragment, and during whose fourteenth year Cyrus became King of Babylon.

the great lord, and Sin, the light of heaven and earth, had appeared on either side of his couch, the former addressing him in the following words: "Nabonidus, King of Babylon, with the horses of thy chariot bring brick, rebuild Ê-khul-khul, the temple of Harrân, that Sin, the great lord, may take up his abode therein." Nabonidus had respectfully pointed out that the town was in the hands of the Scythians, who were subjects of the Medes, but the god had replied: "The Scythian of whom thou speakest, he, his country and the kings his protectors, are no more." Cyrus was the instrument of the fulfilment of the prophecy. Nabonidus took possession of Harrân without difficulty, and immediately put the necessary work in hand. This was, indeed, the sole benefit that he derived from the changes which were taking place, and it is probable that his inaction was the result of the enfeebled condition of the empire. The country over which he ruled, exhausted by the Assyrian conquest, and depopulated by the Scythian invasions, had not had time to recover its forces since it had passed into the hands of the Chaldæans; and the wars which Nebuchadrezzar had been obliged to undertake for the purpose of strengthening his own power, though few in number and not fraught with danger, had tended to prolong the state of weakness into which it had sunk. If the hero of the dynasty who had conquered Egypt had not ventured to measure his strength with the Median princes, and if he had courted the friendship not only of the warlike Cyaxares but of the effeminate Astyages, it would not be prudent for Nabonidus to come into collision with the victorious new-comers from the heart of Iran. Chaldæa doubtless was right in avoiding hostilities, at all events so long as she had to bear the brunt of them alone, but other nations had not the same motives for exercising prudence, and Lydia was fully assured that the moment had come for her to again take up the ambitious designs which the treaty of 585 had forced her to renounce. Alyattes, relieved from anxiety with regard to the Medes, had confined his energies to establishing firmly his kingdom in the regions of Asia Minor extending westwards from the Halys and the Anti-Taurus. The acquisition of Colophon, the destruction of Smyrna, the alliance with the towns of the littoral, had ensured him undisputed possession of the valleys of the Caicus and the Hermus, but the plains of the Mæander in the south, and the mountainous districts of Mysia in the north, were not yet fully brought under his sway. He completed the occupation of the Troad and Mysia about 584, and afterwards made of the entire province an appanage for Adramyttios, who was either his son or his brother.[1] He even carried his arms into Bithynia, where, to enforce his rule, he built several strongholds, one of which, called Alyatta, commanded

[1] The doings of Alyattes in Troas and in Mysia are vouched for by the anecdote related by Plutarch concerning this king's relations with Pittakos. The founding of Adramyttium is attributed to him by Stephen of Byzantium, after Aristotle, who made Adramyttios the brother of Crœsus. Radat gives good reasons for believing that Adramyttios was brother to Alyattes and uncle to Crœsus, and the same person as Adramys, the son of Sadyattes, according to Xanthus of Lydia. Radet gives the year 584 for the date of these events.

the main road leading from the basin of the Rhyndacus to that of the Sangarius, skirting the spurs of Olympus.[1] He experienced some difficulty in reducing Caria, and did not finally succeed in his efforts till nearly the close of his reign in 566. Adramyttios was then dead, and his fief had devolved on his eldest surviving brother or nephew, Crœsus, whose mother was by birth a Carian. This prince had incurred his father's displeasure by his prodigality, and an influential party desired that he should be set aside in favour of his brother Pantaleon, the son of Alyattes by an Ionian. Crœsus, having sown his wild oats, was anxious to regain his father's favour, and his only chance of so doing was by distinguishing himself in the coming war, if only money could be found for paying his mercenaries. Sadyattes, the richest banker in Lydia, who had already had dealings with all the members of the royal family, refused to make him a loan, but Theokharides of Prienê advanced him a thousand gold staters, which enabled Crœsus to enroll his contingent at Ephesus, and to be the first to present himself at the rallying-place for the troops.[2] Caria was annexed to the

[1] Radet places the operations in Bithynia before the Median war, towards 594 at the latest. I think that they are more probably connected with those in Mysia, and that they form part of the various measures taken after the Median war to achieve the occupation of the regions west of the Halys.

[2] A mutilated extract from Xanthus of Lydia in Suidas seems to carry these events back to the time of the war against Prienê, towards the beginning of the reign. The united evidence of the accompanying circumstances proves that they belong to the time of the old age of Alyattes, and makes it very likely that they occurred in 566, the date proposed by Radet for the Carian campaign.

kingdom, but the conditions under which the annexation took place are not known to us;[1] and Crœsus contributed so considerably to the success of the campaign, that he was reinstated in popular favour. Alyattes, however, was advancing in years, and was soon about to rejoin his adversaries Cyaxares and Nebuchadrezzar in Hades. Like the Pharaohs, the kings of Lydia were accustomed

THE TUMULUS OF ALYATTES AND THE ENTRANCE TO THE PASSAGE.[2]

to construct during their lifetime the monuments in which they were to repose after death. Their necropolis was situated not far from Sardes, on the shores of the little lake Gygæa; it was here, close to the resting-place of his ancestors and their wives, that Alyattes chose the spot for his tomb,[3] and his subjects did not lose the

[1] The fragment of Nicolas of Damascus does not speak of the result of the war, but it was certainly favourable, for Herodotus counts the Carians among Crœsus' subjects.

[2] Drawn by Boudier, from the sketch by Spiegelthal.

[3] The only one of these monuments, besides that of Alyattes, which is mentioned by the ancients, belonged to one of the favourites of Gyges, and was called *the Tomb of the Courtesan*. Strabo, by a manifest error, has applied this name to the tomb of Alyattes.

opportunity of proving to what extent he had gained their affections. His predecessors had been obliged to finish their work at their own expense and by forced labour;[1] but in the case of Alyattes the three wealthiest classes of the population, the merchants, the craftsmen, and the courtesans, all united to erect for him an enormous tumulus, the remains of which still rise 220 feet above the plains of the Hermus. The sub-structure consisted of a circular wall of great blocks of limestone resting on the solid rock, and it contained in the centre a vault of grey marble which was reached by a vaulted passage. A huge mound of red clay and yellowish earth was raised above the chamber, surmounted by a small column representing a phallus, and by four stelæ covered with inscriptions, erected at the four cardinal points. It follows the traditional type of burial-places in use among the old Asianic races, but it is constructed with greater

ONE OF THE LYDIAN ORNAMENTS IN THE LOUVRE.[2]

---

[1] This, at least, seems to be the import of the passage in Clearchus of Soli, where that historian gives an account of the erection of the *Tomb of the Courtesan.*

[2] Drawn by Faucher-Gudin, from a photograph.

regularity than most of them; Alyattes was laid within it in 561, after a glorious reign of forty-nine years.[1]

It was wholly due to him that Lydia was for the moment raised to the level of the most powerful states which then existed on the eastern shores of the Mediterranean. He was by nature of a violent and uncontrolled

MOULD FOR JEWELLERY OF LYDIAN ORIGIN.[2]

temper, and during his earlier years he gave way to fits of anger, in which he would rend the clothes of those who came in his way or would spit in their faces, but with advancing years his character became more softened, and he finally earned the reputation of being a just and

---

[1] Herodotus gave fifty-seven years' length of reign to Alyattes, whilst the chronographers, who go back as far as Xanthus of Lydia, through Julius Africanus, attribute to him only forty-nine; historians now prefer the latter figures, at least as representing the maximum length of reign.

[2] Drawn by Faucher-Gudin, from a photograph.

moderate sovereign. The little that we know of his life reveals an energy and steadfastness of purpose quite unusual; he proceeded slowly but surely in his undertakings, and if he did not succeed in extending his domains as far as he had hoped at the beginning of his campaigns against the Medes, he at all events never lost any of the provinces he had acquired. Under his auspices agriculture flourished, and manufactures attained a degree of perfection

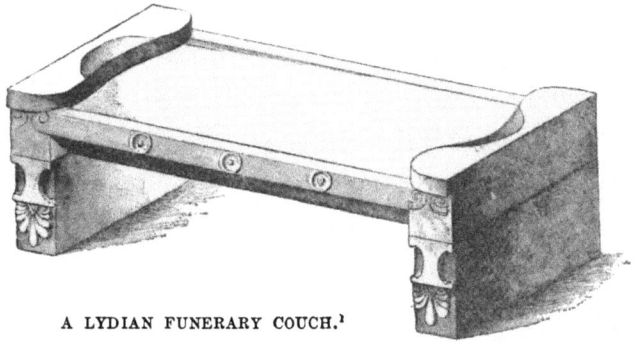

A LYDIAN FUNERARY COUCH.[1]

hitherto unknown. None of the vases in gold, silver, or wrought-iron, which he dedicated and placed among the treasures of the Greek temples, has come down to us, but at rare intervals ornaments of admirable workmanship are found in the Lydian tombs. Those now in the Louvre exhibit, in addition to human figures somewhat awkwardly treated, heads of rams, bulls, and griffins of a singular delicacy and faithfulness to nature. These examples reveal a blending of Grecian types and methods of production with those of Egypt or Chaldæa, the Hellenic being predominant,[2] and the same combination of heterogeneous

[1] Drawn by Faucher-Gudin, from Choisy.

[2] The ornaments, of which we have now no specimens, but only the original moulds cut in serpentine, betray imitation of Assyria and Chaldæa.

elements must have existed in the other domains of industrial art—in the dyed and embroidered stuffs,[1] the vases,[2] and the furniture.[3] Lydia, inheriting the traditions of Phrygia, and like that state situated on the border of two worlds, allied moreover with Egypt as well as Babylon, and in regular communication with the Delta, borrowed from each that which fell in with her tastes or seemed likely to be most helpful to her in her commercial relations. As the country produced gold in considerable quantities, and received still more from extraneous sources, the precious metal came soon to be employed as a means of exchange under other conditions than those which had hitherto prevailed. Besides acting as commission agents

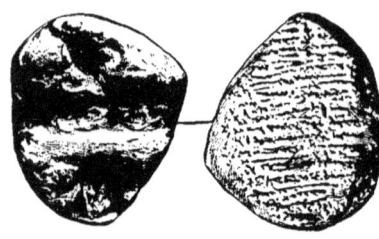

LYDIAN COIN BEARING A RUNNING FOX.[4]

LYDIAN COIN WITH A HARE.[5]

---

[1] The custom of clothing themselves in dyed and embroidered stuffs was one of the effeminate habits with which the poet Xenophanes reproached the Ionians as having been learned from their Lydian neighbours.

[2] M. Perrot points out that one of the vases discovered by G. Dennis at Bintépé is an evident imitation of the Egyptian and Phœnician chevroned glasses. The shape of the vase is one of those found represented, with the same decoration, on Egyptian monuments subsequent to the Middle Empire, where the chevroned lines seem to be derived from the undulations of ribbon-alabaster.

[3] The stone funerary couches which have been discovered in Lydian tombs are evidently copied from pieces of wooden furniture similarly arranged and decorated.

[4] Drawn by Faucher-Gudin, from a specimen in the *Cabinet des Médailles*: a stater of electrum weighing 14·19 grammes.

* [These illustrations are larger than the original pieces.—Tr.]

[5] Drawn by Faucher-Gudin, from a coin in the *Cabinet des Médailles*.

and middle-men for the disposal of merchandise at Sardes, Ephesus, Miletus, Clazomenæ, and all the maritime cities, the Lydians performed at the same time the functions of pawnbrokers, money-changers, and bankers, and they were ready to make loans to private individuals as well as to kings. Obliged by the exigencies of their trade to cut up the large gold ingots into sections sufficiently small to represent the smallest values required in daily life, they did not at first impress upon these portions any stamp as a guarantee of the exact weight or of the purity of the metal: they were estimated, like the *tabonu* of the Egyptians, by actual weighing on the occasion of each business transaction.

LYDIAN COIN WITH A LION.[1]

COIN WITH LION'S HEAD.[1]

The idea at length occurred to them to impress each of these pieces with a common stamp, serving, like the trade-marks employed by certain guilds of artisans, to testify at once to their genuineness and their exact weight: in a word, they were the inventors of money. The most ancient coinage of their mint was like a flattened sphere, more or less ovoid, in form: it consisted at first of electrum, and afterwards of smelted gold, upon which parallel striæ or shallow creases were made by a hammer. There were two kinds of coinage, differing considerably from each other; one consisted of the heavy stater, weighing about 14·20 grammes, perhaps of Phœnician origin, the other of the light stater, of some 10·80 grammes in weight, which doubtless served as money for the local needs of Lydia:

[1] Drawn by Faucher-Gudin, from a coin in the *Cabinet des Médailles*.

THE IRANIAN CONQUEST

both forms were subdivided into pieces representing respectively the third, the sixth, the twelfth, and the twenty-fourth of the value of the original. The stamp which came to be impressed upon the money was in relief, and varied with the banker;* when political communities began to follow the example of individuals, it also bore the name of the city where it was minted. The type of impression once selected, was little modified for fear of exciting mistrust among the people, but it was more finely executed and enlarged so as to cover one of the faces, that which we now call the *ob-verse*. Several subjects entered into the composition of the design, each being impressed by a special punch: thus in the central concavity we find the figure of a running fox, emblem of Apollo Bassareus, and in two similar depressions, one above and the other below the central, appear a horse's or stag's head, and a flower with four petals. Later on the design was simplified, and contained only one, or at most two figures—a hare squatting under a tortuous climbing plant, a roaring lion crouching with its head turned to the left, the grinning muzzle of a lion, the horned profile of an antelope or mouflon sheep: rosettes and flowers, included within a square depression, were then used to replace the striæ and irregular lines of

COIN BEARING HEAD OF MOUFLON GOAT.[1]

MONEY OF CRŒSUS.[1]

* [The best English numismatists do not agree with M. Babelon's "banker" theory. Cf. BARCLAY V. HEAD, *Histo*ria *Nummorum*, p. xxxiv.—TR.]

[1] Drawn by Faucher-Gudin, from a coin in the *Cabinet des Médailles*.

the reverse. These first efforts were without inscriptions; it was not long, however, before there came to be used, in addition to the figures, legends, from which we sometimes learn the name of the banker; we read, for instance, "I am the mark of Phannes," on a stater of electrum struck at Ephesus, with a stag grazing on the right. We are ignorant as to which of the Lydian kings first made use of the new invention, and so threw into circulation the gold and electrum which filled his treasury to overflowing. The ancients say it was Gyges, but the Gygads of their time cannot be ascribed to him; they were, without any doubt, simply ingots marked with the stamp of the banker of the time, and were attributed to Gyges either out of pure imagination or by mistake.[1] The same must be said of the pieces of money which have been assigned to his successors, and, even when we find on them traces of writing, we cannot be sure of their identification; one legend which was considered to contain the name of Sadyattes has been made out, without producing conviction, as involving, instead, that of Clazomenæ. There is no certainty until after the time of Alyattes, that is, in the reign of Crœsus. It is, as a fact, to this prince that we

[1] The gold of Gyges is known to us through a passage in Pollux. Fr. Lenormant attributed to Gyges the coins which Babelon restores to the banks of Asia Minor. Babelon sees in the Gygads only "ingots of gold, struck *possibly* in the name of Gyges, capable of being used as coin, doubtless representing a definitely fixed weight, but still lacking that ultimate perfection which characterises the coinage of civilised peoples: from the standpoint of circulation in the market their shape was defective and inconvenient; their subdivision did not extend to such small fractions as to make all payments easy; they were too large and too dear for easy circulation through many hands."

owe the fine gold and silver coins bearing on the obverse a demi-lion couchant confronting a bull treated similarly.[1] The two creatures appear to threaten one another, and the introduction of the lion recalls a tradition regarding the city of Sardes; it may represent the actual animal which was alleged to have been begotten by King Meles of one of his concubines, and which he caused to be carried solemnly round the city walls to render them impregnable.

Crœsus did not succeed to the throne of his father without trouble. His enemies had not laid down their arms after the Carian campaign, and they endeavoured to rid themselves of him by all the means in use at Oriental courts. The Ionian mother of his rival furnished the slave who kneaded the bread with poison, telling her to mix it with the dough, but the woman revealed the intended crime to her master, who at once took the necessary measures to frustrate the plot; later on in life he dedicated in the temple of Delphi a statue of gold representing the faithful bread-maker.[2] The chief of the rival party seems to have been Sadyattes, the banker from whom Crœsus had endeavoured to borrow money at the beginning of his career, but several of the Lydian nobles, whose exercise of feudal rights had been restricted by the growing authority of the Mermnadæ, either secretly or openly gave their adhesion to Pantaleon, among them being Glaucias of

---

[1] Lenormant ascribed an issue of coins without inscriptions to the kings Ardys, Sadyattes, and Alyattes, but this has since been believed not to have been their work.

[2] Herodotus mentions the statue of the bread-maker, giving no reason why Crœsus dedicated it. The author quoted by Plutarch would have it that in revenge he made his half-brothers eat the poisoned bread.

Sidênê; the Greek cities, always ready to chafe at authority, were naturally inclined to support a claimant born of a Greek mother, and Pindarus the tyrant of Ephesus, and grandson of the Melas who had married the daughter of Gyges, joined the conspirators. As soon as

VIEW OF THE SITE AND RUINS OF EPHESUS.[1]

Alyattes was dead, Crœsus, who was kept informed by his spies of their plans, took action with a rapidity which disconcerted his adversaries. It is not known what became of Pantaleon, whether he was executed or fled the country, but his friends were tortured to death or had to purchase their pardon dearly. Sadyattes was stretched on a rack and torn with carding combs.[2] Glaucias, besieged in his

[1] Drawn by Boudier, from a photograph.
[2] The history of Sadyattes and of his part in the conspiracy results from

fortress of Sidênê, opened its gates after a desperate resistance; the king demolished the walls, and pronounced a solemn curse on those who should thereafter rebuild them. Pindarus, summoned to surrender, refused, but as he had not sufficient troops to defend the entire city, he evacuated the lower quarters, and concentrated all his forces on the defence of the citadel; he refused to open negotiations until after the fall of a tower at the moment when a practicable breach had been made, and succeeded in obtaining an honourable capitulation for himself and his people by a ruse. He dedicated the town to Artemis, and by means of a rope connected the city walls with the temple, which stood nearly a mile away in the suburbs, and then entreated for peace in the name of the goddess. Crœsus was amused at the artifice, and granted favourable conditions to the inhabitants, but insisted on the expulsion of the tyrant. The latter bowed before the decree, and confiding the care of his children and possessions to his friend Pasicles, left for the Peloponnesus with his retinue. Ephesus up to this time had been a kind of allied principality, whose chiefs, united to the royal family of Lydia by marriages from generation to generation, recognised the nominal suzerainty of the reigning king rather than his effective authority. It was in fact a species of protectorate, which, while furthering the commercial interests of Lydia, satisfied at the same time the passion of the Greek cities for autonomy. Crœsus, encouraged by

points of agreement which have been established between various passages in Herodotus and in Nicolas of Damascus, where the person is sometimes named and sometimes not.

his first success, could not rest contented with such a compromise. He attacked, successively, Miletus and the various Ionian, Æolian, and Dorian communities of the littoral, and brought them all under his sway, promising on their capitulation that their local constitutions should be respected if they became direct dependencies of his empire. He placed garrisons in such towns as were strategically important for him to occupy, but everywhere else he razed to the ground the fortresses and ramparts which might afford protection to his enemies in case of rebellion, compelling the inhabitants to take up their abode on the open plain where they could not readily defend themselves.[1] The administration of the affairs of each city was entrusted to either a wealthy citizen, or an hereditary tyrant, or an elected magistrate, who was held responsible for its loyalty; the administrator paid over the tribute to the sovereign's treasurers, levied the specified contingent and took command of it in time of war, settled any quarrels which might occur, and was empowered, when necessary, to exile turbulent and ambitious persons whose words or actions appeared to him to be suspicious. Crœsus treated with generosity those republics which tendered him loyal obedience, and affected a special devotion to their gods. He gave a large number of ex-voto offerings to the much-revered sanctuary of Branchidæ, in the territory of Miletus; he dedicated some golden heifers at the Artemision of Ephesus, and erected the greater number of the columns of that temple at his own expense.[2]

---

[1] He treated thus the Ephesians and the Ilians.
[2] The fragments of columns brought from this temple by Wood and

At one time in his career he appears to have contemplated extending his dominion over the Greek islands, and planned, as was said, the equipment of a fleet, but he soon acknowledged the imprudence of such a project, and confined his efforts to strengthening his advantageous position on the littoral by contracting alliances with the island populations and with the nations of Greece proper.[1] Following the diplomacy of his ancestors, he began by devoting himself to the gods of the country, and took every pains to gain the good graces of Apollo of Delphi. He dispensed his gifts with such liberality that neither his contemporaries nor subsequent generations grew weary of admiring it. On one occasion he is said to have sacrificed three thousand animals, and burnt, moreover, on the pyre the costly contents of a palace—couches covered with silver and gold, coverlets and robes of purple, and golden vials. His subjects were commanded to contribute to the offering, and he caused one hundred and seventeen hollow half-bricks to be cast of the gold which they brought him for this purpose. These bricks were placed in regular layers within the treasury at Delphi where the gifts of Lydia from the time of Alyattes were deposited, and the top of the pile was surmounted by a lion of fine gold of such a size that the pedestal and statue together were worth £1,200,000 of our present money. These, however, formed only a tithe of his gifts;

preserved in the British Museum have on one of the bases the remains of an inscription confirming the testimony of Herodotus.

[1] He seems to have been deterred from his project by a sarcastic remark made, as some say, by Pittakos the Mitylenian, or according to others, by Bias of Priênê.

many of the objects dedicated by him were dispersed half a century (548 B.C.) later when the temple was burnt, and found their way into the treasuries of the Greek states which enjoyed the favour of Apollo—among them being an enormous gold cup sent to Clazomenæ, and four barrels of silver and two bowls, one of silver and one of gold, sent to the Corinthians. The people at Delphi, as well as their god, participated in the royal largesse, and Crœsus distributed to them the sum of two staters per head. No doubt their gratitude led them by degrees to exaggerate the total of the benefits showered upon them, especially as time went on and their recollection of the king became fainter; but even when we reduce the number of the many gifts which they attributed to him, we are still obliged to acknowledge that they surpassed anything hitherto recorded, and that they produced throughout the whole of Greece the effect that Crœsus had desired. The oracle granted to him and to the Lydians the rights of citizenship in perpetuity, the privilege of priority in consulting it before all comers, precedence for his legates over other foreign embassies, and a place of honour at the games and at all religious ceremonies. It was, in fact, the admission of Lydia into the Hellenic concert, and the offerings which Crœsus showered upon the sanctuaries of lesser fame—that of Zeus at Dodona, of Amphiaraos at Oropos, of Trophonios at Lebadæa, on the oracle of Abæ in Phocis, and on the Ismenian Apollo at Thebes—secured a general approval of the act. Political alliances contracted with the great families of Athens, the Alcmæonidæ and Eupatridæ,[1] with

---

[1] Traditions as to Crœsus' relations with Alcmæon are preserved by

the Cypselidæ of Corinth,[1] and with the Heraclidæ of Sparta,[2] completed the policy of bribery which Crœsus had inaugurated in the sacerdotal republics, with the result that, towards 548, being in the position of uncontested patron of the Greeks of Asia, he could count upon the sympathetic neutrality of the majority of their compatriots in Europe, and on the effective support of a smaller number of them in the event of his being forced into hostilities with one or other of his Asiatic rivals.

This, however, constituted merely one side of his policy, and the negotiations which he carried on with his western neighbours were conducted simultaneously with his wars against those of the east. Alyattes had asserted his supremacy over the whole of the country on the western side of the Halys, but it was of a very vague kind, having no definite form, and devoid of practical results as far as several of the districts in the interior were concerned. Crœsus made it a reality, and in less than ten years all the peoples contained within it, the Lycians excepted —Mysians, Phrygians, Mariandynians, Paphlagonians,

---

Herodotus. The king compelled the inhabitants of Lampsacus, his vassals, to release the elder Miltiades, whom they had taken prisoner, and thus earned the gratitude of the Eupatridæ.

[1] Alyattes had been the ally of Periander, as is proved by an anecdote in Herodotus. This friendship continued under Crœsus, for after the fall of the monarchy, when the special treasuries of Lydia were suppressed, the ex-voto offerings of the Lydian kings were deposited in the treasury of Corinth.

[2] According to Theopompus, the Lacedæmonians, wishing to gild the face of the statue of the Amyclæan, Apollo, and finding no gold in Greece, consulted the Delphian prophetess: by her advice they sent to Lydia to buy the precious metal from Crœsus.

Thynians, Bithynians, and Pamphylians—had rendered him homage. In its constitution his empire in no way differed from those which at that time shared the rule of Western Asia; the number of districts administered directly by the sovereign were inconsiderable, and most of the states comprised in it preserved their autonomy. Phrygia had its own princes, who were descendants of Midas,[1] and in the same way Caria and Mysia also retained theirs; but these vassal lords paid tribute and furnished contingents to their liege of Sardes, and garrisons lodged in their citadels as well as military stations or towns founded in strategic positions, such as Prusa[2] in Bithynia, Cibyra, Hyda, Grimenothyræ, and Temenothyræ,[3] kept strict watch over them, securing the while free circulation for caravans or individual merchants throughout the whole country. Crœsus had achieved his conquest just as Media was tottering to its fall under the attacks of the Persians. Their victory placed the Lydian king in a position of great perplexity, since it annulled the treaties concluded after the eclipse of 585, and by releasing him from the obligations then contracted, afforded him an opportunity of extending the limits within which his father had confined himself. Now or never was the time for crossing the Halys in order

[1] This is proved by the history of the Prince Adrastus in Herodotus. Herodotus probably alluded to this colonisation by Crœsus, when he said that the Mysians of Olympus were descendants of Lydian colonists.

[2] Strabo merely says that the Kibyrates were descended from the Lydians who dwelt in Cabalia; since Crœsus was, as far as we know, the only Lydian king who ever possessed this part of Asia, Radet, with good reason, concludes that Kibyra was colonised by him.

[3] Radet has given good reasons for believing that at least some of these towns were enlarged and fortified by Crœsus.

to seize those mineral districts with which his subjects had so long had commercial relations; on the other hand, the unexpected energy of which the Persians had just given proof, their bravery, their desire for conquest, and the valour of their leader, all tended to deter him from the project: should he be victorious, Cyrus would probably not rest contented with the annexation of a few unimportant districts or the imposition of a tribute, but would treat his adversary as he had Astyages, and having dethroned him, would divide Lydia into departments to be ruled by one or other of his partisans. Warlike ideas, nevertheless, prevailed at the court of Sardes, and, taking all into consideration, we cannot deny that they had reason on their side. The fall of Ecbatana had sealed the fate of Media proper, and its immediate dependencies had naturally shared the fortunes of the capital; but the more distant provinces still wavered, and they would probably attempt to take advantage of the change of rule to regain their liberty. Cyrus, obliged to take up arms against them, would no longer have his entire forces at his disposal, and by attacking him at that juncture it might be possible to check his power before it became irresistible. Having sketched out his plan of campaign, Crœsus prepared to execute it with all possible celerity. Egypt and Chaldæa, like himself, doubtless felt themselves menaced; he experienced little difficulty in persuading them to act in concert with him in face of the common peril, and he obtained from both Amasis and Nabonidus promises of effective co-operation. At the same time he had recourse to the Greek oracles, and that of Delphi was instrumental in obtaining for him a treaty of alliance and friendship with Sparta. Negotiations had been carried on so rapidly, that by the end of 548 all was in readiness for a simultaneous movement; Sparta was equipping a fleet, and merely awaited the return of the favourable season to embark her contingent; Egypt had already despatched hers, and her Cypriot vassals were on the point of starting, while bands of Thracian infantry were marching to reinforce the Lydian army. These various elements represented so considerable a force of men, that, had they been ranged on a field of battle, Cyrus would have experienced considerable difficulty in overcoming them. An unforeseen act of treachery obliged the Lydians to hasten their preparations and commence hostilities before the moment agreed on. Eurybatos, an Ephesian, to whom the king had entrusted large sums of money for the purpose of raising mercenaries in the Peloponnesus, fled with his gold into Persia, and betrayed the secret of the coalition. The Achæmenian sovereign did not hesitate to forestall the attack, and promptly assumed the offensive. The transport of an army from Ecbatana to the middle course of the Halys would have been a long and laborious undertaking, even had it kept within the territory of the empire; it would have necessitated crossing the mountain groups of Armenia at their greatest width, and that at a time when the snow was still lying deep upon the ground and the torrents were swollen and unfordable. The most direct route, which passed through Assyria and the part of Mesopotamia south of the Masios, lay for the most part in the hands of the Chaldæans, but their enfeebled condition justified Cyrus's choice of it, and he resolved, in the event of their resistance, to cut his way through sword in hand. He therefore bore down upon Arbela by the gorges of Rowandîz in the month Nisan, making as though he were bound for Karduniash; but before the Babylonians had time to recover from their alarm at this movement, he crossed the river not far from Nineveh and struck into Mesopotamia. He probably skirted the slopes of the Masios, overcoming and killing in the month Iyyâr some petty king, probably the ruler of Armenia,[1] and debouched into Cappadocia. This province was almost entirely in the power of the enemy; Nabonidus had despatched couriers by the shortest route in order to warn his ally, and if necessary to claim his promised help. Crœsus, when he received them, had with him only the smaller portion of his army, the Lydian cavalry, the contingents of his Asiatic subjects, and a few Greek veterans, and it would probably have been wiser to defer the attack till after the disembarkation of the Lacedæmonians; but hesitation at so critical a moment might have discouraged his followers, and decided his fate before any

[1] Floigl, who was the first to refer a certain passage in the *Annals of Nabonidus* to the expedition against Crœsus, restored Is[parda] as the name of the country mentioned, and saw even the capture of Sardes in the events of the month Iyyâr, in direct contradiction to the Greek tradition. The connection between the campaign beyond the Tigris and the Lydian war seems to me incontestable, but the Babylonian chronicler has merely recorded the events which affected Babylonia. Cyrus' object was both to intimidate Nabonidus and also to secure possession of the most direct, and at the same time the easiest, route: by cutting across Mesopotamia, he avoided the difficult marches in the mountainous districts of Armenia. Perhaps we should combine, with the information of the *Annals*, the passage of Xenophon, where it is said that the Armenians refused tribute and service to the King of Persia: Cyrus would have punished the rebels on his way, after crossing the Euphrates.

action had taken place. He therefore collected his troops together, fell upon the right bank of the Halys,[1] devastated the country, occupied Pteria and the neighbouring towns, and exiled the inhabitants to a distance. He had just completed the subjection of the White Syrians when he was met by an emissary from the Persians; Cyrus offered him his life, and confirmed his authority on condition of his pleading for mercy and taking the oath of vassalage.[2] Crœsus sent a proud refusal, which was followed by a brilliant victory, after which a truce of three months was concluded between the belligerents.[3] Cyrus employed the

[1] On this point Herodotus tells a current story of his time: Thales had a trench dug behind the army, which was probably encamped in one of the bends made by the Halys; he then diverted the stream into this new bed, with the result that the Lydians found themselves on the right bank of the river without having had the trouble of crossing it.

[2] Nicolas of Damascus records that Cyrus, after the capture of Sardes, for a short time contemplated making Crœsus a vassal king, or at least a satrap of Lydia.

[3] We have two very different accounts of this campaign, viz. that of Herodotus, and that of Polyænus. According to Herodotus, Crœsus gave battle only once in Pteria, with indecisive result, and on the next day quietly retired to his kingdom, thinking that Cyrus would not dare to pursue him. According to Polyænus, Crœsus, victorious in a first engagement owing to a more or less plausible military stratagem, consented to a truce, but on the day after was completely defeated, and obliged to return to his kingdom with a routed army. Herodotus' account of the fall of Crœsus and of Sardes, borrowed partly from a good written source, Xanthus or Charon of Lampsacus, partly from the tradition of the Harpagidæ, seems to have for its object the soothing of the vanity both of the Persians and of the Lydians, since, if the result of the war could not be contested, the issue of the battle was at least left uncertain. If he has given a faithful account, no one can understand why Crœsus should have retired and ceded White Syria to a rival who had never conquered him. The account given by Polyænus, in spite of the improbability of some of its details, comes from a well-informed author:

respite in attempting to win over the Greek cities of the littoral, which he pictured to himself as nursing a bitter hatred against the Mermnadæ; but it is to be doubted if his emissaries succeeded even in wresting a declaration of neutrality from the Milesians; the remainder, Ionians and Æolians, all continued faithful to their oaths.[1] On the resumption of hostilities, the tide of fortune turned, and the Lydians were crushed by the superior forces of the Persians and the Medes; Crœsus retired under cover of night, burning the country as he retreated, to prevent the enemy from following him, and crossed the Halys with the remains of his battalions. The season was already far advanced; he thought that the Persians, threatened in the rear by the Babylonian troops, would shrink from the prospect of a winter campaign, and he fell back upon Sardes without further lingering in Phrygia. But Nabonidus did not feel himself called upon to show the same devotion that his ally had evinced towards him, or perhaps the priests who governed in his name did not permit him to fulfil his engagements.[2] As soon as peace was proposed, he accepted terms, without once considering the danger to which the Lydians were exposed by his

the defeat of the Lydians in the second battle explains the retreat of Crœsus, who is without excuse in Herodotus' version of the affair. Pompeius Trogus adopted a version similar to that of Polyænus.

[1] Herodotus makes the attempted corruption of the Ionians to date from the beginning of the war, even before Cyrus took the field.

[2] The author followed by Pompeius Trogus has alone preserved the record of this treaty. The fact is important as explaining Crœsus' behaviour after his defeat, but Schubert goes too far when he re-establishes on this ground an actual campaign of Cyrus against Babylon: Radet has come back to the right view in seeing only a treaty made with Nabonidus.

defection. The Persian king raised his camp as soon as all fear of an attack to rearward was removed, and, falling upon defenceless Phrygia, pushed forward to Sardes in spite of the inclemency of the season. No movement could have been better planned, or have produced such startling results. Crœsus had disbanded the greater part of his feudal contingents, and had kept only his body-guard about him, the remainder of his army—natives, mercenaries, and allies—having received orders not to reassemble till the following spring. The king hastily called together all his available troops, both Lydians and foreigners, and confronted his enemies for the second time. Even under these unfavourable conditions he hoped to gain the advantage, had his cavalry, the finest in the world, been able to take part in the engagement. But Cyrus had placed in front of his lines a detachment of camels, and the smell of these animals so frightened the Lydian horses that they snorted and refused to charge.[1] Crœsus was again worsted on the confines of the plain of the Hermus, and taking refuge in the citadel of Sardes, he despatched

[1] Herodotus' mention of the use of camels is confirmed, with various readings, by Xenophon, by Polyænus, and by Ælian; their employment does not necessarily belong to a legendary form of the story, especially if we suppose that the camel, unknown before in Asia Minor, was first introduced there by the Persian army. The site of the battle is not precisely known. According to Herodotus, the fight took place in the great plain before Sardes, which is crossed by several small tributaries of the Hermus, amongst others the Hyllus. Radet recognises that the Hyllus of Herodotus is the whole or part of the stream now called the Kusu-tchai, and he places the scene of action near the township of Adala, which would correspond with Xenophon's Thymbrara. This continues to be the most likely hypothesis. After the battle Crœsus would have fled along the Hermus towards Sardes. Xenophon's story is a pure romance.

couriers to his allies in Greece and Egypt to beg for succour without delay. The Lacedæmonians hurried on the mobilisation of their troops, and their vessels were on the point of weighing anchor, when the news arrived that Sardes had fallen in the early days of December, and that Crœsus himself was a prisoner.[1]

How the town came to be taken, the Greeks themselves never knew, and their chroniclers have given several different accounts of the event.[2] The least improbable is that found in Herodotus. The blockade had lasted, so he tells us, fourteen days, when Cyrus announced that he would richly reward the first man to scale the walls. Many were tempted by his promises, but were unsuccessful in their efforts, and their failure had discouraged all further attempts, when a Mardian soldier, named Hyreades, on duty at the foot of the steep slopes overlooking the Tmolus, saw a Lydian descend from rock to rock in search of his helmet which he had lost, and regain the city by the same way without any great difficulty. He noted

[1] Radet gives the date of the capture of Sardes as about November 15, 546; but the number and importance of the events occurring between the retreat of Crœsus and the decisive catastrophe—the negotiations with Babylon, the settling into winter quarters, the march of Cyrus across Phrygia—must have required a longer time than Radet allots to them in his hypothesis, and I make the date a month later.

[2] Ctesias and Xenophon seem to depend on Herodotus, the former with additional fabulous details concerning his Œbaras, Cyrus' counsellor, which show the probable origin of his additions. Polyænus had at his disposal a different story, the same probably that he used for his account of the campaign in Cappadocia, for in it can be recognised the wish to satisfy, within possible limits, the pride of the Lydians: here again the decisive success is preceded by a check given to Cyrus and a three months' truce.

carefully the exact spot, and in company with a few
comrades climbed up till he reached the ramparts; others
followed, and taking the besieged unawares, they opened
the gates to the main body of the army.[1] Crœsus could
not bear to survive the downfall of his kingdom: he
erected a funeral pyre in the courtyard of his palace, and
took up his position on it, together with his wives, his
daughters, and the noblest youths of his court, surrounded
by his most precious possessions. He could cite the example of more than one vanquished monarch of the ancient
Asiatic world in choosing such an end, and one of the
fabulous ancestors of his race, Sandon-Herakles, had
perished after this fashion in the midst of the flames.
Was the sacrifice carried out? Everything leads us to
believe that it was, but popular feeling could not be
resigned to the idea that a prince who had shown such
liberality towards the gods in his prosperity should be
abandoned by them in the time of his direst need. They
came to believe that the Lydian monarch had expiated
by his own defeat the crime by the help of which his
ancestor Gyges had usurped the throne. Apollo had
endeavoured to delay the punishment till the next generation, that it might fall on the son of his votary, but he
had succeeded in obtaining from fate a respite of three
years only. Even then he had not despaired, and had
warned Crœsus by the voice of the oracles. They had
foretold him that, in crossing the Halys, the Lydians
would destroy a great empire, and that their power would

[1] About three and a half centuries later Sardes was captured in the
same way by one of the generals of Antiochus the Great.

last till the day when a mule should sit upon the throne of Media. Crœsus, blinded by fate, could not see that Cyrus, who was of mixed race, Persian by his father and Median by his mother, was the predicted mule. He therefore crossed the Halys, and a great empire fell, but it was his own. At all events, the god might have desired to show that to honour his altars and adorn his temple was in itself, after all, the best of treasures. "When Sardes, suffering the vengeance of Zeus, was conquered by the army of the Persians, the god of the golden sword, Apollo, was the guardian of Crœsus. When the day of despair arrived, the king could not resign himself to tears and servitude; within the brazen-walled court he erected a funeral pyre, on which, together with his chaste spouse and his bitterly lamenting daughters of beautiful locks, he mounted; he raised his hands towards the depths of the ether and cried: "Proud fate, where is the gratitude of the gods, where is the prince, the child of Leto? Where is now the house of Alyattes? . . . The ancient citadel of Sardes has fallen, the Pactolus of golden waves runs red with blood; ignominiously are the women driven from their well-decked chambers! That which was once my hated foe is now my friend, and the sweetest thing is to die!' Thus he spoke, and ordered the softly moving eunuch[1] to set fire to the wooden structure. The maidens shrieked and threw their arms around their mother, for

[1] The word translated "softly moving eunuch" is here perhaps a proper name: the slave whose duty it was to kindle the pyre was called Abrobatas in the version of the story chosen by Bacchylides, while that adopted by the potter whose work is reproduced on the opposite page, calls him Euthymos.

the death before them was that most hated by mortals. But just when the sparkling fury of the cruel fire had spread around, Zeus, calling up a black-flanked cloud, extinguished the yellow flame. Nothing is incredible of that which the will of the gods has decreed: Apollo of

CRŒSUS ON HIS PYRE.[1]

Delos, seizing the old man, bore him, together with his daughters of tender feet, into the Hyperborean land as a reward for his piety, for no mortal had sent richer offerings to the illustrious Pythô!" This miraculous ending delighted the poets and inspired many fine lines, but history could with difficulty accommodate itself to such a materialistic intervention of a divine being, and

[1] Drawn by Faucher-Gudin, from a photograph of the original in the Museum of the Louvre.

sought a less fabulous solution. The legend which appeared most probable to the worthy Herodotus did not even admit that the Lydian king took his own life; it was Cyrus who condemned him, either with a view of devoting the first-fruits of his victory to the immortals, or to test whether the immortals would save the rival whose piety had been so frequently held up to his admiration. The edges of the pyre had already taken light, when the Lydian king sighed and thrice repeated the name of Solon. It was a tardy recollection of a conversation in which the Athenian sage had stated, without being believed, that none can be accounted truly happy while they still live. Cyrus, applying it to himself, was seized with remorse or pity, and commanded the bystanders to quench the fire, but their efforts were in vain. Thereupon Crœsus implored the pity of Apollo, and suddenly the sky, which up till then had been serene and clear, became overcast; thick clouds collected, and rain fell so heavily that the burning pile was at once extinguished.[1] Well treated by his conqueror, the Lydian king is said to have become his friend and most loyal counsellor; he accepted from him the fief of Barênê in Media, often accompanied him in his campaigns, and on more than one occasion was of great service to him by the wise advice which he gave.

[1] The story told by Nicolas of Damascus comes down probably from Xanthus of Lydia, but with many additions borrowed directly from Herodotus and rhetorical developments by the author himself. Most other writers who tell the story depend for their information, either directly or indirectly, on Herodotus: in later times it was supposed that the Lydian king was preserved from the flames by the use of some talisman such as the Ephesian letters.

We may well ask what would have taken place had he gained the decisive victory over Cyrus that he hoped. Chaldæa possessed merely the semblance of her former greatness and power, and if she still maintained her hold over Mesopotamia, Syria, Phœnicia, and parts of Arabia, it was because these provinces, impoverished by the Assyrian conquest, and entirely laid waste by the Scythians, had lost the most energetic elements of their populations, and felt themselves too much enfeebled to rise against their suzerain. Egypt, like Chaldæa, was in a state of decadence, and even though her Pharaohs attempted to compensate for the inferiority of their native troops by employing foreign mercenaries, their attempts at Asiatic rule always issued in defeat, and just as the Babylonian sovereigns were unable to reduce them to servitude, so they on their part were powerless to gain an advantage over the sovereigns of Babylon. Hence Lydia, in her youth and vigour, would have found little difficulty in gaining the ascendency over her two recent allies, but beyond that she could not hope to push her success; her restricted territory, sparse population, and outlying position would always have debarred her from exercising any durable dominion over them, and though absolute mistress of Asia Minor, the countries beyond the Taurus were always destined to elude her grasp. If the Achæmenian, therefore, had confined himself, at all events for the time being, to the ancient limits of his kingdom, Egypt and Chaldæa would have continued to vegetate each within their respective area, and the triumph of Crœsus would, on the whole, have caused but little change in the actual balance of power in the East.

The downfall of Crœsus, on the contrary, marked a decisive era in the world's history. His army was the only one, from the point of numbers and organisation, which was a match for that of Cyrus, and from the day of its dispersion it was evident that neither Egypt nor Chaldæa had any chance of victory on the battle-field. The subjection of Babylon and Harrân, of Hamath, Damascus, Tyre and Sidon, of Memphis and Thebes, now became merely a question of time, and that not far distant; the whole of Asia, and that part of Africa which had been the oldest cradle of human civilisation, were now to pass into the hands of one man and form a single empire, for the benefit of the new race which was issuing forth in irresistible strength from the recesses of the Iranian table-land. It was destined, from the very outset, to come into conflict with an older, but no less vigorous race than itself, that of the Greeks, whose colonists, after having swarmed along the coasts of the Mediterranean, were now beginning to quit the seaboard and penetrate wherever they could into the interior. They had been on friendly terms with that dynasty of the Mermnadæ who had shown reverence for the Hellenic gods; they had, as a whole, disdained to

A PERSIAN KING FIGHTING WITH GREEKS.[1]

[1] Drawn by Faucher-Gudin, from an intaglio reproduced in the Antiquités du Bosphore cimmérien.

betray Crœsus, or to turn upon him when he was in difficulties beyond the Halys; and now that he had succumbed to his fate, they considered that the ties which had bound them to Sardes were broken, and they were determined to preserve their independence at all costs. This spirit of insubordination would have to be promptly dealt with and tightly curbed, if perpetual troubles in the future were to be avoided. The Asianic peoples soon rallied round their new master—Phrygians, Mysians, the inhabitants on the shores of the Black Sea, and those of the Pamphylian coast;[1] even Cilicia, which had held its own against Chaldæa, Media, and Lydia, was now brought under the rising power, and its kings were henceforward obedient to the Persian rule.[2] The two leagues of the Ionians and Æolians had at first offered to recognise Cyrus as their suzerain under the same conditions as those with which Crœsus had been satisfied; but he had consented to accept it only in the case of Miletus, and had demanded from the rest an unconditional surrender. This they had refused, and, uniting in a common cause perhaps for the first time in their existence, they had resolved to take up arms. As the Persians possessed no fleet, the Greeks had nothing to fear from the side of the Ægean, and the severity of the winter prevented any attack being made

[1] None of the documents actually say this, but the general tenor of Herodotus' account seems to show clearly that, with the exception of the Greek cities of the Carians and Lycians, all the peoples who had formed part of the Lydian dominion under Crœsus submitted, without any appreciable resistance, after the taking of Sardes.
[2] Herodotus mentions a second Syennesis king of Cilicia forty years later at the time of the Ionian revolt.

from the land side till the following spring. They meanwhile sought the aid of their mother-country, and despatched an embassy to the Spartans; the latter did not consider it prudent to lend them troops, as they would have done in the case of Crœsus, but they authorised Lakrines, one of their principal citizens, to demand of the great king

THE PRESENT SITE OF MILETUS.[1]

that he should respect the Hellenic cities, under pain of incurring their enmity. Cyrus was fully occupied with the events then taking place in the eastern regions of Iran; Babylon had not ventured upon any move after having learned the news of the fall of Sardes, but the Bactrians and the Sakæ had been in open revolt during the whole of the year that he had been detained in the extreme west,

[1] Drawn by Boudier, from a photograph.

THE SUBMISSION OF CARIA AND LYCIA

and a still longer absence might risk the loss of his prestige in Media, and even in Persia itself.[1] The threat of the Lacedæmonians had little effect upon him; he inquired as to what Sparta and Greece were, and having been informed, he ironically begged the Lacedæmonian envoy to thank his compatriots for the good advice with which they had honoured him; "but," he added, "take care that I do not soon cause you to babble, not of the ills of the Ionians, but of your own." He confided the government of Sardes to one of his officers, named Tabalos, and having entrusted Paktyas, one of the Lydians who had embraced his cause, with the removal of the treasures of Crœsus to Persia, he hastily set out for Ecbatana. He had scarcely accomplished half of his journey when a revolt broke out in his rear; Paktyas, instead of obeying his instructions, intrigued with the Ionians, and, with the mercenaries he had hired from them, besieged Tabalos in the citadel of Sardes. If the place capitulated, the entire conquest would have to be repeated; fortunately it held out, and its resistance gave Cyrus time to send its governor reinforcements, commanded by Mazares the Median. As soon as they approached the city, Paktyas, conscious that he had lost the day, took refuge at Kymê. Its inhabitants, on being summoned to deliver him up, refused, but helped him to escape to Mytilene, where the inhabitants of the island

[1] The tradition followed by Ctesias maintained that the submission of the eastern peoples was an accomplished fact when the Lydian war began. That adopted by Herodotus placed this event after the fall of Crœsus; at any rate, it showed that fear of the Bactrians and the Sakæ, as well as of the Babylonians and Egyptians was the cause that hastened Cyrus' retreat.

attempted to sell him to the enemy for a large sum of money. The Kymæans saved him a second time, and conveyed him to the temple of Athene Poliarchos at Chios. The citizens, however, dragged him from his retreat, and delivered him over to the Median general in exchange for Atarneus, a district of Mysia, the possession of which they were disputing with the Lesbians.[1] Paktyas being a prisoner, the Lydians were soon recalled to order, and Mazares was able to devote his entire energies to the reduction of the Greek cities; but he had accomplished merely the sack of Priênê,[2] and the devastation of the suburbs of Magnesia on the Mæander, when he died from some illness. The Median Harpagus, to whom tradition assigns so curious a part as regards Astyages and the infant Cyrus, succeeded him as governor of the ancient Lydian kingdom, and completed the work which he had begun. The first two places to be besieged were Phocæa and Teos, but their inhabitants preferred exile to slavery; the Phocæans sailed away to found Marseilles in the western regions of the Mediterranean, and the people of Teos settled along the coast of Thracia, near to the gold-mines of the Pangæus, and there built Abdera on the site of an ancient Clazomenian colony. The other Greek towns were either taken by assault or voluntarily opened their gates, so that

[1] A passage which has been preserved of Charon of Lampsacus sums up in a few words the account given by Herodotus of the adventures of Paktyas, but without mentioning the treachery of the islanders: he confines himself to saying Cyrus caught the fugitive after the latter had successively left Chios and Mytilene.

[2] Herodotus attributes the taking of this city to the Persian Tabules, who is evidently the Tabalos of Herodotus.

THE SUBMISSION OF CARIA AND LYCIA 83

ere long both Ionians and Æolians were, with the exception of the Samians, under Persian rule. The very position of the latter rendered them safe from attack; without a fleet they could not be approached, and the only people who could have furnished Cyrus with vessels were the Phœnicians, who were not as yet under his power. The rebellion having been suppressed in this quarter, Harpagus made a descent into Caria; the natives hastened to place themselves under the Persian yoke, and the Dorian colonies scattered along the coast, Halicarnassus, Cnidos, and the islands of Cos and Rhodes, followed their examples, but Lycia refused to yield without a struggle.

A LYCIAN CITY UPON ITS INACCESSIBLE ROCK.[1]

Its steep mountain chains, its sequestered valleys, its towns and fortresses perched on inaccessible rocks, all rendered it easy for the inhabitants to carry on a successful petty warfare against the enemy. The inhabitants of Xanthos, although very inferior in numbers, issued down into the plain and disputed the victory with the invaders for a considerable time; at length their defeat and the capitulation of their town induced the remainder of the Lycians to lay down arms, and brought about the final pacification of the peninsula. It was

[1] The rock and tombs of Tlôs, drawn by Boudier, from the view in Fellows.

parcelled out into several governorships, according to its ethnographical affinities; as for instance, the governorship of Lydia, that of Ionia, that of Phrygia,[1] and others whose names are unknown to us. Harpagus appeared to have resided at Sardes, and exercised vice-regal functions over the various districts, but he obtained from the king an extensive property in Lycia and in Caria, which subsequently caused these two provinces to be regarded as an appanage of his family.

While thus consolidating his first conquest, Cyrus penetrated into the unknown regions of the far East. Nothing would have been easier for him than to have fallen upon Babylon and overthrown, as it were by the way, the decadent rule of Nabonidus; but the formidable aspect which the empire still presented, in spite of its enfeebled condition, must have deceived him, and he was unwilling to come into conflict with it until he had made a final reckoning with the restless and unsettled peoples between the Caspian and the slopes on the Indian side of the table-land of Iran. As far as we are able to judge, they were for the most part of Iranian extraction, and had the same religion, institutions, and customs as the Medes and Persians. Tradition had already referred the origin of Zoroaster, and the scene of his preaching, to Bactriana, that land of heroes whose exploits formed the theme of Persian epic song. It is not known, as we have already had occasion to remark, by what ties it was

[1] Herodotus calls a certain Mitrobates satrap of Daskylion; he had perhaps been already given this office by Cyrus. Orœtes had been made governor of Ionia and Lydia by Cyrus.

ANNEXATION OF REGIONS EAST OF THE IRAN 85

bound to the empire of Cyaxares, nor indeed if it ever had been actually attached to it. We do not possess, unfortunately, more than almost worthless scraps of information on this part of the reign of Cyrus, perhaps the most important period of it, since then, for the first time, peoples, who had been hitherto strangers to the Asiatic world were brought within its influence. If Ctesias is to be credited, Bactriana was one of the first districts to be conquered. Its inhabitants were regarded as being among the bravest of the East, and furnished the best soldiers. They at first obtained some successes, but laid down arms on hearing that Cyrus had married a daughter of Astyages.[1] This tradition was prevalent at a time when the Achæmenians were putting forward the theory that they, and Cyrus before them, were the legitimate successors of the old Median sovereigns; they welcomed every legend which tended to justify their pretensions, and this particular one was certain to please them, since it attributed the submission of Bactriana not to a mere display of brute force, but to the recognition of an hereditary right. The annexation of this province entailed, as a matter of course, that of Margiana, of the Khoramnians,[2] and of Sogdiana. Cyrus constructed fortresses in all these districts, the most celebrated being that of Kyropolis, which commanded one of the principal fords of the Iaxartes.[3] The steppes of

[1] This is the campaign which Ctesias places before the Lydian war, but which Herodotus relegates to a date after the capture of Sardes.

[2] Ctesias must have spoken of the submission of these peoples, for a few words of a description which he gave of the Khoramnians have been preserved to us.

[3] Tomaschek identifies Kyra or Kyropolis with the present Ura-Tepe,

Siberia arrested his course on the north, but to the east, in the mountains of Chinese Turkestan, the Sakæ, who were renowned for their wealth and bravery, did not escape his ambitious designs. The account which has come down to us of his campaigns against them is a mere romance of love and adventure, in which real history plays a very small part. He is said to have attacked and defeated them at the first onset, taking their King Amorges prisoner; but this capture, which Cyrus considered a decisive advantage, was supposed to have turned the tide of fortune against him. Sparêthra, the wife of Amorges, rallied the fugitives round her, defeated the invaders in several engagements, and took so many of their men captive, that they were glad to restore her husband to her in exchange for the prisoners she had made. The struggle finally ended, however, in the subjection of the Sakæ; they engaged to pay tribute, and thenceforward constituted the advance-guard of the Iranians against the Nomads of the East. Cyrus, before quitting their neighbourhood, again ascended the table-land, and reduced Ariana, Thatagus, Harauvati, Zaranka, and the country of Cabul; and we may well ask if he found leisure to turn southwards beyond Lake Hamun and reach the shores of the Indian Ocean. One tradition, of little weight, relates that, like Alexander at a later date, he lost his army in the arid deserts of Gedrosia; the one fact that remains is that the conquest of Gedrosia was achieved, but the details of it are lost. The period covered by his campaigns

but distinguishes it from the Kyreskhata of Ptolemy, to which he assigns a site near Usgent.

was from five to six years, from 545 to 539, but Cyrus returned from these expeditions into the unknown only to plan fresh undertakings. There remained nothing now to hinder him from marching against the Chaldæans, and the discord prevailing at Babylon added to his chance of success. Nabonidus's passion for archæology had in no way lessened since the opening of his reign. The temple restorations prompted by it absorbed the bulk of his revenues. He made excavations in the sub-structures of the most ancient sanctuaries, such as Larsam, Uruk, Uru, Sippar, and Nipur; and when his digging was rewarded by the discovery of cylinders placed there by his predecessors, his delight knew no bounds. Such finds constituted the great events of his life, in comparison with which the political revolutions of Asia and Africa diminished in importance day by day. It is difficult to tell whether this indifference to the weighty affairs of government was as complete as it appears to us at this distance of time. Certain facts recorded in the official chronicles of that date go to prove that, except in name and external pomp, the king was a nonentity. The real power lay in the hands of the nobles and generals, and Bel-sharuzur, the king's son, directed affairs for them in his father's name. Nabonidus meanwhile resided in a state of inactivity at his palace of Tima, and it is possible that his condition may have really been that of a prisoner, for he never left Tima to go to Babylon, even on the days of great festivals, and his absence prevented the celebration of the higher rites of the national religion, with the procession of Bel and its accompanying ceremonies, for several consecutive years. The people suffered from these quarrels in high places; not only the native Babylonians or Kaldâ, who were thus deprived of their accustomed spectacles, and whose piety was scandalised by these dissensions, but also the foreign races dispersed over Mesopotamia, from the confluence of the Khabur to the mouths of the Euphrates. Too widely scattered or too weak to make an open delaration of their independence, their hopes and their apprehensions were alternately raised by the various reports of hostilities which reached their ears. The news of the first victories of the Persians aroused in the exiled Jews the idea of speedy deliverance, and Cyrus clearly appeared to them as the hero chosen by Jahveh to reinstate them in the country of their forefathers.

The number of the Jewish exiles, which perhaps at first had not exceeded 20,000,[1] had largely increased in the half-century of their captivity, and even if numerically they were of no great importance, their social condition entitled them to be considered as the *élite* of all Israel. There had at first been the two kings, Jehoiachin and Zedekiah, their families, the aristocracy of Judah, the priests and pontiff of the temple, the prophets,

---

[1] The body of exiles of 597 consisted of ten thousand persons, of whom seven thousand belonged to the wealthy, and one thousand to the artisan class, while the remainder consisted of people attached to the court (2 *Kings* xxiv. 14–16). In the body of 587 are reckoned three thousand and twenty-three inhabitants of Judah, and eight hundred and thirty-two dwellers in Jerusalem. But the body of exiles of 581 numbers only seven hundred and forty-five persons (*Jer.* lii. 30). These numbers are sufficiently moderate to be possibly exact, but they are far from being certain.

the most skilled of the artisan class and the soldiery. Though distributed over Babylon and the neighbouring cities, we know from authentic sources of only one of their settlements, that of Tell-Abib on the Chebar,[1] though many of the Jewish colonies which flourished thereabouts in Roman times could undoubtedly trace their origin to the days of the captivity; one legend found in the Talmud affirmed that the synagogue of Shafyâthîb, near Nehardaa, had been built by King Jehoiachin with stones brought from the ruins of the temple at Jerusalem. These communities enjoyed a fairly complete autonomy, and were free to administer their own affairs as they pleased, provided that they paid their tribute or performed their appointed labours without complaint. The shêkhs, or elders of the family or tribe, who had played so important a part in their native land, still held their respective positions; the Chaldæans had permitted them to retain all the possessions which they had been able to bring with them into exile, and recognised them as the rulers of their people, who were responsible to their conquerors for the obedience of those under them, leaving them entire liberty to exercise their authority so long as they maintained order and tranquillity among their subordinates.[2] How the latter existed, and what industries they pursued in order to earn their daily bread, no writer of the time has left

[1] *Ezek.* iii. 15. The Chebar or Kebar has been erroneously identified with the Khabur; cuneiform documents show that it was one of the canals near Nipur.

[2] Cf. the assemblies of these chiefs at the house of Ezekiel and their action (viii. 1; xiv. 1; xx. 1).

on record. The rich plain of the Euphrates differed so widely from the soil to which they had been accustomed in the land of Judah, with its bare or sparsely wooded hills, slopes cultivated in terraces, narrow and ill-watered wadys, and tortuous and parched valleys, that they must have felt themselves much out of their element in their Chaldæan surroundings. They had all of them, however, whether artisans, labourers, soldiers, gold-workers, or merchants, to earn their living, and they succeeded in doing so, following meanwhile the advice of Jeremiah, by taking every precaution that the seed of Israel should not be diminished.[1] The imagination of pious writers of a later date delighted to represent the exiled Jews as giving way to apathy and vain regrets: " By the rivers of Babylon, there we sat down, yea, we wept, when we remembered Zion. Upon the willows in the midst thereof we hanged up our harps. For there they that led us captive required of us songs, and they that wasted us required of us mirth, saying, Sing us one of the songs of Zion. How shall we sing the Lord's song in a strange land?"[2] This was true of the priests and scribes only. A blank had been made in their existence from the moment when the conqueror had dragged them from the routine of daily rites which their duties in the temple service entailed upon them. The hours which had been formerly devoted to their offices were now expended in bewailing the misfortunes of their nation, in accusing themselves and others, and in demanding what crime had merited this punishment, and why Jahveh, who had

[1] *Jer.* xxix. 1-7.   [2] *Ps.* cxxxvii. 1-4.

so often shown clemency to their forefathers, had not extended His forgiveness to them. It was, however, by the long-suffering of God that His prophets, and particularly Ezekiel, were allowed to make known to them the true cause of their downfall. The more Ezekiel in his retreat meditated upon their lot, the more did the past appear to him as a lamentable conflict between divine justice and Jewish iniquity. At the time of their sojourn in Egypt, Jahveh had taken the house of Jacob under His protection, and in consideration of His help had merely demanded of them that they should be faithful to Him. "Cast ye away every man the abominations of his eyes, and defile not yourselves with the idols of Egypt: I am the Lord your God." The children of Israel, however, had never observed this easy condition, and this was the root of their ills; even before they were liberated from the yoke of Pharaoh, they had betrayed their Protector, and He had thought to punish them: " But I wrought for My name's sake, that it should not be profaned in the sight of the nations, among whom they were, in whose sight I made myself known unto them. . . . So I caused them to go forth out of the land of Egypt, and brought them into the wilderness. And I gave them My statutes, and showed them My judgments, which if a man do, he shall live in them. Moreover also I gave them My sabbaths, to be a sign between Me and them . . . but the house of Israel rebelled against Me." As they had acted in Egypt, so they acted at the foot of Sinai, and again Jahveh could not bring Himself to destroy them; He confined Himself to decreeing that none of those who had offended Him should enter the Promised Land, and He extended His goodness to their children. But these again showed themselves no wiser than their fathers; scarcely had they taken possession of the inheritance which had fallen to them, "a land flowing with milk and honey . . . the glory of all lands," than when they beheld "every high hill and every thick tree . . . they offered there their sacrifices, and there they presented the provocation of their offering, there also they made their sweet savour, and they poured out there their drink offerings." Not contented with profaning their altars by impious ceremonies and offerings, they further bowed the knee to idols, thinking in their hearts, "We will be as the nations, as the families of the countries, to serve wood and stone." "As I live, saith the Lord God, surely with a mighty hand and with a stretched out arm, and with fury poured out, will I be King over you."[1] However just the punishment, Ezekiel did not believe that it would last for ever. The righteousness of God would not permit future generations to be held responsible for ever for the sins of generations past and present. "What mean ye, that ye use this proverb concerning the land of Israel, saying, The fathers have eaten sour grapes, and the children's teeth are set on edge? As I live, saith the Lord God, ye shall not have occasion to use this proverb any more in Israel! Behold, all souls are Mine; as the soul of the father, so also the soul of the son is Mine; the soul that sinneth it shall die. But if a man be just . . . he shall surely live, saith the Lord

[1] *Ezek.* xx.

God." Israel, therefore, was master of his own destiny. If he persisted in erring from the right way, the hour of salvation was still further removed from him; if he repented and observed the law, the Divine anger would be turned away. "Therefore ... O house of Israel ... cast away from you all your transgressions wherein ye have transgressed; and make you a new heart and a new spirit; for why will ye die, O house of Israel? For I have no pleasure in the death of him that dieth ... wherefore turn yourselves and live."[1] There were those who objected that it was too late to dream of regeneration and of hope in the future: "Our bones are dried up and our hope is lost; we are clean cut off." The prophet replied that the Lord had carried him in the spirit and set him down in the midst of a plain strewn with bones. "So I prophesied ... and as I prophesied there was a noise ... and the bones came together, bone to his bone. And I beheld, and lo, there were sinews upon them, and flesh came up and skin covered them above; but there was no breath in them. Then said (the Lord) unto me, Prophesy unto the wind, prophesy, son of man, and say to the wind, Thus saith the Lord God: Come from the four winds, O breath, and breathe upon these slain, that they may live. So I prophesied as He commanded me, and the breath came into them and they lived, and stood up upon their feet, an exceeding great army. Then He said unto me ... these bones are the whole house of Israel. ... Behold, I will open your graves and cause you to come up out of your graves, O my

[1] *Ezek.* xviii.

people; and I will bring you into the land of Israel. ...
And I will put My Spirit in you and ye shall live, and
I will place you in your own land; and ye shall know
that I the Lord hath spoken it and performed it, saith the
Lord."[1]

A people raised from such depths would require a
constitution, a new law to take the place of the old, from
the day when the exile should cease. Ezekiel would
willingly have dispensed with the monarchy, as it had been
tried since the time of Samuel with scarcely any good
results. For every Hezekiah or Josiah, how many kings of
the type of Ahaz or Manasseh had there been! The Jews
were nevertheless still so sincerely attached to the house of
David, that the prophet judged it inopportune to exclude it
from his plan for their future government. He resolved to
tolerate a king, but a king of greater piety and with less
liberty than the compiler of the Book of Deuteronomy had
pictured to himself, a servant of the servants of God, whose
principal function should be to provide the means of
worship. Indeed, the Lord Himself was the only Sovereign
whom the prophet fully accepted, though his concept of
Him differed greatly from that of his predecessors: from
that, for instance, of Amos—the Lord God who would do
nothing without revealing "His secret unto His servants
the prophets;"[2] or of Hosea—who desired "mercy, and
not sacrifice; and the knowledge of God more than burnt
offerings."[3] The Jahveh of Ezekiel no longer admitted any
intercourse with the interpreters of His will. He held
"the son of man" at a distance, and would consent to

[1] *Ezek.* xxxvii. 1–14. [2] *Amos* iii. 7. [3] *Hos.* vi. 6.

communicate with him only by means of angels who were His messengers. The love of His people was, indeed, acceptable to Him, but He preferred their reverence and fear, and the smell of the sacrifice offered according to the law was pleasing to His nostrils. The first care of the returning exiles, therefore, would be to build Him a house upon the holy mountain. Ezekiel called to mind the temple of Solomon, in which the far-off years of his youth were spent, and mentally rebuilt it on the same plan, but larger and more beautiful; first the outer court, then the inner court and its chambers, and lastly the sanctuary, the dimensions of which he calculates with scrupulous care: "And the breadth of the entrance was ten cubits; and the sides of the entrance were five cubits on the one side and five cubits on the other side: and he measured the length thereof, forty cubits; and the breadth, twenty cubits"— and so forth, with a wealth of technical details often difficult to be understood.[1] And as a building so well proportioned should be served by a priesthood worthy of it, the sons of Zadok only were to bear the sacerdotal office, for they alone had preserved their faith unshaken; the other Levites were to fill merely secondary posts, for not only had they shared in the sins of the nation, but they had shown a bad example in practising idolatry. The duties and prerogatives of each one, the tithes and offerings, the sacrifices, the solemn festivals, the preparation of the feasts,—all was foreseen and prearranged with scrupulous exactitude.[2] Ezekiel was, as we have seen, a priest; the smallest details were as dear to him as the noblest offices of

---

[1] *Ezek.* xl. 5–xlvi. 24. [2] *Ezek.* xliv. 1–xlvi. 24

his calling, and the minute ceremonial instructions as to the killing and cooking of the sacrificial animals appeared to him as necessary to the future prosperity of his people as the moral law. Towards the end, however, the imagination of the seer soared above the formalism of the sacrificing priest; he saw in a vision waters issuing out of the very threshold of the divine house, flowing towards the Dead Sea through a forest of fruit trees, "whose leaf shall not wither, neither shall the fruit thereof fail." The twelve tribes of Israel, alike those of whom a remnant still existed as well as those which at different times had become extinct, were to divide the regenerated land by lot among them—Dan in the extreme north, Reuben and Judah in the south; and they would unite to found once more, around Mount Sion, that new Jerusalem whose name henceforth was to be Jahveh-shammah, "The Lord is there."[1] The influence of Ezekiel does not seem to have extended beyond a restricted circle of admirers. Untouched by his preaching, many of the exiles still persisted in their worship of the heathen gods; most of these probably became merged in the bulk of the Chaldæan population, and were lost, as far as Israel was concerned, as completely as were the earlier exiles of Ephraim under Tiglath-pileser III. and Sargon. The greater number of the Jews, however, remained faithful to their hopes of future greatness, and applied themselves to discerning in passing events the premonitory signs of deliverance. "Like as a woman with child, that draweth near the time

[1] *Ezek.* xlvii., xlviii. The image of the river seems to be borrowed from the *vessel of water* of Chaldæan mythology.

ACCESSION OF NABONIDUS

of her delivery, is in pain, and crieth out in her pangs; so have we been before Thee, O Lord. . . . Come, my people, enter thou into thy chambers, and shut thy doors about thee: hide thyself for a little moment, until the indignation be overpast. For, behold, the Lord cometh forth out of His place to punish the inhabitants of the earth for their iniquity: the earth also shall disclose her blood, and shall no more cover her slain."[1] The condition of the people improved after the death of Nebuchadrezzar. Amil-marduk took Jehoiachin out of the prison in which he had languished for thirty years, and treated him with honour:[2] this was not as yet the restoration that had been promised, but it was the end of the persecution. A period of court intrigues followed, during which the sceptre of Nebuchadrezzar changed hands four times in less than seven years; then came the accession of the peaceful and devout Nabonidus, the fall of Astyages, and the first victories of Cyrus. Nothing escaped the vigilant eye of the prophets, and they began to proclaim that the time was at hand, then to predict the fall of Babylon, and to depict the barbarians in revolt against her, and Israel released from the yoke by the all-powerful will of the Persians. "Thus saith the Lord to His anointed, to Cyrus, whose right hand I have holden to subdue nations before him, and I will loose the loins of kings; to open the doors before him, and the gates shall not be shut; I will go before thee and make the rugged places plain: I will break in pieces the doors of brass, rend in sunder the bars of iron: and I will give thee

---

[1] An anonymous prophet, about 570, in *Isa.* xxvi. 17, 20, 21.
[2] 2 *Kings* xxv. 27-30; cf. *Jer.* lii. 31-34.

the treasures of darkness, and hidden riches of secret places, that thou mayest know that I am the Lord which call thee by thy name, even the God of Israel. For Jacob My servant's sake, and Israel My chosen, I have called thee by thy name: I have surnamed thee, though thou hast not known Me."[1] Nothing can stand before the victorious prince whom Jahveh leads: "Bel boweth down, Nebo stoopeth; their idols are upon the beasts, and upon the cattle: the things that ye carried about are made a load, a burden to the weary beast. They stoop, they bow down together; they could not deliver the burden, but themselves are gone into captivity."[2] "O virgin daughter of Babylon, sit on the ground without a throne, O daughter of the Chaldæans: for thou shalt no more be called tender and delicate. Take the millstones and grind meal: remove thy veil, strip off the train, uncover the leg, pass through the rivers. They nakedness shall be uncovered, yea, thy shame shall be seen. . . . Sit thou silent, and get thee into darkness, O daughter of the Chaldæans: for thou shalt no more be called the lady of kingdoms."[3]

The task which Cyrus had undertaken was not so difficult as we might imagine. Not only was he hailed with delight by the strangers who thronged Babylonia, but the Babylonians themselves were weary of their king, and the majority of them were ready to welcome the Persian who would rid them of him, as in old days they hailed the Assyrian kings who delivered them from their Chaldæan lords. It is possible that towards the end of his reign

---

[1] *Second Isaiah*, in *Isa.* xlv. 1-4. [2] *Second Isaiah*, in *Isa.* xlvi. 1, 2.
[3] *Second Isaiah*, in *Isa.* xlvii. 1-5.

Nabonidus partly resumed the supreme power;[1] but anxious for the future, and depending but little on human help, he had sought a more powerful aid at the hands of the gods. He had apparently revived some of the old forgotten cults, and had applied to their use revenues which impoverished the endowment of the prevalent worship of his own time. As he felt the growing danger approach, he remembered those towns of secondary grade —Uru, Uruk, Larsam, and Eridu—all of which, lying outside Nebuchadrezzar's scheme of defence, would be sacrificed in the case of an invasion: he had therefore brought away from them the most venerated statues, those in which the spirit of the divinity was more particularly pleased to dwell, and had shut them up in the capital, within the security of its triple rampart.[2] This attempt to concentrate the divine powers, accentuating as it did the supremacy of Bel-Marduk over his compeers, was doubtless flattering to his pride and that of his priests, but was ill received by the rest of the sacerdotal class and by the populace. All these divine guests had not only to be lodged, but required to be watched over, decked, fed, and fêted, together with their respective temple retinues; and the prestige and honour of the local Bel, as well as his revenues, were likely to suffer in consequence. The clamour of the gods in the celestial heights soon re-echoed

---

[1] This seems to follow from the part which he plays in the final crisis, as told in the *Cylinder of Cyrus* and in the *Annals*.

[2] The chronicler adds that the gods of Sippar, Kutha, and Borsippa were not taken to Babylon; and indeed, these cities being included within the lines of defence of the great city, their gods were as well defended from the enemy as if they had been in Babylon itself.

throughout the land; the divinities complained of their sojourn at Babylon as of a captivity in Ê-sagilla; they lamented over the suppression of their daily sacrifices, and Marduk at length took pity on them. He looked upon the countries of Sumir and Akkad, and saw their sanctuaries in ruins and their towns lifeless as corpses; "he cast his eyes over the surrounding regions; he searched them with his glance and sought out a prince, upright, after his own heart, who should take his hands. He proclaimed by name Cyrus, King of Anshân, and he called him by his name to universal sovereignty." Alike for the people of Babylon and for the exiled Jew, and also doubtless for other stranger-colonies, Cyrus appeared as a deliverer chosen by the gods; his speedy approach was everywhere expected, if not with the same impatience, at least with an almost joyful resignation. His plans were carried into action in the early months of 538, and his habitual good fortune did not forsake him at this decisive moment of his career. The immense citadel raised by Nebuchadrezzar in the midst of his empire, in anticipation of an attack by the Medes, was as yet intact, and the walls rising one behind another, the moats, and the canals and marshes which protected it, had been so well kept up or restored since his time, that their security was absolutely complete; a besieging army could do little harm—it needed a whole nation in revolt to compass its downfall. A whole nation also was required for its defence, but the Babylonians were not inclined to second the efforts of their sovereign. Nabonidus concentrated his troops at the point most threatened, in the angle comprised near Opis between the

Medic wall and the bend of the Tigris, and waited in inaction the commencement of the attack. It is supposed that Cyrus put two bodies of troops in motion: one leaving Susa under his own command, took the usual route of all Elamite invasions in the direction of the confluence of the Tigris and the Dîyala; the other commanded by Gobryas, the satrap of Gutium, followed the course of the Adhem or the Diyala, and brought the northern contingents to the rallying-place. From what we know of the facts as a whole, it would appear that the besieging force chose the neighbourhood of the present Bagdad to make a breach in the fortifications. Taking advantage of the months when the rivers were at their lowest, they drew off the water from the Diyala and the Tigris till they so reduced the level that they were able to cross on foot; they then cut their way through the ramparts on the left bank, and rapidly transported the bulk of their forces into the very centre of the enemy's position. The principal body of the Chaldæan troops were still at Opis, cut off from the capital; Cyrus fell upon them, overcame them on the banks of the Zalzallat in the early days of Tammuz, urging forward Gobryas meanwhile upon Babylon itself.[1] On the 14th of Tammuz, Nabonidus evacuated Sippar, which at once fell into the hands of the Persian outposts; on the 16th Gobryas entered Babylon without striking a blow, and Nabonidus surrendered himself a prisoner.[2] The victorious

[1] For the strategic interpretation of the events of this campaign I have generally adopted the explanations of Billerbeck. Herodotus' account with regard to the river Gyndes is probably a reminiscence of alterations made in the river-courses at the time of the attack in the direction of Bagdad.

[2] The *Cylinder of Cyrus*, l. 17, expressly says so: "Without combat or

army had received orders to avoid all excesses which would offend the people; they respected the property of the citizens and of the temples, placed a strong detachment around Ê-sagilla to protect it from plunder, and no armed soldier was allowed within the enclosure until the king had determined on the fate of the vanquished. Cyrus arrived after a fortnight had elapsed, on the 3rd of Marchesvân, and his first act was one of clemency. He prohibited all pillage, granted mercy to the inhabitants, and entrusted the government of the city to Gobryas. Belsharuzur, the son of Nabonidus, remained to be dealt with, and his energetic nature might have been the cause of serious difficulties had he been allowed an opportunity of rallying the last partisans of the dynasty around him. Gobryas set out to attack him, and on the 11th of Marchesvân succeeded in surprising and slaying him. With him perished the last hope of the Chaldæans, and the nobles and towns, still hesitating on what course to pursue, now vied with each other in their haste to tender submission. The means of securing their good will, at all events for the moment, was clearly at hand, and it was used without any delay: their gods were at once restored to them. This exodus extended over nearly two months, during Marchesvân and Adar, and on its termination a proclamation of six days of mourning, up to the 3rd of Nisân, was made for the death of Bel-sharuzur, and as an atonement for the faults of Nabonidus, after which, on the 4th of Nisân, the notables of the city were called together in the temple of

battle did Marduk make him enter Babylon." The *Annals of Nabonidus* confirm this testimony of the official account.

Nebo to join in the last expiatory ceremonies. Cyrus did not hesitate for a moment to act as Tiglath-pileser III. and most of the Sargonids had done; he "took the hands of Bel," and proclaimed himself king of the country, but in order to secure the succession, he associated his son Cambyses with himself as King of Babylon. Mesopotamia having been restored to order, the provinces in their turn transferred their allegiance to Persia; "the kings enthroned in their palaces, from the Upper Sea to the Lower, those of Syria and those who dwell in tents, brought their weighty tribute to Babylon and kissed the feet of the suzerain." Events had followed one another so quickly, and had entailed so little bloodshed, that popular imagination was quite disconcerted: it could not conceive that an empire of such an extent and of so formidable an appearance should have succumbed almost without a battle, and three generations had not elapsed before an entire cycle of legends had gathered round the catastrophe. They related how Cyrus, having set out to make war, with provisions of all kinds for his household, and especially with his usual stores of water from the river Choaspes, the only kind of which he deigned to drink, had reached the banks of the Gyndes. While seeking for a ford, one of the white horses consecrated to the sun sprang into the river, and being overturned by the current, was drowned before it could be rescued. Cyrus regarded this accident as a personal affront, and interrupted his expedition to avenge it. He employed his army during one entire summer in digging three hundred and sixty canals, and thus caused the principal arm of the stream to run dry, and he did not resume his march upon Babylon till the following spring, when the level of the water was low enough to permit of a woman crossing from one bank to the other without wetting her knees. The Babylonians at first attempted to prevent the blockade of the place, but being repulsed in their *sorties*, they retired within the walls, much to Cyrus's annoyance, for they were provisioned for several years. He therefore undertook to turn the course of the Euphrates into the Bahr-i-Nejîf, and having accomplished it, he crept into the centre of the city by the dry bed of the river. If the Babylonians had kept proper guard, the Persians would probably have been surrounded and caught like fish in a net; but on that particular day they were keeping one of their festivals, and continued their dancing and singing till they suddenly found the streets alive with the enemy.

Babylon suffered in no way by her servitude, and far from its being a source of unhappiness to her, she actually rejoiced in it; she was rid of Nabonidus, whose sacrilegious innovations had scandalised her piety, and she possessed in Cyrus a legitimate sovereign since he had "taken the hands of Bel." It pleased her to believe that she had conquered her victor rather than been conquered by him, and she accommodated herself to her Persian dynasty after the same fashion that she had in turn accustomed herself to Cossæan or Elamite, Ninevite or Chaldæan dynasties in days gone by.[1]* Nothing in or around the city was changed, and she remained what she had been since the fall of Assyria, the real capital of the regions situated between the Mediterranean and the

* See Note 1, on next page.

Zagros. It seems that none of her subjects—whether Syrians, Tyrians, Arabs, or Idumæans—attempted to revolt against their new master, but passively accepted him, and the Persian dominion extended uncontested as far as the isthmus of Suez; Cyprus even, and such of the Phœnicians as were still dependencies of Egypt, did homage to her without further hesitation. The Jews alone appeared only half satisfied, for the clemency shown by Cyrus to their oppressors disappointed their hopes and the predictions of their prophets. They had sung in anticipation of children killed before their fathers' eyes, of houses pillaged, of women violated, and Babylon, the glory of the empire and the beauty of Chaldæan pride, utterly destroyed like Sodom and Gomorrha when overthrown by Jahveh. "It shall never be inhabited, neither shall it be dwelt in from generation to generation: neither shall the Arabian pitch tent there; neither shall shepherds make their flocks to

[1] The table of the last kings of Babylon, according to the Canon of Ptolemy and the monuments, is given below—

747–733. NABONAZIR [NABONASSAR].	693–692. NIRGAL-USHEZÎB.
733–731. NABU-NADÎNZÎRU.	692–689. MUSHEZÎB-MARDUK.
731. NABU-SHUMUKÎN.	689–681. [SENNACHERIB].
731–728. UKÎNZÎR.	681–667. ESARHADDON.
728–727. PULU [TIGLATH-PILESER III.].	667–647. SHAMASH-SHUMUKÎN.
727–721. ULULAÎ [SHALMANESER V.].	647–625. KANDALANU [ASSUR-BANI-PAL].
721–709. MARDUK-ABALIDDÎNA.	625–604. NABU-BALUZUR.
709–704. SARGON.	604–561. NEBUCHADREZZAR II.
704–702. [SENNACHERIB].	561–559. AMÎL-MARDUK.
702. MARDUK-ZAKÎRSHUMU.	559–555. NERGAL-SHARUZUR.
702. MARDUK-ABALIDDÎNA.	555. LABASHI-MARDUK.
702–699. BELIBNI.	558–538. NABONIDUS.
699–693. ASSUR-NADIN-SHUMU.	

lie down there. But wild beasts of the desert shall lie there; and their houses shall be full of doleful creatures; and ostriches shall dwell there, and satyrs shall dance there. And wolves shall cry in their castles, and jackals in the pleasant palaces."[1] Cyrus, however, was seated on the throne, and the city of Nebuchadrezzar, unlike that of Sargon and Sennacherib, still continued to play her part in the world's history. The revenge of Jerusalem had not been as complete as that of Samaria, and her sons had to content themselves with obtaining the cessation of their exile. It is impossible to say whether they had contributed to the downfall of Nabonidus otherwise than by the fervency of their prayers, or if they had rendered Cyrus some service either in the course of his preparations or during his short campaign. They may have contemplated taking up arms in his cause, and have been unable to carry the project into execution owing to the rapidity with which events took place. However this may be, he desired to reward them for their good intentions, and in the same year as his victory, he promulgated a solemn edict, in which he granted them permission to return to Judah and to rebuild not only their city, but the temple of their God. The inhabitants of the places where they were living were charged to furnish them with silver, gold, materials, and cattle, which would be needed by those among them who should claim the benefits of the edict; they even had restored to them, by order of the king, what remained in the Babylonian treasury of the vessels of gold and silver which had belonged to

[1] An anonymous prophet in *Isa.* xiii. 19-22.

the sanctuary of Jahveh. The heads of the community received the favour granted to them from such high quarters, without any enthusiasm. Now that they were free to go, they discovered that they were well off at Babylon. They would have to give up their houses, their fields, their business, their habits of indifference to politics, and brave the dangers of a caravan journey of three or four months' duration, finally encamping in the midst of ruins in an impoverished country, surrounded by hostile and jealous neighbours; such a prospect was not likely to find favour with many, and indeed it was only the priests, the Levites, and the more ardent of the lower classes who welcomed the idea of the return with a touching fervour. The first detachment organised their departure in 536, under the auspices of one of the princes of the royal house, named Shauash-baluzur (Sheshbazzar), a son of Jehoiachin.[1] It comprised only a small number of families, and contained doubtless a few of the captives of Nebuchadrezzar who in their childhood had seen the temple standing and had been present at its destruction.

[1] The name which is written Sheshbazzar in the Hebrew text of the Book of Ezra (i. 9, 11; v. 14, 16) is rendered Sasabalassaros in Lucian's recension of the Septuagint, and this latter form confirms the hypothesis of Hoonacker, which is now universally accepted, that it corresponds to the Babylonian Shamash-abaluzur. It is known that Shamash becomes Shauash in Babylonian; thus Saosdukhînos comes from Shamash-shumukîn: similarly Shamash-abaluzur has become Shauash-abaluzur. Imbert has recognised Sheshbazzar, Shauash-abaluzur in the Shenazzar mentioned in 1 *Chron.* iii. 8, as being one of the sons of Jeconiah, and this identification has been accepted by several recent historians of Israel. It should be remembered that Shauash-abaluzur and Zerubbabel have long been confounded one with the other.

The returning exiles at first settled in the small towns of Judah and Benjamin, and it was not until seven months after their arrival that they summoned courage to clear the sacred area in order to erect in its midst an altar of sacrifice.[1] They formed there, in the land of their fathers, a little colony, almost lost among the heathen nations of former times—Philistines, Idumæans, Moabites, Ammonites, and the settlers implanted at various times in what had been the kingdom of Israel by the sovereigns of Assyria and Chaldæa. Grouped around the Persian governor, who alone was able to protect them from the hatred of their rivals, they had no hope of prospering, or even of maintaining their position, except by exhibiting an unshaken fidelity to their deliverers. It was on this very feeling that Cyrus mainly relied when he granted them permission to return to their native hills, and he was actuated as much by a far-seeing policy as from the promptings of instinctive generosity. It was with satisfaction that he saw in that distant province, lying on the frontier of the only enemy yet left to him in the old world, a small band, devoted perforce to his interests, and whose very existence depended entirely on that of his empire. He no doubt extended the same favour to the other exiles in Chaldæa who demanded it of him, but we do not know how many of

[1] The history of this first return from captivity is summarily set forth in *Ezra* i.; cf. v. 13–17; vi. 3–5, 15. Its authenticity has been denied: with regard to this point and the questions relating to Jewish history after the exile, the modifications which have been imposed on the original plan of this work have obliged me to suppress much detail in the text and the whole of the bibliography in the notes.

them took advantage of the occasion to return to their native countries, and this exodus of the Jews still remains, so far as we know, a unique fact. The administration continued the same as it had been under the Chaldæans; Aramæan was still the official language in the provincial dependencies, and the only change effected was the placing of Persians at the head of public offices, as in Asia Minor, and allowing them a body of troops to support their authority.[1] One great state alone remained of all those who had played a prominent part in the history of the East. This was Egypt; and the policy which her rulers had pursued since the development of the Iranian power apparently rendered a struggle with it inevitable. Amasis had taken part in all the coalitions which had as their object the perpetuation of the balance of the powers in Western Asia; he had made a treaty with Crœsus, and it is possible that his contingents had fought in the battles before Sardes; Lydia having fallen, he did all in his power to encourage Nabonidus in his resistance. As soon as he found himself face to face with Cyrus, he understood that a collision was imminent, and did his best in preparing to meet it. Even if Cyrus had forgotten the support which had been freely given to his rivals, the wealth of Egypt was in itself sufficient to attract the Persian hordes to her frontiers.

A century later, the Egyptians, looking back on the past with a melancholy retrospection, confessed that

[1] The presence of Persian troops in Asia Minor is proved by the passage in Herodotus where he says that Orœtes had with him 1000 Persians as his body-guard.

"never had the valley been more flourishing or happier than under Amasis; never had the river shown itself more beneficent to the soil, nor the soil more fertile for mankind, and the inhabitated towns might be reckoned at 20,000 in number." The widespread activity exhibited under Psammetichus II., and Apries, was redoubled under the usurper, and the quarries of Turah,[1] Silsileh,[2] Assuan, and even those of Hammamât, were worked as in the palmy days of the Theban dynasties. The island of Philæ, whose position just below the cataract attracted to it the attention of the military engineers, was carefully fortified and a temple built upon it, the materials of which were used later on in the masonry of the sanctuary of Ptolemaic times. Thebes exhibited a certain outburst of vitality under the impulse given by Ankhnasnofiribri and by Shashonqu, the governor of her palace;[3] two small chapels, built in the centre of the town, still witness to the queen's devotion to Amon, of whom she was the priestess. Wealthy private individuals did their best to emulate their sovereign's example, and made for themselves at Shêkh Abd-el-Gurnah and at Assassif those rock-hewn tombs which rival those of the best periods in their extent and the beauty of their bas-reliefs.[4] Most of the cities of the Saîd were in such a state

---

[1] A stele of his forty-fourth year still exists in the quarries of the Mokattam.

[2] According to Herodotus, it was from the quarries of Elephantinê that Amasis caused to be brought the largest blocks which he used in the building of Sais.

[3] Her tomb still exists at Deir el-Medineh, and the sarcophagus, taken from the tomb in 1833, is now in the British Museum.

[4] The most important of these tombs is that of Petenit, the father of

THE BUILDINGS OF AMASIS

of decadence that it was no longer possible to restore to them their former prosperity, but Abydos occupied too important a place in the beliefs connected with the future world, and attracted too many pilgrims, to permit of its being neglected. The whole of its ancient necropolis had been rifled by thieves during the preceding centuries, and the monuments were nearly as much buried by sand as in our own times. The dismantled fortress now known as the Shunêt ez-Zebîb served as the cemetery for the ibises of Thoth, and for the stillborn children of the sacred singing-women, while the two Memnonia of Seti and Ramses, now abandoned by their priests, had become mere objects of respectful curiosity, on which devout Egyptians or passing travellers —

AN OSIRIS STRETCHED FULL LENGTH ON THE GROUND.[1]

Phœnicians, Aramæans, Cypriots, Carians, and Greeks from Ionia and the isles—came to carve their names.[2] Amasis confided the work of general restoration to one of the principal personages of his court, Pefzââunît, Prince of Saïs, who devoted his attention chiefly to two buildings—the

Shashonqu, who was associated with Ankhnasnofiribri in the government of Thebes.

[1] Drawn by Faucher-Gudin, after Mariette. The monument is a statuette measuring only 15 centimetres in length; it has been reproduced to give an idea of the probable form of the statue seen by Herodotus.

[2] The position occupied by the graffiti on certain portions of the walls show that in these places in the temple of Seti there was already a layer of sand varying from one to three metres in depth.

great sanctuary of Osiris, which was put into good condition throughout, and the very ancient necropolis of Omm-el-Gaâb, where lay hidden the *álquhah*, one of the sepulchres of the god; he restored the naos, the table of offerings, the barques, and the temple furniture, and provided for the sacred patrimony by an endowment of fields, vineyards, palm groves, and revenues, so as to ensure to the sanctuary offerings in perpetuity. It was a complete architectural resurrection. The nomes of Middle Egypt, which had suffered considerably during the Ethiopian and Assyrian wars, had some chance of prosperity now that their lords were relieved from the necessity of constantly fighting for some fresh pretender. Horu, son of Psammetichus, Prince of the Oleander nome, rebuilt the ancient sanctuary of Harshafaîtu at Heracleopolis, and endowed it with a munificence which rivalled that of Pefzââunît at Abydos. The king himself devoted his resources chiefly to works at Memphis and in the Delta. He founded a temple of Isis at Memphis, which Herodotus described as extending over an immense area and being well worth seeing; unfortunately nothing now remains of it, nor of the recumbent colossus, sixty feet in length, which the king placed before the court of Phtah, nor of the two gigantic statues which he raised in front of the temple, one on each side of the door. Besides these architectural works, Amasis invested the funerary ceremonies of the Apis-bulls with a magnificence rarely seen before his time, and the official stelæ which he carved to the memory of the animals who died in his reign exhibit a perfection of style quite unusual. His labours at Memphis, however, were eclipsed by the

THE TWO GODDESSES OF LAW; ANI ADORING OSIRIS; THE TRIAL OF THE CONSCIENCE; TOTH AND THE FEATHER OF THE LAW.

admirable work which he accomplished at Sais. The propylæa which he added to the temple of Nit "surpassed most other buildings of the same kind, as much by their height and extent, as by the size and quality of the materials;" he had, moreover, embellished them by a fine

AMASIS IN ADORATION BEFORE THE BULL APIS.[1]

colonnade, and made an approach to them by an avenue of sphinxes. In other parts of the same building were to be seen two superb obelisks, a recumbent figure similar to that at Memphis, and a monolithic naos of rose granite brought from the quarries of Elephantinê. Amasis had a special predilection for this kind of monument. That which he erected at Thmuis is nearly twenty-three feet

[1] Drawn by Faucher-Gudin, from a photograph taken in the Louvre.

in height,[1] and the Louvre contains another example, which though smaller still excites the admiration of the

THE NAOS OF AMASIS AT THMUIS.[2]

modern visitor.[3] The naos of Sais, which amazed

[1] The exact measurements are 23½ ft. in height, 12 ft. 9 ins. in width, and 10 ft. 6 ins. in depth. The naos of Saft el-Hinneh must have been smaller, but it is impossible to determine its exact dimensions.

[2] Drawn by Boudier, from the sketch of Burton.

[3] It measures 9 ft. 7 ins. in height, 3 ft. 1 in. in width, and 3 ft. 8 ins.

Herodotus, was much larger than either of the two already mentioned, or, indeed, than any known example. Tradition states that it took two thousand boatmen three years to convey it down from the first cataract. It measured nearly thirty feet high in the interior, twenty-four feet in depth, and twelve feet in breadth; even when hollowed out to contain the emblem of the god, it still weighed nearly 500,000 kilograms. It never reached its appointed place in the sanctuary. The story goes that " the architect, at the moment when the monument had been moved as far as a certain spot in the temple, heaved a sigh, oppressed with the thought of the time expended on its transport and weary of the arduous work. Amasis overheard the sigh, and taking it as an omen, he commanded that the block should be dragged no further. Others relate that one of the overseers in charge of the work was crushed to death by the monument, and for this reason it was left standing on the spot," where for centuries succeeding generations came to contemplate it.[1]

Amasis, in devoting his revenues to such magnificent works, fully shared the spirit of the older Pharaohs, and his labours were flattering to the national vanity, even though many lives were sacrificed in their accomplishment;

in depth. It had been erected in the nome of Athribis, and afterwards taken to Alexandria about the Ptolemaic era; it was discovered under water in one of the ports of the town at the beginning of this century, and Drovetti, who recovered it, gave it to the Museum of the Louvre in 1825.

[1] The measurements given by Herodotus are so different from those of any naos as yet discovered, that I follow Kenrick in thinking that Herodotus saw the monument of Amasis lying on its side, and that he took for the height what was really the width.

but the glory which they reflected on Egypt did not have the effect of removing the unpopularity in which he was personally held. The revolution which overthrew Apries had been provoked by the hatred of the native party towards the foreigners; he himself had been the instrument by which it had been accomplished, and it would have been only natural that, having achieved a triumph in spite of the Greeks and the mercenaries, he should have wished to be revenged on them, and have expelled them from his dominions. But, as a fact, nothing of the kind took place, and Amasis, once crowned, forgot the wrongs he had suffered as an aspirant to the royal dignity : no sooner was he firmly seated on the throne, than he recalled the strangers, and showed that he had only friendly intentions with regard to them. His predecessors had received them into favour, he, in fact, showed a perfect infatuation for them, and became as complete a Greek as it was possible for an Egyptian to be. His first care had been to make a treaty with the Dorians of Cyrene, and he displayed so much tact in dealing with them, that they forgave him for the skirmish of Irasa, and invited him to act as arbitrator in their dissensions. A certain Arkesilas II. had recently succeeded the Battos who had defeated the Egyptian troops, but his suspicious temper had obliged his brothers to separate themselves from him, and they had founded further westwards the independent city of Barca. On his threatening to evict them, they sent a body of Libyans against him. Fighting ensued, and he was beaten close to the town of Leukon. He lost 7000 hoplites in the engagement, and the disaster aroused so much ill-feeling against him that Laarchos, another of his brothers, strangled him. Laarchos succeeded him amid the acclamations of the soldiery; but not long after, Eryxô and Polyarchos, the wife and brother-in-law of his victim, surprised and assassinated him in his turn. The partisans of Laarchos then had recourse to the Pharaoh, who showed himself disposed to send them help; but his preparations were suspended owing to the death of his mother. Polyarchos repaired to Egypt before the royal mourning was ended, and pleaded his cause with such urgency that he won over the king to his side; he obtained the royal investiture for his sister's child, who was still a minor, Battos III., the lame, and thus placed Cyrene in a sort of vassalage to the Egyptian crown.[1] The ties which connected the two courts were subsequently drawn closer by marriage; partly from policy and partly from a whim, Amasis espoused a Cyrenian woman named Ladikê, the daughter, according to some, of Arkesilas or of Battos, according to others,

---

[1] Herodotus narrates these events without mentioning Amasis, and Nicolas of Damascus adopted Herodotus' account with certain modifications taken from other sources. The intervention of Amasis is mentioned only by Plutarch and by Polyænus; but the record of it had been handed down to them by some more ancient author—perhaps by Akesandros; or perhaps, in the first instance, by Hellanicos of Lesbos, who gave a somewhat detailed account of certain points in Egyptian history. The passage of Herodotus is also found incorporated in accounts of Cyrenian origin: his informants were interested in recalling deeds which reflected glory on their country, like the defeat of Apries at Irasa, but not in the memory of events so humiliating for them as the sovereign intervention of Pharaoh only a few years after this victory. And besides, the merely pacific success which Amasis achieved was not of a nature to leave a profound mark on the Egyptian mind. It is thus easy to explain how it was that Herodotus makes no allusion to the part played by Egypt in this affair.

of a wealthy private individual named Kritobulos.[1] The Greeks of Europe and Asia Minor fared no less to their own satisfaction at his hand than their compatriots in Africa; following the example of his ally Crœsus, he entered into relations with their oracles on several occasions, and sent them magnificent presents. The temple of Delphi having been burnt down in 548, the Athenian family of the Alcmæonides undertook to rebuild it from the ground for the sum of three hundred talents, of which one-fourth was to be furnished by the Delphians. When these, being too poor to pay the sum out of their own resources, made an appeal to the generosity of other friendly powers, Amasis graciously offered them a thousand talents of Egyptian alum, then esteemed the most precious of all others. Alum was employed in dyeing, and was an expensive commodity in the markets of Europe; the citizens of Delphi were all the more sensible of Pharaoh's generosity, since the united Greeks of the Nile valley contributed only twenty *minæ* of the same mineral as their quota. Amasis erected at Cyrene a statue of his wife Ladikê, and another of the goddess Neît, gilded from head to foot, and to these he added his own portrait, probably painted on a wooden panel.[2] He gave to Athene of Lindos two stone statues and a corselet of linen of marvellous

---

[1] The very fact of the marriage is considered by Wiedemann as a pure legend, but there is nothing against its authenticity; the curious story of the relations of the woman with Amasis told by the Cyrenian commentators is the only part which need be rejected.

[2] The text of Herodotus can only mean a painted panel similar to those which have been found on the mummies of the Græco-Roman era in the Fayum.

fineness;¹ and Hera of Samos received two wooden statues, which a century later Herodotus found still intact. The Greeks flocked to Egypt from all quarters of the world in such considerable numbers that the laws relating to them had to be remodelled in order to avoid conflicts with the natives.

The townships founded a century earlier along the Pelusiac arm of the Nile had increased still further since the time of Necho, and to their activity was attributable the remarkable prosperity of the surrounding region. But the position which they occupied on the most exposed side of Egypt was regarded as permanently endangering the security of the country : her liberty would be imperilled should they revolt during a war with the neighbouring empire, and hand over the line of defence which was garrisoned by them to the invader. Amasis therefore dispossessed their inhabitants, and transferred them to Memphis and its environs. The change benefited him in two ways, for, while securing himself from possible treason, he gained a faithful guard for himself in the event of risings taking place in his turbulent capital. While he thus distributed these colonists of ancient standing to his best interests, he placed those of quite recent date in the part of the Delta furthest removed from Asia, where surveillance was most easy, in the triangle, namely, lying

[1] It seems that one of these statues is that which, after being taken to Constantinople, was destroyed in a fire in 476 A.D. Fragments of the corselet still existed in the first century of our era, but inquisitive persons used to tear off pieces to see for themselves whether, as Herodotus assures us, each thread was composed of three hundred and sixty-five strands, every one visible with the naked eye.

to the west of Sais, between the Canopic branch of the Nile, the mountains, and the sea-coast. The Milesians had established here some time previously, on a canal connected with the main arm of the river, the factory of Naucratis, which long remained in obscurity, but suddenly developed at the beginning of the XXVIth dynasty, when Sais became the favourite residence of the Pharaohs. This town Amasis made over to the Greeks so that they might make it the commercial and religious centre of their communities in Egypt. Temples already existed there, those of Apollo and Aphrodite, together with all the political and religious institutions indispensable to the constitution of an Hellenic city; but the influx of immigrants was so large and rapid, that, after the lapse of a few years, the entire internal organism and external aspect of the city were metamorphosed. New buildings rose from the ground with incredible speed —the little temple of the Dioskuri, the protectors of the sailor, the temple of the Samian Hera, that of Zeus of

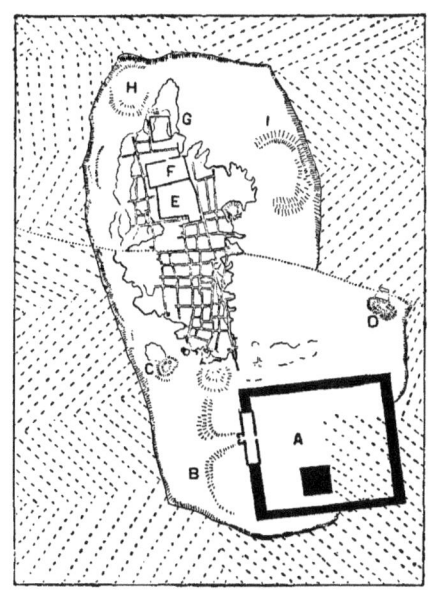

THE PRESENT SITE OF NAUCRATIS.[1]

---

[1] Reduced by Faucher-Gudin from the plan published by Petrie. The site of the Hellenion is marked A, the modern Arab village B, the temenos of Hera and Apollo E, that of the Dioskuri F, and that of Aphrodite G.

Ægina, and that of Athene;[1] ere long the great temenos, the Hellenion, was erected at the public expense by nine Æolian, Ionian, and Dorian towns of Asia Minor, to serve as a place of assembly for their countrymen, as a storehouse, as a sanctuary, and, if need be, even as a refuge and fortress, so great was its area and so thick its walls.[2] It was not possible for the constitution of Naucratis to be very homogeneous, when a score of different elements assisted in its composition. It appears to have been a compromise between the institutions of the Dorians and those of the Ionians. Its supreme magistrates were called timuchi, but their length of office and functions are alike unknown to us. The inspectors of the emporia and markets could be elected only by the citizens of the nine towns, and it is certain that the chief authority was not entirely in the hands either of the timuchi or the inspectors; perhaps each quarter of the town had its council taken from among the oldest residents. A prytanæum was open to all comers where assemblies and banquets were held on feast-days; here were celebrated at the public expense the festivals of Dionysos and Apollo Komæos. Amasis made the city a free port, accessible at all times to whoever should present themselves with peaceable intent, and the privileges which he granted naturally brought about the closing of all the other seaports of Egypt. When a

[1] The temple of Athene, the Nit of the Saite nome, is as yet known only by an inscription in Petrie.

[2] The site has been rediscovered by Petrie at the southern extremity of and almost outside the town; the walls were about 48 feet thick and 39 feet high, and the rectangular area enclosed by them could easily contain fifty thousand men.

Greek ship, pursued by pirates, buffeted by storms, or disabled by an accident at sea, ran ashore at some prohibited spot on the coast, the captain had to appear before the nearest magistrate, in order to swear that he had not violated the law wilfully, but from the force of circumstances. If his excuse appeared reasonable, he was permitted to make his way to the mouth of the Canopic branch of the Nile; but when the state of the wind or tide did not allow of his departure, his cargo was transferred to boats of the locality, and sent to the Hellenic settlement by the canals of the Delta. This provision of the law brought prosperity to Naucratis; the whole of the commerce of Egypt with the Greek world passed through her docks, and in a few years she became one of the wealthiest emporia of the Mediterranean. The inhabitants soon overflowed the surrounding country, and covered it with villas and townships. Such merchants as refused to submit to the rule of their own countrymen found a home in some other part of the valley which suited them, and even Upper Egypt and the Libyan desert were subject to their pacific inroads. The Milesians established depôts in the ancient city of Abydos;[1] the Cypriots and Lesbians, and the people of Ephesus, Chios, and Samos, were scattered over the islands formed by the network of canals and arms of the Nile, and delighted in giving

---

[1] In Stephen of Byzantium the name of the town is said to be derived from that of the Milesian Abydos who founded it, probably on the testimony of Aristagoras. Letronne has seen that the historian meant a factory established by the Milesians probably in the reign of Amasis, at the terminus of the route leading to the Great Oasis.

them the names of their respective countries;[1] Greeks of diverse origin settled themselves at Neapolis, not far from Panopolis; and the Samians belonging to the Æschrionian tribe penetrated as far as the Great Oasis; in fact, there was scarcely a village where Hellenic traders were not found, like the *bakals* of to-day, selling wine, perfumes, oil, and salted provisions to the natives, practising usury in all its forms, and averse from no means of enriching themselves as rapidly as possible. Those who returned to their mother-country carried thither strange tales, which aroused the curiosity and cupidity of their fellow-citizens; and philosophers, merchants, and soldiers alike set out for the land of wonders in pursuit of knowledge, wealth, or adventures. Amasis, ever alert upon his Asiatic frontier, and always anxious to strengthen himself in that quarter against a Chaldæan or Persian invasion, welcomed them with open arms: those who remained in the country obtained employment about his person, while such as left it not to return, carried away with them the memory of his kindly treatment, and secured for him in Hellas alliances of which he might one day stand in need. The conduct of Amasis was politic, but it aroused the ill-feeling of his subjects against him. Like the Jews under Hezekiah, the Babylonians under Nabonidus, and all other decadent races threatened by ruin, they attributed their decline, not to their own vices, but to the machinations

---

[1] The compiler confines himself to stating that there were in the Nile islands called Ephesus, Chios, Samos, Lesbos, Cyprus, and so on; the explanation I have given in the text accounts for this curious fact quite simply.

of an angry god, and they looked on favours granted to strangers as a sacrilege. Had not the Greeks brought their divinities with them? Did they not pervert the simple country-folk, so that they associated the Greek religion with that of their own country? Money was scarce; Amasis had been obliged to debit the rations and pay of his mercenaries to the accounts of the most venerated Egyptian temples—those of Sais, Heliopolis, Bubastis, and Memphis; and each of these institutions had to rebate so much per cent. on their annual revenues in favour of the barbarians, and hand over to them considerable quantities of corn, cattle, poultry, stuffs, woods, perfumes, and objects of all kinds. The priests were loud in their indignation, the echo of which still rang in the ears of the faithful some centuries later, and the lower classes making common cause with their priests, a spirit of hatred was roused among the populace as bitter as that which had previously caused the downfall of Apries. As the fear of the army prevented this feeling from manifesting itself in a revolt, it found expression in the secret calumnies which were circulated against the king, and misrepresented the motives of all his actions. Scores of malicious stories were repeated vilifying his character. It was stated that before his accession he was much addicted to eating and drinking, but that, suffering from want of money, he had not hesitated in procuring what he wished for by all sorts of means, the most honest of which had been secret theft. When made king, he had several times given way to intoxication to such an extent as to be incapable of attending to public business; his ministers were then obliged to relate moral tales to him to bring him to a state of reason. Many persons having taunted him with his low extraction, he had caused a statue of a divinity to be made out of a gold basin in which he was accustomed to wash his feet, and he had exposed it to the adoration of the faithful. When it had been worshipped by them for some time, he revealed the origin of the idol, and added "that it had been with himself as with the foot-pan. . . . If he were a private person formerly, yet now he had come to be their king, and so he bade them honour and reverence him." Towards the middle and end of his reign he was as much detested as he had been beloved at the outset.

He had, notwithstanding, so effectively armed Egypt that the Persians had not ventured to risk a collision with her immediately after their conquest of Babylon. Cyrus had spent ten years in compassing the downfall of Nabonidus, and, calculating that that of Amasis would require no less a period of time, he set methodically to work on the organisation of his recently acquired territory; the cities of Phœnicia acknowledged him as their suzerain, and furnished him with what had hitherto been a coveted acquisition, a fleet. These preliminaries had apparently been already accomplished, when the movements of the barbarians suddenly made his presence in the far East imperative. He hurried thither, and was mysteriously lost to sight (529). Tradition accounts for his death in several ways. If Xenophon is to be credited, he died peaceably on his bed, surrounded by his children, and edifying those present by his wisdom and his almost superhuman resignation.[1] Berosus tells us that he was killed in a campaign against the Dahæ; Ctesias states that, having been wounded in a skirmish with the Derbikes, one of the savage tribes of Bactriana, he succumbed to his injuries three days after the engagement. According to the worthy Herodotus, he asked the hand of Tomyris, Queen of the Massagetæ, in marriage, and was refused with disdain. He declared war against her to avenge his wounded vanity, set out to fight with her beyond the Araxes, in the steppes of Turkestan, defeated the advance-guard of cavalry, and took prisoner the heir to the crown, Spargapises, who thereupon ran himself through with his sword. "Then Tomyris collected all the forces of her kingdom, and gave him (Cyrus) battle. Of all the combats in which barbarians have engaged among themselves, I reckon this to have been the fiercest. The following, as I understand, was the manner of it:—First, the two armies stood apart and shot their arrows at each other; then, when their quivers were empty, they closed and fought hand to hand with lances and daggers; and thus they continued fighting for a length of time, neither choosing to give ground. At length the Massagetæ prevailed. The greater part of the army of the Persians was destroyed. Search was made among the slain by order of the queen for the body of Cyrus; and when it was found, she took a skin, and, filling it full of human blood, she dipped the head of Cyrus in the gore, saying, as

---

[1] A similar legend, but later in date, told how Cyrus, when a hundred years old, asked one day to see his friends. He was told that his son had had them all put to death: his grief at the cruelty of Cambyses caused his death in a few days.

she thus insulted the corse, 'I live and have conquered thee in fight, and yet by thee am I ruined, for thou tookest my son with guile; but thus I make good my threat, and give thee thy fill of blood.'" The engagement was not as serious as the legend would have us believe, and the growth of the Persian power was in no way affected by it. It cost Cyrus his life, but his army experienced no serious disaster, and his men took the king's body and brought it to Pasargadæ. He had a palace there, the remains of which can still be seen on the plain of Murgâb. The edifice was unpretentious, built upon a rectangular plan, with two porches of four columns on the longer sides, a lateral chamber at each of the four angles, and a hypostyle hall in the centre, divided lengthways by two rows of columns which supported the roof. The walls were decorated with bas-reliefs, and wherever the inscriptions have not been destroyed, we can read in cuneiform characters in the three languages which thenceforward formed the official means of communication of the empire—Persian, Medic, and Chaldæan—the name, title, and family of the royal occupant. Cyrus himself is represented in a standing posture on the pilasters, wearing a costume in which Egyptian and Assyrian features are curiously combined. He is clothed from neck to ankle in the close-fitting fringed tunic of the Babylonian and Ninevite sovereigns; his feet are covered with laced boots, while four great wings, emblems of the supreme power, overshadow his shoulders and loins, two of them raised in the air, the others pointing to the earth; he wears on his head the Egyptian skull-cap, from which rises one of the most complicated head-dresses of the royal wardrobe of the Pharaohs. The monarch raises his right hand with the gesture of a man speaking to an assembled people, and as if repeating the legend traced above his image: "I am Cyrus, the king, the Achæmenian." He was buried not far off, in

CYRUS THE ACHÆMENIAN.[1]

the monumental tomb which he had probably built for himself in a square enclosure, having a portico on three of its sides; a small chamber, with a ridge roof, rises from a base composed of six receding steps, so arranged as to appear of unequal height. The doorway is narrow, and so low that a man of medium statue finds some difficulty in entering. It is surmounted by a hollow moulding, quite Egyptian in style, and was closed by a two-leaved stone door. The golden coffin rested on a couch of the same metal, covered with precious stuffs; and a circular table, laden with drinking-vessels and ornaments enriched with precious stones, completed the furniture of the chamber. The body of the conqueror remained undisturbed on this

[1] Drawn by Boudier, from the photograph by Dieulafoy.

spot for two centuries under the care of the priests; but while Alexander was waging war on the Indian frontier, the Greek officers, to whom he had entrusted the government of Persia proper, allowed themselves to be tempted by the enormous wealth which the funerary chapel was

THE TOMB OF CYRUS.[1]

supposed to contain. They opened the coffin, broke the couch and the table, and finding them too heavy to carry away easily, they contented themselves with stealing the drinking-vessels and jewels. Alexander on his return visited the place, and caused the entrance to be closed with a slight wall of masonry; he intended to restore the monument to its former splendour, but he himself perished

[1] Drawn by Faucher-Gudin, from the heliogravure of Dieulafoy.

shortly after, and what remained of the contents probably soon disappeared. After the death of Cyrus, popular imagination, drawing on the inexhaustible materials furnished by his adventurous career, seemed to delight in making him the ideal of all a monarch should be; they attributed to him every virtue—gentleness, bravery, moderation, justice, and wisdom. There is no reason to doubt that he possessed the qualities of a good general—activity, energy, and courage, together with the astuteness and the duplicity so necessary to success in Asiatic conquest—but he does not appear to have possessed in the same degree the gifts of a great administrator. He made no changes in the system of government which from the time of Tiglath-pileser III. onwards had obtained among all Oriental sovereigns; he placed satraps over the towns and countries of recent acquisition, at Sardes and Babylon, in Syria and Palestine, but without clearly defining their functions or subjecting them to a supervision sufficiently strict to ensure the faithful performance of their duties. He believed that he was destined to found a single empire in which all the ancient empires were to be merged, and he all but carried his task to a successful close: Egypt alone remained to be conquered when he passed away.

His wife Kassandanê, a daughter of Pharnaspes, and an Achæmenian like himself, had borne him five children; two sons, Cambyses[1] and Smerdis,[2] and three daughters,

[1] The Persian form of the name rendered Kambyses by the Greeks was Kâbuzîyâ or Kambuzîya. Herodotus calls him the son of Kassandanê, and the tradition which he has preserved is certainly authentic. Ctesias has

Atossa, Roxana, and Artystonê.¹ Cambyses was probably born about 558, soon after his father's accession, and he was his legitimate successor, according to the Persian custom which assigned the crown to the eldest of the sons born in the purple. He had been associated, as we have seen, in the Babylonian regal power immediately after the victory over Nabonidus, and on the eve of his departure for the fatal campaign against the Massagetæ his father, again in accordance with the Persian law, had appointed him regent. A later tradition, preserved by Ctesias, relates that on this occasion the territory had been divided between the two sons: Smerdis, here called Tanyoxarkes, having received as his share Bactriana, the Khoramnians, the Parthians, and the Carmanians, under the suzerainty of his brother. Cambyses, it is clear, inherited the whole

erroneously stated that his mother was Amytis, the daughter of Astyages, and Dinon, also erroneously, the Egyptian women Nitêtis; Diodorus Siculus and Strabo make him the son of Meroê.

² The original form was Bardiya or Barzîya, "the laudable," and the first Greek transcript known, in Æschylus, is Mardos, or, in the scholiasts on the passage, Merdias, which has been corrupted into Marphios by Hellanikos and into Merges by Pompeius Trogus. The form Smerdis in Herodotus, and in the historians who follow him, is the result of a mistaken assimilation of the Persian name with the purely Greek one of Smerdis or Smerdies.

¹ Herodotus says that Atossa was the daughter of Kassandanê, and the position which she held during three reigns shows that she must have been so; Justi, however, calls her the daughter of Amytis. A second daughter is mentioned by Herodotus, the one whom Cambyses killed in Egypt by a kick; he gives her no name, but she is probably the same as the Roxana who according to Ctesias bore a headless child. The youngest, Artystonê, was the favourite wife of Darius. Josephus speaks of a fourth daughter of Cyrus called Meroê, but without saying who was the mother of this princess.

empire, but intrigues gathered round Smerdis, and revolts broke out in the provinces, incited, so it was said, whether rightly or wrongly, by his partisans.[1] The new king was possessed of a violent, merciless temper, and the Persians subsequently emphasised the fact by saying that Cyrus had been a father to them, Cambyses a master. The rebellions were repressed with a vigorous hand, and finally Smerdis disappeared by royal order, and the secret of his fate was so well kept, that it was believed, even by his mother and sisters, that he was merely imprisoned in some obscure Median fortress.[2] The ground being cleared of his rival, and

[1] Herodotus speaks of peoples subdued by Cambyses in Asia, and this allusion can only refer to a revolt occurring after the death of Cyrus, before the Egyptian expedition; these troubles are explicitly recorded in Xenophon.

[2] The inscription of Behistun says distinctly that Cambyses had his brother Bardiya put to death before the Egyptian expedition; on the other hand, Herodotus makes the murder occur during the Egyptian expedition and Ctesias after this expedition. Ctesias' version of the affair adds that Cambyses, the better to dissimulate his crime, ordered the murderer Sphendadates to pass himself off as Tanyoxarkes, as there was a great resemblance between the two: Sphendadates—the historian goes on to say—was exiled to Bactriana, and it was not until five years afterwards that the mother of the two princes heard of the murder and of the substitution. These additions to the story are subsequent developments suggested by the traditional account of the Pseudo-Smerdis. In recent times several authorities have expressed the opinion that all that is told us of the murder of Smerdis and about the Pseudo-Smerdis is merely a legend, invented by Darius or those about him in order to justify his usurpation in the eyes of the people: the Pseudo-Smerdis would be Smerdis himself, who revolted against Cambyses, and was then, after he had reigned a few months, assassinated by Darius. Winckler acknowledges "that certainty is impossible in such a case;" and, in reality, all ancient tradition is against his hypothesis, and it is best to accept Herodotus' account, with all its contradictions, until contemporaneous documents enable us to decide what to accept and what to reject in it

affairs on the Scythian frontier reduced to order, Cambyses took up the projects against Egypt at the exact point at which his predecessor had left them. Amasis, who for ten years had been expecting an attack, had taken every precaution in his power against it, and had once more patiently begun to make overtures of alliance with the Hellenic cities; those on the European continent did not feel themselves so seriously menaced as to consider it to their interest to furnish him with any assistance, but the Greeks of the independent islands, with their chief, Polycrates, tyrant of Samos, received his advances with alacrity. Polycrates had at his disposal a considerable fleet, the finest hitherto seen in the waters of the Ægean, and this, combined with the Egyptian navy, was not any too large a force to protect the coasts of the Delta, now that the Persians had at their disposition not only the vessels of the Æolian and Ionian cities, but those of Phœnicia and Cyprus. A treaty was concluded, bringing about an exchange of presents and amenities between the two princes which lasted as long as peace prevailed, but was ruptured at the critical moment by the action of Polycrates, though not actually through his own fault. The aristocratic party, whose chiefs were always secretly plotting his overthrow, had given their adherence to the Persians, and their conduct became so threatening about the time of the death of Cyrus, that Polycrates had to break his engagements with Egypt in order to avert a catastrophe.[1] He made a treaty with

---

[1] Herodotus laid the blame for the breach of the treaty to the King of Egypt, and attributed to his fear of the constant good fortune of Polycrates.

the Persian king, and sent a squadron of forty galleys to join the fleet then being equipped in the Phœnician ports.[1] Amasis, therefore, when war at last broke out, found himself left to face the enemy alone. The struggle was inevitable, and all the inhabitants of the eastern coasts of the Mediterranean had long foreseen its coming. Without taking into consideration the danger to which the Persian empire and its Syrian provinces were exposed by the proximity of a strong and able power such as Egypt, the hardy and warlike character of Cambyses would naturally have prompted him to make an attempt to achieve what his predecessors, the warrior-kings of Nineveh and Babylon, had always failed to accomplish successfully. Policy ruled his line of action, and was sufficient to explain it, but popular imagination sought other than the very natural causes which had brought the most ancient and most recent of the great empires of the world into opposition; romantic reasons were therefore invented to account for the great drama which was being enacted, and the details supplied varied considerably, according as the tradition was current in Asia or Africa. It was said that a physician lent to Cyrus by Amasis, to treat him for an affection of the eyes, was the cause of all the evil. The unfortunate man, detained at Susa and chafing at his exile, was

The latter's accession to power is fixed at about the year 540 by some, by others in the year 537, or in the year 533–2; his negotiations with Amasis must be placed somewhere during the last fifteen years of the Pharaoh.

[1] Herodotus records two opposing traditions: one that the Samians joined in the Egyptian campaign, the other that they went only as far as the neighbourhood of Karpathos.

said to have advised Cambyses to ask for the daughter of Pharaoh in marriage, hoping either that Amasis would grant the request, and be dishonoured in the eyes of his subjects for having degraded the solar race by a union with a barbarian, or that he would boldly refuse, and thus arouse the hatred of the Persians against himself. Amasis, after a slight hesitation, substituted Nitêtis, a daughter of Apries, for his own child. It happened that one day in sport Cambyses addressed the princess by the name of her supposed father, whereupon she said, "I perceive, O king, that you have no suspicion of the way in which you have been deceived by Amasis; he took me, and having dressed me up as his own daughter, sent me to you. In reality I am the daughter of Apries, who was his lord and master until the day that he revolted, and, in concert with the rest of the Egyptians, put his sovereign to death." The deceit which Cambyses thus discovered had been put upon him irritated him so greatly as to induce him to turn his arms against Egypt. So ran the Persian account of the tale, but on the banks of the Nile matters were explained otherwise. Here it was said that it was to Cyrus himself that Nitêtis had been married, and that she had borne Cambyses to him; the conquest had thus been merely a revenge of the legitimate heirs of Psammetichus upon the usurper, and Cambyses had ascended the throne less as a conqueror than as a Pharaoh of the line of Apries. It was by this childish fiction that the Egyptians in their decadence consoled themselves before the stranger for their loss of power. Always proud of their ancient prowess, but incapable of imitating the deeds of their forefathers, they none the less pretended that they could neither be vanquished nor ruled except by one of themselves, and the story of Nitêtis afforded complete satisfaction to their vanity. If Cambyses were born of a solar princess, Persia could not be said to have imposed a barbarian king upon Egypt, but, on the contrary, that Egypt had cleverly foisted her Pharaoh upon Persia, and through Persia upon half the universe.

One obstacle still separated the two foes—the desert and the marshes of the Delta. The distance between the outposts of Pelusium and the fortress of Ienysos[1] on the Syrian frontier was scarcely fifty-six miles, and could be crossed by an army in less than ten days.[2] Formerly the width of this strip of desert had been less, but the Assyrians, and after them the Chaldæans, had vied with each other in laying waste the country, and the absence of any settled population now rendered the transit difficult. Cambyses had his head-quarters at Gaza, at the extreme limit of his own dominions,[3] but he was at a loss how to face this solitary region without incurring the risk of seeing half his men buried beneath its sands, and his uncertainty was delaying his departure when a stroke of fortune

[1] The Ienysos of Herodotus is now Khân Yunes.

[2] In 1799, Napoleon's army left Kattiyeh on the 18th of Pluviose, and was at Gaza on the 7th of Ventose, after remaining from the 21st to the 30th of Pluviose before El-Arish besieging that place.

[3] This seems to follow from the tradition, according to which Cambyses left his treasures at Gaza during the Egyptian campaign, and the town was thence called *G*aza, "the treasury." The etymology is false, but the fact that suggested it is probably correct, considering the situation of Gaza and the part it must necessarily play in an invasion of Egypt.

relieved him from his difficulty. Phanes of Halicarnassus, one of the mercenaries in the service of Egypt, a man of shrewd judgment and an able soldier, fell out with Amasis for some unknown reason, and left him to offer his services to his rival. This was a serious loss for Egypt, since Phanes possessed considerable authority over the mercenaries, and was better versed in Egyptian affairs than any other person. He was pursued and taken within sight of the Lycian coast, but he treated his captors to wine and escaped from them while they were intoxicated. He placed Cambyses in communication with the shêkh of the scattered tribes between Syria and the Delta. The Arab undertook to furnish the Persian king with guides, as one of his predecessors had done in years gone by for Esarhaddon, and to station relays of camels laden with water along the route that the invading army was to follow. Having taken these precautions, Cambyses entrusted the cares of government and the regulation of his household to Oropastes,[1] one of the Persian magi, and gave the order to

[1] Herodotus calls this individual Patizeithes, and Dionysius of Miletus, who lived a little before Herodotus, gives Panzythes as a variant of this name: the variant passed into the Syncellus as Pauzythes, but the original form Patikhshâyathiya is a title signifying *viceroy*, *regent*, or *minister*, answering to the modern Persian *Padishah:* Herodotus, or the author he quotes, has taken the name of the office for that of the individual. On the other hand, Pompeius Trogus, who drew his information from good sources, mentions, side by side with Cometes or Gaumata, his brother Oropastes, whose name Ahura-upashta is quite correct, and may mean, *Him whom Ahura helps*. It is generally admitted that Pompeius Trogus, or rather Justin, has inverted the parts they played, and that his Cometes is the Pseudo-Smerdis, and not, as he says, Oropastes; it was, then, the latter who was the usurper's brother, and it is his name of Oropastes which should be substituted for that of the Patizeithes of Herodotus.

march forward. On arriving at Pelusium, he learned that his adversary no longer existed. Amasis had died after a short illness, and was succeeded by his son Psammetichus III. This change of command, at the most critical moment, was almost in itself a disaster. Amasis, with his consummate experience of men and things, his intimate knowledge of the resources of Egypt, his talents as a soldier and a general, his personal prestige, his Hellenic leanings, commanded the confidence of his own men and the respect of foreigners; but what could be expected of his unknown successor,[1] and who could say whether he were equal to the heavy task which fate had assigned to him? The whole of the Nile valley was a prey to gloomy presentiment. Egypt was threatened not only, as

PSAMMETICHUS III.[2]

---

[1] Psammetichus III. has left us very few monuments, which is accounted for by the extreme shortness of his reign. For the same reason doubtless several writers of classical times have ignored his existence, and have made the conquest of Egypt take place under Amasis. Ctesias calls the Pharaoh Amyrtæus, and gives the same name to those who rebelled against the Persians in his own time, and he had an account of the history of the conquest entirely different from that of Herodotus.

[2] Drawn by Boudier, from a photograph of the original in the Louvre.

in the previous century, by the nations of the Tigris and Euphrates, but all Asia, from the Indus to the Hellespont, was about to fall on her to crush her. She was destitute of all human help and allies, and the gods themselves appeared to have forsaken her. The fellahîn, inspired with vague alarm, recognised evil omens in all around them. Rain is rare in the Thebaid, and storms occur there only twice or three times in a century: but a few days after the accession of Psammetichus, a shower of fine rain fell at Thebes, an event, so it was stated with the exaggeration characteristic of the bearers of ill news, which had never before occurred.[1] Pharaoh hastened to meet the invader with all the men, chariots, and native bowmen at his disposal, together with his Libyan and Cyrenæan auxiliaries, and the Ionians, Carians, and Greeks of the isles and mainland. The battle took place before Pelusium, and was fought on both sides with brave desperation, since defeat meant servitude for the Egyptians, and for the Persians, cut off by the desert from possible retreat, captivity or annihilation. Phanes had been obliged to leave his children behind him, and Pharaoh included them in his suite, to serve, if needful, as hostages. The Carians

---

[1] The inhabitants of the Said have, up to our own time, always considered rain in the valley as an ill-omened event. They used to say in the beginning of the nineteenth century, when speaking of Napoleon's expedition, "We knew that misfortune threatened us, because it rained at Luxor shortly before the French came." Wilkinson assures us that rain is not so rare at Thebes as Herodotus thought: he speaks of five or six showers a year, and of a great storm on an average every ten years. But even he admits that it is confined to the mountain district, and does not reach the plain: I never heard of rain at Luxor during the six winters that I spent in Upper Egypt.

and Ionians, who felt themselves disgraced by the defection of their captain, called loudly for them just before the commencement of the action. They were killed immediately in front of the lines, their father being a powerless onlooker; their blood was thrown into a cask half full of wine, and the horrible mixture was drunk by the soldiers, who then furiously charged the enemy's battalions. The issue of the struggle was for a long time doubtful, but the Egyptians were inferior in numbers; towards evening their lines gave way and the flight began.[1] All was not, however, lost, if Psammetichus had but followed the example of Taharqa, and defended the passage of the various canals and arms of the river, disputing the ground inch by inch with the Persians, and gaining time meanwhile to collect a fresh army. The king lost his presence of mind, and without attempting to rally what remained of his regiments, he hastened to take refuge within the White Wall. Cambyses halted a few days to reduce Pelusium,[2] and in the mean time sent a vessel of Mitylene to summon Memphis to capitulate: the infuriated populace, as soon as they got wind of the message, massacred the herald and the crew, and dragged their bleeding limbs through the streets. The city held out for a considerable

---

[1] According to Herodotus, eighty years later the battle-field used to be shown covered with bones, and it was said that the Egyptians could be distinguished from the Persians by the relative hardness of their skulls.

[2] Polyænus hands down a story that Cambyses, in order to paralyse the resistance of the besieged, caused cats, dogs, ibises, and other sacred animals to march at the head of his attacking columns: the Egyptians would not venture to use their arms for fear of wounding or killing some of their gods.

time; when at length she opened her gates, the remaining inhabitants of the Saîd who had hesitated up to then, hastened to make their submission, and the whole of Egypt as far as Philæ became at one stroke a Persian province. The Libyans did not wait to be summoned to bring their tribute; Cyrene and Barca followed their example, but their offerings were so small that the conqueror's irritation was aroused, and deeming himself mocked, he gave way to his anger, and instead of accepting them, he threw them to his soldiers with his own hand (B.C. 525).[1] This sudden collapse of a power whose exalted position had defied all attacks for centuries, and the tragic fate of the king who had received his crown merely to lose it, filled contemporary beholders with astonishment and pity. It was said that, ten days after the capitulation of Memphis, the victorious king desired out of sport to test the endurance of his prisoner. Psammetichus beheld his daughter and the daughters of his nobles pass before him, half naked, with jars on their shoulders, and go down to the Nile to fetch water from the river like common slaves; his son and two thousand young men of the same age, in chains and with ropes round their necks, also defiled before him on their way to die as a revenge for the murder of the Mitylenians; yet he never for a moment lost his royal imperturbability. But when one of his former companions in pleasure chanced to pass, begging for alms and clothed in rags, Psammetichus suddenly broke out into weeping,

---

[1] The question as to the year in which Egypt was subdued by Cambyses has long divided historians: I still agree with those who place the conquest in the spring of 525.

and lacerated his face in despair. Cambyses, surprised at this excessive grief in a man who up till then had exhibited such fortitude, demanded the reason of his conduct. " Son of Cyrus," he replied, ." the misfortunes of my house are too unparalleled to weep over, but not the affliction of my friend. When a man, on the verge of old age, falls from luxury and abundance into extreme poverty, one may well lament his fate." When the speech was reported to Cambyses, he fully recognised the truth of it. Crœsus, who was also present, shed tears, and the Persians round him were moved with pity. Cambyses, likewise touched, commanded that the son of the Pharaoh should be saved, but the remission of the sentence arrived too late. He at all events treated Pharaoh himself with consideration, and it is possible that he might have replaced him on the throne, under an oath of vassalage, had he not surprised him in a conspiracy against his own life. He thereupon obliged him to poison himself by drinking bulls' blood, and he confided the government of the Nile valley to a Persian named Aryandes.

No part of the ancient world now remained unconquered except the semi-fabulous kingdom of Ethiopia in the far-off south. Cities and monarchies, all the great actors of early times, had been laid in the dust one after another—Tyre, Damascus, Carchemish, Urartu, Elam, Assyria, Jerusalem, Media, the Lydians, Babylon, and finally Egypt; and the prey they had fought over so fiercely and for so many centuries, now belonged in its entirety to one master for the first time as far as memory could reach back into the past. Cambyses, following in the footsteps of Cyrus, had pursued his victorious way successfully, but it was another matter to consolidate his conquests and to succeed in governing within the limits of one empire so many incongruous elements—the people of the Caucasus and those of the Nile valley, the Greeks of the Ægean and the Iranians, the Scythians from beyond the Oxus and the Semites of the banks of the Euphrates or of the Mediterranean coast; and time alone would show whether this heritage would not fall to pieces as quickly as it had been built up. The Asiatic elements of the empire appeared, at all events for the moment, content with their lot, and Babylon showed herself more than usually resigned; but Egypt had never accepted the yoke of the stranger willingly, and the most fortunate of her Assyrian conquerors had never exercised more than a passing supremacy over her. Cambyses realised that he would never master her except by governing her himself for a period of several years, and by making himself as Egyptian as a Persian could be without offending his own subjects at home. He adopted the titles of the Pharaohs, their double cartouche, their royal costume, and their solar filiation; as much to satisfy his own personal animosity as to conciliate the Egyptian priests, he repaired to Sais, violated the tomb of Amasis, and burnt the mummy after offering it every insult.[1] He removed his

[1] Herodotus gives also a second account, which declares that Cambyses thus treated the body, not of Amasis, but of some unknown person whom he took for Amasis. The truth of the story is generally contested, for the deed would have been, as Herodotus himself remarks, contrary to Persian ideas about the sanctity of fire. I think that by his cruel treatment of the mummy, Cambyses wished to satisfy the hatred of the natives against the Greek-loving king, and so render himself more acceptable to them. The

troops from the temple of Nît, which they had turned into a barrack to the horror of the faithful, and restored at his own expense the damage they had done to the building. He condescended so far as to receive instruction in the local religion, and was initiated in the worship of the goddess by the priest Uzaharrîsnîti. This was, after all, a pursuance of the policy employed by his father towards the Babylonians, and the projects which he had in view necessitated his gaining the confidence of the people at all costs. Asia having no more to offer him, two almost untried fields lay open to his ambition—Africa and Europe —the Greek world and what lay beyond it, the Carthaginian world and Ethiopia. The necessity of making a final reckoning with Egypt had at the outset summoned him to Africa, and it was therefore in that continent that he determined to carry on his conquests. Memphis was necessarily the base of his operations, the only point from which he could direct the march of his armies in a westerly or southerly direction, and at the same time keep in touch with the rest of his empire, and he would indeed have been imprudent had he neglected anything which could make him acceptable to its inhabitants. As soon as he felt he had gained their sympathies, he despatched two expeditions, one to Carthage and one to Ethiopia. Cyrene had spontaneously offered him her homage; he now further secured it by sending thither with all honour Ladikê, the

destruction of the mummy entailing that of the soul, his act gave the Saitic population a satisfaction similar to that experienced by the refined cruelty of those who, a few centuries ago, killed their enemies when in a state of deadly sin, and so ensure not only their dismissal from this world, but also their condemnation in the next.

widow of Amasis, and he apparently contemplated taking advantage of the good will of the Cyrenians to approach Carthage by sea. The combined fleets of Ionia and Phœnicia were without doubt numerically sufficient for this undertaking, but the Tyrians refused to serve against their own colonies, and he did not venture to employ the Greeks alone in waters which were unfamiliar to them. Besides this, the information which he obtained from those about him convinced him that the overland route would enable him to reach his destination more surely if more slowly; it would lead him from the banks of the Nile to the Oases of the Theban desert, from there to the Ammonians, and thence by way of the Libyans bordering on the Syrtes and the Liby-phœnicians. He despatched an advance-guard of fifty thousand men from Thebes to occupy the Oasis of Ammon and to prepare the various halting-places for the bulk of the troops. The fate of these men has never been clearly ascertained. They crossed the Oasis of El-Khargeh and proceeded to the north-west in the direction of the oracle. The natives afterwards related that when

THE NAOPHOROS STATUETTE OF THE VATICAN.[1]

[1] Drawn by Faucher-Gudin, from a photograph: the head and hands are a restoration of the eighteenth century, in the most inappropriate Græco-Roman style.

they had arrived halfway, a sudden storm of wind fell upon them, and the entire force was buried under mounds of sand during a halt. Cambyses was forced to take their word; in spite of all his endeavours, no further news of his troops was forthcoming, except that they never reached the temple, and that none of the generals or soldiers ever again saw Egypt (524). The expedition to Ethiopia was not more successful. Since the retreat of Tanuatamanu, the Pharaohs of Napata had severed all direct relations with Asia; but on being interfered with by Psammetichus I. and II., they had repulsed the invaders, and had maintained their frontier almost within sight of Philæ.[1] In Nubia proper they had merely a few outposts stationed in the ruins of the towns of the Theban period—at Derr, at Pnubsu, at Wady-Halfa, and at Semneh; the population again becoming dense and the valley fertile to the south of this spot. Kush, like Egypt, was divided into two regions —To-Qonusît, with its cities of Danguru,[2] Napata, Astamuras, and Barua; and Alo,[3] which extended along the White and the Blue Nile in the plain of Sennaar: the Asmakh, the descendants of the Mashauasha emigrants of the time of Psammetichus I., dwelt on the southern border of Alo. A number of half-savage tribes, Maditi and

---

[1] The northern boundary of Ethiopia is given us approximately by the lists of temples in the inscriptions of Harsiatef and of Nastosenen: Pnubsu is mentioned several times as receiving gifts from the king, which carries the permanent dominion of the Ethiopian kings as far as the second cataract.

[2] Now Old Dongola.

[3] Berua is the Meroê of Strabo, Astaboras the modern Ed-Dameîr, and Alo the kingdom of Aloah of the mediæval Arab geographers.

THE EGYPTIAN KINGDOM OF ETHIOPIA 147

Rohrehsa, were settled to the right and to the left of the territory watered by the Nile, between Darfur, the mountains of Abyssinia, and the Red Sea; and the warlike

ETHIOPIAN GROUP.[1]

disposition of the Ethiopian kings found in these tribes an inexhaustible field for obtaining easy victories and abundant spoil. Many of these sovereigns—Piônkhi,

[1] Drawn by Boudier, from the photograph by Berghoff.

Alaru, Harsiatef, Nastosenen—whose respective positions in the royal line are still undetermined, specially distinguished themselves in these struggles, but the few monuments they have left, though bearing witness to their military enterprise and ability, betray their utter decadence in everything connected with art, language, and religion. The ancient Egyptian syllabary, adapted to the needs of a barbarous tongue, had ended by losing its elegance; architecture was degenerating, and sculpture slowly growing more and more clumsy in appearance. Some of the work, however, is not wanting in a certain rude nobility—as, for instance, the god and goddess carved side by side in a block of grey granite. Ethiopian worship had become permeated with strange superstitions, and its creed was degraded, in spite of the strictness with which the priests supervised its application and kept watch against every attempt to introduce innovations. Towards the end of the seventh century some of the families attached to the temple of Amon at Napata had endeavoured to bring about a kind of religious reform; among other innovations they adopted the practice of substituting for the ordinary sacrifice, new rites, the chief feature of which was the offering of the flesh of the victim raw, instead of roasted with fire. This custom, which was doubtless borrowed from the negroes of the Upper Nile, was looked upon as a shameful heresy by the orthodox. The king repaired in state to the temple of Amon, seized the priests who professed these seditious beliefs, and burnt them alive. The use of raw meat, nevertheless, was not discontinued, and it gained such ground in the course of ages that even Christianity was unable to suppress it; up to the present time, the *brindê*, or piece of beef cut from the living animal and eaten raw, is considered a delicacy by the Abyssinians.

The isolation of the Ethiopians had rather increased than lowered their reputation among other nations. Their transitory appearance on the battle-fields of Asia had left a deep impression on the memories of their opponents. The tenacity they had displayed during their conflict with Assyria had effaced the remembrance of their defeat. Popular fancy delighted to extol the wisdom of Sabaco,[1] and exalted Taharqa to the first rank among the conquerors of the old world; now that Kush once more came within the range of vision, it was invested with a share of all these virtues, and the inquiries Cambyses made concerning it were calculated to make him believe that he was about to enter on a struggle with a nation of demigods rather than of men. He was informed that they were taller, more beautiful, and more vigorous than all other mortals, that their age was prolonged to one hundred and twenty years and more, and that they possessed a marvellous fountain whose waters imparted perpetual youth to their bodies. There existed near their capital a meadow, perpetually furnishing an inexhaustible supply of food and drink; whoever would might partake of this "Table of the Sun," and eat to his fill.[2] Gold was so abundant that

---

[1] The eulogy bestowed on him by Herodotus shows the esteem in which he was held even in the Saite period; later on he seems to have become two persons, and so to have given birth to the good Ethiopian king Aktisanes.

[2] Pausanias treats it as a traveller's tale. Heeren thought that he saw in Herodotus' account a reference to intercourse by signs, so frequent in

it was used for common purposes, even for the chains of their prisoners; but, on the other hand, copper was rare and much prized. Cambyses despatched some spies chosen from among the Ichthyophagi of the Red Sea to explore this region, and acting on the report they brought back, he left Memphis at the head of an army and a fleet.[1] The expedition was partly a success and partly a failure. It followed the Nile valley as far as Korosko, and then struck across the desert in the direction of Napata;[2] but

Africa. The "Table of the Sun" would thus have been a kind of market, whither the natives would come for their provisions, using exchange to procure them. I am inclined rather to believe the story to be a recollection, partly of the actual custom of placing meats, which the first comer might take, on the tombs in the necropolis, partly of the mythical "Meadow of Offerings" mentioned in the funerary texts, to which the souls of the dead and the gods alike had access. This divine region would have transferred to our earth by some folk-tale, like the judgment of the dead, the entrance into the solar bark, and other similar beliefs.

[1] Herodotus' text speaks of an army only, but the accounts of the wars between Ethiopia and Egypt show that the army was always accompanied by the necessary fleet.

[2] It is usually thought that the expedition marched by the side of the Nile as far as Napata; to support this theory the name of a place mentioned in Pliny is quoted, Cambusis at the third cataract, which is supposed to contain the name of the conqueror. This town, which is sometimes mentioned by the classical geographers, is called Kambîusît in the Ethiopic texts, and the form of the name makes its connection with the history of Cambyses easy. I think it follows, from the text of Herodotus, that the Persians left the grassy land, the river-valley, at a given moment, to enter the sand, *i.e.* the desert. Now this is done to-day at two points— near Korosko to rejoin the Nile at Abu-Hammed, and near Wady-Halfah to avoid the part of the Nile called the "Stony belly," Batn el-Hagar. The Korosko route, being the only one suitable for the transit of a body of troops, and also the only route known to Herodotus, seems, I think, likely to be the one which was followed in the present instance; at all events, it fits in best with the fact that Cambyses was obliged to retrace his steps hurriedly, when he had accomplished hardly a fifth of the journey.

provisions ran short before a quarter of the march had been achieved, and famine obliged the invaders to retrace their steps after having endured terrible sufferings.[1] Cambyses had to rest content with the acquisition of those portions of Nubia adjoining the first cataract—the same, in fact, that had been annexed to Egypt by Psammetichus I. and II. (523). The failure of this expedition to the south, following so closely on the disaster which befell that of the west, had a deplorable effect on the mind of Cambyses. He had been subject, from childhood, to attacks of epilepsy, during which he became a maniac and had no control over his actions. These reverses of fortune aggravated the disease, and increased the frequency and length of the attacks.[2] The bull Apis had died shortly before the close of the Ethiopian campaign, and the Egyptians, after mourning for him during the prescribed number of weeks, were bringing his successor with rejoicings into the temple

[1] Many modern historians are inclined to assume that Cambyses' expedition was completely successful, and that its result was the overthrow of the ancient kingdom of Nepata and the foundation of that of Meroê. Cambyses would have given the new town which he built there the name of his sister Meroê. The traditions concerning Cambusis and Meroê belong to the Alexandrine era, and rest only on chance similarities of sound. With regard to the Ethiopian province of the Persian empire and to the Ethiopian neighbours of Egypt whom Cambyses subdued, the latter are not necessarily Ethiopians of Napata. Herodotus himself says that the Ethiopians dwelt in the country above Elephantinê, and that half of what he calls the island of Takhompsô was inhabited by Ethiopians: the subjugated Ethiopians and their country plainly correspond with the Dodekaschênos of the Græco-Roman era.

[2] Recent historians admit neither the reality of the illness of Cambyses nor the madness resulting from it, but consider them Egyptian fables, invented out of spite towards the king who had conquered and persecuted them.

of Phtah, when the remains of the army re-entered Memphis. Cambyses, finding the city holiday-making, imagined that it was rejoicing over his misfortunes. He summoned the magistrates before him, and gave them over to the executioner without deigning to listen to their explanations. He next caused the priests to be brought to him, and when they had paraded the Apis before him, he plunged his dagger into its flank with derisive laughter: "Ah, evil people! So you make for yourselves divinities of flesh and blood which fear the sword! It is indeed a fine god that you Egyptians have here; I will have you to know, however, that you shall not rejoice overmuch at having deceived me!" The priests were beaten as impostors, and the bull languished from its wound and died in a few days;[1] its priests buried it, and chose another in its place without the usual ceremonies, so as not to exasperate the anger of the tyrant,[2] but the horror evoked by this double sacrilege

---

[1] Later historians improved upon the account of Herodotus, and it is said in the *De Iside*, that Cambyses killed the Apis and threw him to the dogs. Here there is probably a confusion between the conduct of Cambyses and that attributed to the eunuch Bagoas nearly two centuries later, at the time of the second conquest of Egypt by Ochus.

[2] Mariette discovered in the Serapæum and sent to the Louvre fragments of the epitaph of an Apis buried in Epiphi in the sixth year of Cambyses, which had therefore died a few months previously. This fact contradicts the inference from the epitaph of the Apis that died in the fourth year of Darius, which would have been born in the fifth year of Cambyses, if we allow that there could not have been two Apises in Egypt at once. This was, indeed, the usual rule, but a comparison of the two dates shows that here it was not followed, and it is therefore simplest, until we have further evidence, to conclude that at all events in cases of violence, such as sacrilegious murder, there could have been two Apises at once, one

raised passions against Cambyses which the ruin of the country had failed to excite. The manifestations of this antipathy irritated him to such an extent that he completely changed his policy, and set himself from that time forward to act counter to the customs and prejudices of the Egyptians. They consequently regarded his memory with a vindictive hatred. The people related that the gods had struck him with madness to avenge the murder of the Apis, and they attributed to him numberless traits of senseless cruelty, in which we can scarcely distinguish truth from fiction. It was said that, having entered the temple of Phtah, he had ridiculed the grotesque figure under which the god was represented, and had commanded the statues to be burnt. On another occasion he had ordered the ancient sepulchres to be opened, that he might see what was the appearance of the mummies. The most faithful members of his family and household, it was said, did not escape his fury. He killed his own sister Roxana, whom he had married, by a kick in the abdomen; he slew the son of Prexaspes with an arrow; he buried alive twelve influential Persians; he condemned Crœsus to death, and then repented, but punished the officers who had failed to execute the sentence pronounced against the Lydian king.[1] He had no longer any reason for remaining in Egypt, since he had failed in his undertakings; yet he did not quit the country, and through repeated delays his departure was

discharging his functions, and the other unknown, living still in the midst of the herds.

[1] The whole of this story of Crœsus is entirely fabulous.

retarded a whole year. Meanwhile his long sojourn in Africa, the report of his failures, and perhaps whispers of his insanity, had sown the seeds of discontent in Asia; and as Darius said in after-years, when recounting these events, "untruth had spread all over the country, not only in Persia and Media, but in other provinces." Cambyses himself felt that a longer absence would be injurious to his interests; he therefore crossed the isthmus in the spring of 521, and was making his way through Northern Syria, perhaps in the neighbourhood of Hamath,[1] when he learned that a revolution had broken out, and that its rapid progress threatened the safety of his throne and life. Tradition asserted that a herald appeared before him and proclaimed aloud, in the hearing of the whole army, that Cambyses, son of Cyrus, had ceased to reign, and summoned whoever had till that day obeyed him to acknowledge henceforth Smerdis, son of Cyrus, as their lord. Cambyses at first believed that his brother had been spared by the assassins, and now, after years of concealment, had at length declared himself; but he soon received proofs that his orders had been faithfully accomplished, and it is said that he wept at the remembrance of the fruitless crime. The usurper was Gaumâta, one of the Persian Magi, whose resemblance

---

[1] Herodotus calls the place where Cambyses died Agbatana (Ecbatana). Pliny says that the town of Carmel was thus named at first; but the place here mentioned cannot well have been in that direction. It has been identified with Batanæa in the country between the Orontes and the Euphrates, but the most likely theory is the one suggested by a passage in Stephen of Byzantium, that the place in question is the large Syrian city of Hamath. Josephus makes him die at Damascus.

to Smerdis was so remarkable that even those who were cognisant of it invariably mistook the one for the other,[1] and he was brother to that Oropastes to whom Cambyses had entrusted the administration of his household before setting out for Egypt.[2] Both of them were aware of the fate of Smerdis; they also knew that the Persians were ignorant of it, and that every one at court, including the mother and sisters of the prince, believed that he was still alive. Gaumâta headed a revolt in the little town of Pasyauvadâ on the 14th of Viyakhna, in the early days of March, 521, and he was hailed by the common people from the moment of his appearance. Persia, Media, and the Iranian provinces pronounced in his favour, and solemnly enthroned him three months later, on the 9th of Garmapada; Babylon next accepted him, followed by Elam and the regions of the Tigris. Though astounded at first by such a widespread defection, Cambyses soon recovered his presence of mind, and was about to march forward at the head of the troops who were still loyal to him, when he mysteriously disappeared. Whether

[1] Greek tradition is unanimous on this point, but the inscription of Behistun does not mention it.

[2] The inscription of Behistun informs us that the usurper's name was Gaumâta. Pompeius Trogus alone, probably following some author who made use of Charon of Lampsacus, handed down this name in the form Cometes or Gometes, which his abbreviator Justin carelessly applied to the second brother. Ctesias gives the Mage the name Sphendadates, which answers to the Old Persian Spentôdata, "he who is given by the Holy One," *i.e.* by Ahura-mazdâ. The supporters of the Mage gave him this name, as an heroic champion of the Mazdæan faith who had destroyed such sanctuaries as were illegal, and identified him with Spentôdata, son of Wistâspa.

he was the victim of a plot set on foot by those about him, is not known. The official version of the story given by Darius states that he died by his own hand, and it seems to insinuate that it was a voluntary act, but another account affirms that he succumbed to an accident;[1] while mounting his horse, the point of his dagger pierced his thigh in the same spot in which he had stabbed the Apis of the Egyptians. Feeling himself seriously wounded, he suddenly asked the name of the place where he was lying, and was told it was "Agbatana" (Ecbatana). "Now, long before this, the oracle of Buto had predicted that he should end his days in Agbatana, and he, believing it to be the Agbatana in Media where were his treasures, understood that he should die there in his old age; whereas the oracle meant Agbatana in Syria. When he heard the name, he perceived his error. He understood what the god intended, and cried, 'It is here, then, that Cambyses, son of Cyrus, must perish!'" He expired about three weeks after, leaving no posterity and having appointed no successor.[2]

[1] It has been pointed out, for the purpose of harmonising the testimony of Herodotus with that of the inscription of Behistun, that although the latter speaks of the death of Cambyses by his own hand, it does not say whether that death was voluntary or accidental.

[2] The story of a person whose death has been predicted to take place in some well-known place, and who has died in some obscure spot of the same name, occurs several times in different historians, e.g. in the account of the Emperor Julian, and in that of Henry III. of England, who had been told that he would die in Jerusalem, and whose death took place in the Jerusalem Chamber at Westminster. Ctesias has preserved an altogether different tradition—that Cambyses on his return from Babylon wounded himself while carving a piece of wood for his amusement, and died eleven days after the accident.

What took place in the ensuing months still remains an enigma to us. The episode of Gaumâta has often been looked on as a national movement, which momentarily restored to the Medes the supremacy of which Cyrus had robbed them; but it was nothing of the sort. Gaumâta was not a Mede by birth: he was a Persian, born in Persia, in the township of Pisyauvadâ, at the foot of Mount Arakadrish, and the Persians recognised and supported him as much as did the Medes. It has also been thought that he had attempted to foment a religious revolution,[1] and, as a matter of fact, he destroyed several temples in a few months. Here, however, the reform touched less upon a question of belief than on one of fact. The unity of the empire presupposed the unity of the royal fire, and wherever that fire was burning another could not be lighted without sacrilege in the eyes of the faithful. The pyres that Gaumâta desired to extinguish were, no doubt, those which the feudal families had maintained for their separate use in defiance of the law, and the measure which abolished them had a political as well as a religious side. The little we can glean of the line of action adopted by Smerdis does not warrant the attribution to him of the vast projects which some modern writers credit him with. He naturally sought to strengthen himself on the throne, which by a stroke of good fortune he had ascended, and whatever he did tended solely to this end. The name and the

[1] Most of the ancient writers shared this opinion, and have been followed therein by many modern writers. Rawlinson was the first to show that Gaumâta's movement was not Median, and that he did not in the least alter the position of the Persians in the empire: but he allows the Magian usurpation to have been the prelude to a sort of religious reform.

character that he had assumed secured him the respect and fidelity of the Iranians: "there was not one, either among the Medes or the Persians, nor among the members of the Achæmenian race, who dreamed of disputing his power" in the early days of his reign. The important thing in his eyes was, therefore, to maintain among his subjects as long as possible the error as to his identity. He put to death all, whether small or great, who had been in any way implicated in the affairs of the real Smerdis, or whom he suspected of any knowledge of the murder. He withdrew from public life as far as practicable, and rarely allowed himself to be seen. Having inherited the harem of his predecessors, together with their crown, he even went so far as to condemn his wives to a complete seclusion. He did not venture to hope, nor did those in his confidence, that the truth would not one day be known, but he hoped to gain, without loss of time, sufficient popularity to prevent the revelation of the imposture from damaging his prospects. The seven great houses which he had dispossessed would, in such a case, refuse to rally round him, and it was doubtless to lessen their prestige that he extinguished their pyres; but the people did not trouble themselves as to the origin of their sovereign, if he showed them his favour and took proper precautions to secure their good will. He therefore exempted the provinces from taxes and military service for a period of three years. He had not time to pursue this policy, and if we may believe tradition, the very precautions which he took to conceal his identity became the cause of his misfortunes. In the royal harem there were, together with the daughters of Cyrus, relatives of all the Persian nobility, and the order issued to stop all their communications with the outer world had excited suspicion: the avowals which had escaped Cambyses before the catastrophe were now called to mind, and it was not long before those in high places became convinced that they had been the dupes of an audacious imposture. A conspiracy broke out, under the leadership of the chiefs of the seven clans, among whom was numbered Darius, the son of Hystaspes, who was connected, according to a genealogy more or less authentic, with the family of the Achæmenides:[1] the conspirators surprised Gaumâta in his palace of Sikayauvatish, which was situated in the district of Nisaya, not far from Ecbatana, and assassinated him on the 10th of Bâgayâdîsh, 521 B.C. The exact particulars of this scene were never known, but popular imagination soon supplied the defect, furnishing a full and complete account of all that took place. In the first place, Phædimê, daughter of Otanes,

DARIUS, SON OF HYSTASPES.[2]

---

[1] The passage in the Behistun inscription, in which Darius sets forth his own genealogy, has received various interpretations. That of Oppert seems still the most probable, that the text indicates two parallel branches of Achæmenides, which flourished side by side until Cambyses died and Darius ascended the throne. Such a genealogy, however, appears to be fictitious, invented solely for the purpose of connecting Darius with the ancient royal line, with which in reality he could claim no kinship, or only a very distant connection.

[2] Drawn by Faucher-Gudin, from M. Dieulafoy.

one of the seven, furnished an authentic proof of the fraud which had been perpetrated. Her father had opportunely recalled the marvellous resemblance between Smerdis and the Magian, and remembered at the same time that the latter had been deprived of his ears in punishment for some misdeed: he therefore sent certain instructions to Phædimê, who, when she made the discovery, at the peril of her life, that her husband had no ears, communicated the information to the disaffected nobles. The conspirators thereupon resolved to act without delay; but when they arrived at the palace, they were greeted with an extraordinary piece of intelligence. The Magi, disquieted by some vague rumours which were being circulated against them, had besought Prexaspes to proclaim to the people that the reigning monarch was indeed Smerdis himself. But Prexaspes, instead of making the desired declaration, informed the multitude that the son of Cyrus was indeed dead, for he himself had murdered him at the bidding of Cambyses, and, having made this confession, he put himself to death, in order to escape the vengeance of the Magi. This act of Prexaspes was an additional inducement to the conspirators to execute their purpose. The guard stationed at the gates of the palace dared not refuse admission to so noble a company, and when the throne-room was reached and the eunuchs forbade further advance, the seven boldly drew their swords and forced their way to the apartment occupied by the two Magi. The usurpers defended themselves with bravery, but succumbed at length to the superior number of their opponents, after having wounded two of the conspirators. Gobryas pinioned Gaumâta with his arms, and in such a way that Darius hesitated to make the fatal thrust for fear of wounding his comrade; but the latter bade him strike at all hazards, and by good fortune the sword did not even graze him. The crime accomplished, the seven conspirators agreed to choose as king that member of their company whose horse should first neigh after sunrise: a stratagem of his groom caused the election to fall on Darius. As soon as he was duly enthroned, he instituted a festival called the "magophonia," or "massacre of the Magi," in commemoration of the murder which had given him the crown.

His first care was to recompense the nobles to whom he owed his position by restoring to them the privileges of which they had been deprived by the pseudo-Smerdis, namely,.the right of free access to the king, as well as the right of each individual to a funeral pyre; but the usurper had won the affection of the people, and even the inhabitants of those countries which had been longest subject to the Persian sway did not receive the new sovereign favourably. Darius found himself, therefore, under the necessity of conquering his dominions one after the other.[1] The Persian empire, like those of the Chaldæans and Medes, had consisted hitherto of nothing but a fortuitous collection of provinces under military rule, of vassal kingdoms, and of semi-independent cities and tribes; there was no fixed

[1] The history of the early part of the reign of Darius is recorded in the great inscription which the king caused to be cut in three languages on the rocks of Behistun. The order of the events recorded in it is not always easy to determine. I have finally adopted, with some modifications, the arrangement of Marquart, which seems to me to give the clearest "conspectus" of these confused wars.

division of authority, and no regular system of government for the outlying provinces. The governors assigned by Cyrus and Cambyses to rule the various provinces acquired by conquest, were actual viceroys, possessing full control of an army, and in some cases of a fleet as well, having at their disposal considerable revenues both in money and in kind, and habituated, owing to their distance from the capital, to settle pressing questions on their own responsibility, subject only to the necessity of making a report to the sovereign when the affair was concluded, or when the local resources were insufficient to bring it to a successful issue. For such free administrators the temptation must have been irresistible to break the last slender ties which bound them to the empire, and to set themselves up as independent monarchs. The two successive revolutions which had taken place in less than a year, convinced such governors, and the nations over which they bore rule, that the stately edifice erected by Cyrus and Cambyses was crumbling to pieces, and that the moment was propitious for each of them to carve out of its ruins a kingdom for himself; the news of the murder, rapidly propagated, sowed the seeds of revolt in its course—in Susiana, at Babylon, in Media, in Parthia, in Margiana, among the Sattagydes, in Asia Minor, and even in Egypt itself[1]—which showed itself in some places in an open and undisguised form, while

---

[1] In the *Behistun Inscription*, it is stated that insurrections broke out in all these countries while Darius was at Babylon; that is to say, while he was occupied in besieging that city, as is evident from the order of the events narrated.

REVOLUTIONS IN SUSIANA, CHALDÆA, AND MEDIA 163

in others it was contemptuously veiled under the appearance of neutrality, or the pretence of waiting to see the issue of events. The first to break out into open rebellion were the neighbouring countries of Elam and Chaldæa: the death of Smerdis took place towards the end of September, and a fortnight later saw two rebel chiefs enthroned —a certain Athrîna at Susa, and a Nadinta-bel at Babylon.[1] Athrîna, the son of Umbadaranma, was a scion of the dynasty dispossessed by the successors of Sargon in the preceding century, but nevertheless he met with but lukewarm assistance from his own countrymen;[2] he was taken prisoner before a month had passed, and sent to Darius, who slew him with his own hand. Babylon was not so easily mastered. Her chosen sovereign claimed to be the son of Nabonidus, and had, on ascending the throne, assumed the illustrious name of Nebuchadrezzar; he was not supported, moreover, by only a few busybodies, but carried the whole population with him. The Babylonians, who had at first welcomed Cyrus so warmly, and had fondly imagined that they had made him one of themselves, as they had made so many of their conquerors for centuries past, soon realised their mistake. The differences of language, manners, spirit, and religion between themselves

[1] The latest known document of the pseudo-Smerdis is dated the 1st of Tisri at Babylon, and the first of Nebuchadrezzar III. are dated the 17th and 20th of the same month. The revolt of Babylon, then, must be placed between the 1st and 17th of Tisri; that is, either at the end of September or the beginning of October, 521 B.C.

[2] The revolt cannot have lasted much more than six weeks, for on the 26th of Athriyâdiya following, that is to say, at the beginning of December, Darius had already joined issue with the Babylonians on the banks of the Tigris.

and the Persians were too fundamental to allow of the naturalisation of the new sovereign, and of the acceptance by the Achæmenides of that fiction of a double personality to which Tiglath-pileser III., Shalmaneser, and even Assurbani-pal had submitted. Popular fancy grew weary of Cyrus, as it had already grown weary in turn of all the foreigners it had at first acclaimed—whether Elamite, Kaldâ, or Assyrian—and by a national reaction the self-styled son of Nabonidus enjoyed the benefit of a devotion proportionately as great as the hatred which had been felt twenty years before for his pretended sire. The situation might become serious if he were given time to consolidate his power, for the loyalty of the ancient provinces of the Chaldæan empire was wavering, and there was no security that they would not feel inclined to follow the example of the capital as soon as they should receive news of the sedition. Darius, therefore, led the bulk of his forces to Babylon without a day's more delay than was absolutely necessary, and the event proved that he had good reason for such haste. Nebuchadrezzar III. had taken advantage of the few weeks which had elapsed since his accession, to garrison the same positions on the right bank of the Tigris, as Nabonidus had endeavoured to defend against Cyrus at the northern end of the fortifications erected by his ancestor. A well-equipped flotilla patrolled the river, and his lines presented so formidable a front that Darius could not venture on a direct attack. He arranged his troops in two divisions, which he mounted partly on horses, partly on camels, and eluding the vigilance of his adversary by attacking him simultaneously on many sides, succeeded in gaining the opposite bank of the river. The Chaldæans, striving in vain to drive him back into the stream, were at length defeated on the 27th of Athriyâdiya, and they retired in good order on Babylon. Six days later, on the 2nd of Anâmaka, they fought a second battle at Zazanu, on the bank of the Euphrates, and were again totally defeated. Nebuchadrezzar escaped with a handful of cavalry, and hastened to shut himself up in his city. Darius soon followed him, but if he cherished a hope that the Babylonians would open their gates to him without further resistance, as they had done to Cyrus, he met with a disappointment, for he was compelled to commence a regular siege and suspend all other operations, and that, too, at a moment when the provinces were breaking out into open insurrection on every hand.[1] The attempt of

[1] The account given by Darius seems to imply that no interval of time elapsed between the second defeat of Nebuchadrezzar III. and the taking of Babylon, so that several modern historians have rejected the idea of an obstinate resistance. Herodotus, however, speaks of the long siege the city sustained, and the discovery of tablets dated in the first and even the second year of Nebuchadrezzar III. shows that the siege was prolonged into the second year of this usurper, at least until the month of Nisân (March–April), 520 B.C. No evidence can be drawn from the tablets dated in the reign of Darius, for the oldest yet discovered, which is dated in the month Sebat (Jan.–Feb.), in the year of his accession, and consequently prior to the second year of Nebuchadrezzar, comes from Abu-habba. On the other hand, the statement that all the revolts broke out while Darius was "at Babylon" does not allow of the supposition that all the events recorded before his departure for Media could have been compressed into the space of three or four months. It seems, therefore, more probable that the siege lasted till 519 B.C., as it can well have done if credit be given to the mention of "twenty-one months at least" by Herodotus ; perhaps the siege was brought to an end in the May of that year, as calculated by Marquart.

the Persian adventurer Martîya to stir up the Susians to revolt in his rear failed, thanks to the favourable disposition of the natives, who refused to recognise in him Ummanîsh, the heir of their national princes. Media, however, yielded unfortunately to the solicitations of a

DARIUS PIERCING A REBEL WITH HIS LANCE BEFORE A GROUP OF FOUR PRISONERS.[1]

certain Fravartîsh, who had assumed the personality of Khshatrita of the race of Cyaxares, and its revolt marked almost the beginning of a total break-up of the empire. The memory of Astyages and Cyaxares had not yet faded so completely as to cause the Median nobles to relinquish the hope of reasserting the supremacy of Media; the opportunity for accomplishing this aim now seemed all

[1] Drawn by Faucher-Gudin, from the impression of an intaglio at St. Petersburg.

the more favourable, from the fact that Darius had been obliged to leave this province almost immediately after the assassination of the usurper, and to take from it all the troops that he could muster for the siege of Babylon. Several of the nomadic tribes still remained faithful to him, but all the settled inhabitants of Media ranged themselves under the banner of the pretender, and the spirit of insurrection spread thereupon into Armenia and Assyria. For one moment there was a fear lest it should extend to Asia Minor also, where Orœtes, accustomed, in the absence of Cambyses, to act as an autonomous sovereign, displayed little zeal in accommodating himself to the new order of things. There was so much uncertainty as to the leanings of the Persian guard of Orœtes, that Darius did not venture to degrade the satrap officially, but despatched Bagæus to Sardes with precise instructions, which enabled him to accomplish his mission by degrees, so as not to risk a Lydian revolt. His first act was to show the guard a rescript by which they were relieved from attendance on Orœtes, and "thereupon they immediately laid down their spears." Emboldened by their ready obedience, Bagæus presented to the secretary a second letter, which contained his instructions: "The great king commands those Persians who are in Sardes to kill Orœtes." "Whereupon," it is recorded, "they drew their swords and slew him."[1] A revolt in Asia Minor was thus

[1] The context of Herodotus indicates that the events narrated took place shortly after the accession of Darius. Further on Herodotus mentions, as contemporaneous with the siege of Babylon, events which took place after the death of Orœtes; it is probable, therefore, that the scene described by Herodotus occurred in 520 B.C. at the latest.

averted, at a time when civil war continued to rage in the centre of Iran.

The situation, however, continued critical. Darius could not think of abandoning the siege of Babylon, and of thus both losing the fruits of his victories and seeing Nebuchadrezzar reappear in Assyria or Susiana. On the other hand, his army was a small one, and he would incur great risks in detaching any of his military chiefs for a campaign against the Mede with an insufficient force. He decided, however, to adopt the latter course, and while he himself presided over the blockade, he simultaneously despatched two columns—one to Media, under the command of the Persian Vidarna, one of the seven; the other to Armenia, under the Armenian Dâdarshîsh. Vidarna, encountered Khshatrita near Marush, in the mountainous region of the old Namri, on the 27th of Anâmaka, and gave him battle; but though he claimed the victory, the result was so indecisive that he halted in Kambadênê, at the entrance to the gorges of the Zagros mountains, and was there obliged to await reinforcements before advancing further. Dâdarshish, on his side, gained three victories over the Armenians—one near Zuzza on the 8th of Thuravâhara, another at Tigra ten days later, and the third on the 2nd of Thâigarshîsh, at a place not far from Uhyâma—but he also was compelled to suspend operations and remain inactive pending the arrival of fresh troops. Half the year was spent in inaction on either side, for the rebels had not suffered less than their opponents, and, while endeavouring to reorganise their forces, they opened negotiations with

THE TAKING OF BABYLON

the provinces of the north-east with the view of prevailing on them to join their cause. Darius, still detained before Babylon, was unable to recommence hostilities until the end of 520 B.C. He sent Vaumisa to replace Dâdarshîsh as the head of the army in Armenia, and the new general distinguished himself at the outset by winning a decisive victory on the 15th of Anâmaka, near Izitush in Assyria; but the effect which he hoped to secure from this success was neutralised almost immediately by grievous defections. Sagartia, in the first place, rose in rebellion at the call of a pretended descendant of Cyaxares, named Chitrañtakhma; Hyrcania, the province governed by Hystaspes, the father of Darius, followed suit and took up the cause of Khshatrita, and soon after Margiana broke out into revolt at the instigation of a certain Frâda. Even Persia itself deserted Darius, and chose another king instead of a sovereign whom no one seemed willing to acknowledge. Many of the mountain tribes could not yet resign themselves to the belief that the male line of Cyrus had become extinct with the death of Cambyses. The usurpation of Gaumâta and the accession of Darius had not quenched their faith in the existence of Smerdis: if the Magian were an impostor, it did not necessarily follow that Smerdis had been assassinated, and when a certain Vahyazdâta rose up in the town of Târavâ in the district of Yautiyâ, and announced himself as the younger son of Cyrus, they received him with enthusiastic acclamations. A preliminary success gained by Hystaspes at Vispauzatîsh, in Parthia, on the 22nd of Viyakhna, 519 B.C., prevented the guerilla bands of Hyrcania from joining forces with the

Medes, and some days later the fall of Babylon at length set Darius free to utilise his resources to the utmost. The long resistance of Nebuchadrezzar furnished a fruitful theme for legend: a fanciful story was soon substituted for the true account of the memorable siege he had sustained. Half a century later, when his very name was forgotten, the heroism of his people continued to be extolled beyond measure. When Darius arrived before the ramparts he found the country a desert, the banks of the canals cut through, and the gardens and pleasure-houses destroyed. The crops had been gathered and the herds driven within the walls of the city, while the garrison had reduced by a massacre the number of non-combatants, the women having all been strangled, with the exception of those who were needed to bake the bread. At the end of twenty months the siege seemed no nearer to its close than at the outset, and the besiegers were on the point of losing heart, when at length Zopyrus, one of the seven, sacrificed himself for the success of the blockading army. Slitting his nose and ears, and lacerating his back with the lash of a whip, he made his way into the city as a deserter, and persuaded the garrison to assign him a post of danger under pretence of avenging the ill-treatment he had received from his former master. He directed some successful sallies on points previously agreed upon, and having thus lulled to rest any remaining feelings of distrust on the part of the garrison, he treacherously opened to the Persians the two gates of which he was in charge; three thousand Babylonians were impaled, the walls were razed to the ground, and the survivors of the struggle were exiled and replaced by strange colonists.¹ The only authentic fact about this story is the length of the siege. Nebuchadrezzar was put to death, and Darius, at length free to act, hastened to despatch one of his lieutenants, the Persian Artavardiya, against Vahyazdâta, while he himself marched upon the Medes with the main body of the royal army.² The rebels had hitherto been confronted by the local militia, brave but inexperienced troops, with whom they had been able to contend on a fairly equal footing: the entry into the field of the veteran regiments of Cyrus and Cambyses changed the aspect of affairs, and promptly brought the campaign to a successful issue. Darius entered Media by the defiles of Kerend, reinforced Vidarna in Kambadênê, and crushed the enemy near the town of Kundurush, on the 20th of Adukanîsh, 519 B.C. Khshatrita fled towards the north with some few horsemen, doubtless hoping to reach the recesses of Mount Elburz, and to continue there the struggle; but he was captured at Ragâ and carried to Ecbatana. His horrible punishment was proportionate to the fear he had inspired: his nose, ears, and tongue were cut off, and his eyes gouged out, and in this mutilated condition he was placed in chains at the gate of the palace,

¹ Ctesias places the siege of Babylon forty years later, under Xerxes I.; according to him, it was Megabysus, son of Zopyrus, who betrayed the city. Polyænus asserts that the stratagem of Zopyrus was adopted in imitation of a Sakian who dwelt beyond the Oxus. Latin writers transferred the story to Italy, and localised it at Gabii: but the Roman hero, Sextus Tarquinius, did not carry his devotion to the point of mutilating himself.

² *Behistun Inscr.*: "Then I sent the army of the Persians and Medes which was with me. One named Artavardiya, a Persian, my servant, I made their general; the rest of the Persian army went to Media with me."

to demonstrate to his former subjects how the Achæmenian king could punish an impostor. When the people had laid this lesson sufficiently to heart, Khshatrita was impaled; many of his principal adherents were ranged around him and suffered the same fate, while the rest were decapitated as an example. Babylon and Media being thus successfully vanquished, the possession of the empire was assured to Darius, whatever might happen in other parts of his territory, and henceforth the process of repressing disaffection went on unchecked. Immediately after the decisive battle of Kundurush, Vaumisa accomplished the pacification of Armenia by a victory won near Autiyâra, and Artavardiya defeated Vahyazdâta for the first time at Rakhâ in Persia. Vahyazdâta had committed the mistake of dividing his forces and sending a portion of them to Arachosia. Vivâna, the governor of this province, twice crushed the invaders, and almost at the same time the Persian Dâdardîsh of Bactriana was triumphing over Frâda and winning Margiana back to allegiance. For a moment it seemed as if the decisive issue of the struggle might be prolonged for months, since it was announced that the appearance of a new pseudo-Smerdis on the scene had been followed by the advent of a second pseudo-Nebuchadrezzar in Chaldæa. Darius left only a weak garrison at Babylon when he started to attack Khshatrita: a certain Arakha, an Armenian by birth, presenting himself to the Babylonian people as the son of Nabonidus, caused himself to be proclaimed king in December, 519 B.C.; but the city was still suffering so severely from the miseries of the long siege, that it was easy for the Mede Vindafrâ to reduce it promptly to submission after a month or six weeks of semi-independence. This was the last attempt at revolt. Chitrañtakhma expiated his crimes by being impaled, and Hystaspes routed the Hyrcanian battalions at Patigrabana in Parthia: Artavardiya having defeated Vahyazdâta, near Mount Paraga, on the 6th of Garmapada, 618 B.C., besieged him in his fortress of Uvâdeshaya, and was not long in effecting his capture. The civil war came thus to an end.

It had been severe, but it had brought into such prominence the qualities of the sovereign that no one henceforth dared to dispute his possession of the crown. A man of less energetic character and calm judgment would have lost his head at the beginning of the struggle, when almost every successive week brought him news of a fresh rebellion—in Susiana, Babylon, Media, Armenia, Assyria, Margiana, Hyrcania, and even Persia itself, not to speak of the intrigues in Asia Minor and Egypt; he would have scattered his forces to meet the dangers on all sides at once, and would assuredly have either succumbed in the struggle, or succeeded only by chance after his fate had trembled in the balance for years. Darius, however, from the very beginning knew how to single out the important points upon which to deal such vigorous blows as would ensure him the victory with the least possible delay. He saw that Babylon, with its numerous population, its immense wealth and prestige, and its memory of recent supremacy, was the real danger to his empire, and he never relaxed his hold on it until it was subdued, leaving his generals to deal with the other nations, the Medes included, and satisfied if each of them could but hold his adversary in check without gaining any decided advantage over him. The event justified his decision. When once Babylon had fallen, the remaining rebels were no longer a source of fear; to defeat Khshatrita was the work of a few weeks only, and the submission of the other provinces followed as a natural consequence on the ruin of Media.[1]

REBELS BROUGHT TO DARIUS BY AHURA-MAZDÂ.[2]

After consummating his victories, Darius caused an inscription in commemoration of them to be carved on the rocks in the pass of Bagistana [Behistun], one of the most frequented routes leading from the basin of the Tigris to the tableland of Iran. There his figure is still to be seen

---

[1] Mention of some new wars is made towards the end of the inscription, but the text here is so mutilated that the sense can no longer be easily determined.

[2] This is the scene depicted on the rock of Behistun.

standing, with his foot resting on the prostrate body of an enemy, and his hand raised in the attitude of one addressing

THE ROCKS OF BEHISTUN.[1]

an audience, while nine figures march in file to meet him,

[1] Drawn by Boudier, from Flandin and Coste.

their arms tied behind their backs, and cords round their necks, representing all the pretenders whom he had fought and put to death—Athrîna, Nadinta-bel, Khshatrita, Vahyazdâta, Arakha, and Chitrañtakhma; an inscription, written in the three official languages of the court, recounts at full length his mighty deeds. The drama did not, however, come to a close with the punishment of Vahyazdâta, for though no tribe or chieftain remained now in open revolt, many of those who had taken no active share in the rebellion had, by their conduct during the crisis, laid themselves open to grave suspicions, and it seemed but prudent to place them under strict surveillance or to remove them from office altogether. Orœtes had been summarily despatched, and his execution did not disturb the peace of Asia Minor; but Aryandes, to whose rule Cambyses had entrusted the valley of the Nile, displayed no less marked symptoms of disaffection, and deserved the same fate. Though he had not ventured to usurp openly the title of king, he had arrogated to himself all the functions and rights of royalty, and had manifested as great an independence in his government as if he had been an actual Pharaoh. The inhabitants of Cyrene did not approve of the eagerness displayed by their tyrant Arkesilas III. to place himself under the Persian yoke: after first expelling and then recalling him, they drove him away a second time, and at length murdered him at Barca, whither he had fled for refuge. Pheretimê came to Egypt to seek the help of Aryandes, just as Laarchos had formerly implored the assistance of Amasis, and represented to him that her son had fallen a victim to his devotion to his suzerain. It was a good opportunity to put to ransom one of the wealthiest countries of Africa; so the governor sent to the Cyrenaica all the men and vessels at his disposal. Barca was the only city to offer any resistance, and the Persian troops were detained for nine months motionless before its walls, and the city then only succumbed through treachery. Some detachments forced their way as far as the distant town of Euesperides,[1] and it is possible that Aryandes dreamt for a moment of realising the designs which Cambyses had formed against Carthage. Insufficiency of supplies stayed the advance of his generals; but the riches of their ally, Cyrene, offered them a strong temptation, and they were deliberating how they might make this wealth their own before returning to Memphis, and were, perhaps, on the point of risking the attempt, when they received orders to withdraw. The march across the desert proved almost fatal to them. The Libyans of Marmarica, attracted by the spoils with which the Persian troops were laden, harassed them incessantly, and inflicted on them serious losses; they succeeded, however, in arriving safely with their prisoners, among whom were the survivors of the inhabitants of Barca. At this time the tide of fortune was setting strongly in favour of Darius: Aryandes, anxious to propitiate that monarch, despatched these wretched captives to Persia as a trophy of his success, and Darius sent them into Bactriana, where they founded a new Barca.[2] But

[1] This is the town which later on under the Lagidæ received the name of Berenice, and which is now called Benghazi.

[2] It is doubtless to these acts of personal authority on the part of

this tardy homage availed him nothing. Darius himself visited Egypt and disembarrassed himself of his troublesome subject by his summary execution, inflicted, some said, because he had issued coins of a superior fineness to those of the royal mint,[1] while, according to others, it was because he had plundered Egypt and so ill-treated the Egyptians as to incite them to rebellion. After the suppression of this rival, Darius set himself to win the affection of his Egyptian province, or, at least, to render its servitude bearable. With a country so devout and so impressed with its own superiority over all other nations, the best means of accomplishing his object was to show profound respect for its national gods and its past glory. Darius, therefore, proceeded to shower favours on the priests, who had been subject to persecution ever since the disastrous campaign in Ethiopia. Cambyses had sent into exile in Elam the chief priest of Sais—that Uzaharrîsnîti who had initiated him into the sacred rites; Darius gave permission to this important personage to return to his native land, and commissioned him to repair the damage inflicted by the madness of the son of Cyrus. Uzaharrîsnîti, escorted back with honour to his native

Aryandes that Darius alludes in the Behistun Inscription, when he says, "While I was before Babylon, the following provinces revolted against me—Persia and Susiana, the Medes and Assyria, and the Egyptians . . ."

[1] It is not certain that Aryandes did actually strike any coinage in his own name, and perhaps Herodotus has only repeated a popular story current in Egypt in his days. If this money actually existed, its coinage was but a pretext employed by Darius; the true motive of the condemnation of Aryandes was certainly an armed revolt, or a serious presumption of revolutionary intentions.

city, re-established there the colleges of sacred scribes, and restored to the temple of Nît the lands and revenues which had been confiscated. Greek tradition soon improved upon the national account of this episode, and asserted that Darius took an interest in the mysteries of Egyptian theology, and studied the sacred books, and that on his arrival at Memphis in 517 B.C., immediately after the death of an Apis, he took part publicly in the general mourning, and promised a reward of a hundred talents of gold to whosoever should discover the successor of the bull. According to a popular story still current when Herodotus travelled in Egypt, the king visited the temple of Pthah before leaving Memphis, and ordered his statue to be erected there beside that of Sesostris. The priests refused to obey this command, for, said they, "Darius has not equalled the deeds of Sesostris: he has not conquered the Scythians, whom Sesostris overcame." Darius replied that "he hoped to accomplish as much as Sesostris had done, if he lived as long as Sesostris," and so conciliated the patriotic pride of the priests. The Egyptians, grateful for his moderation, numbered him among the legislators whose memory they revered, by the side of Menes, Asykhis, Bocchoris, and Sabaco.

The whole empire was now obedient to the will of one man, but the ordeal from which it had recently escaped showed how loosely the elements of it were bound together, and with what facility they could be disintegrated. The system of government in force hitherto was that introduced into Assyria by Tiglath-pileser III., which had proved so eminently successful in the time of Sargon and his descendants;

Babylon and Ecbatana had inherited it from Nineveh, and Persepolis had in turn adopted it from Ecbatana and Babylon. It had always been open to objections, of which by no means the least was the great amount of power and independence accorded by it to the provincial governors; but this inconvenience had been little felt when the empire was of moderate dimensions, and when no province permanently annexed to the empire lay at any very great distance from the capital for the time being. But this was no longer the case, now that Persian rule extended over nearly the whole of Asia, from the Indus to the Thracian Bosphorus, and over a portion of Africa also. It must have seemed far from prudent to set governors invested with almost regal powers over countries so distant that a decree despatched from the palace might take several weeks to reach its destination. The heterogeneity of the elements in each province was a guarantee of peace in the eyes of the sovereign, and Darius carefully abstained from any attempt at unification: not only did he allow vassal republics, and tributary kingdoms and nations to subsist side by side, but he took care that each should preserve its own local dynasty, language, writing, customs, religion, and peculiar legislation, besides the right to coin money stamped with the name of its chief or its civic symbol. The Greek cities of the coast maintained their own peculiar constitutions which they had enjoyed under the Mermnadæ; Darius merely required that the chief authority among them should rest in the hands of the aristocratic party, or in those of an elective or hereditary tyrant whose personal interest secured his fidelity. The

THE DIVISION OF THE EMPIRE INTO SATRAPIES 181

Carians,[1] Lycians,[2] Pamphylians, and Cilicians[3] continued under the rule of their native princes, subject only to the usual obligations of the *corvée*, taxation, and military service as in past days; the majority of the barbarous tribes which inhabited the Taurus and the mountainous regions in the centre of Asia Minor were even exempted from all definite taxes, and were merely required to respect

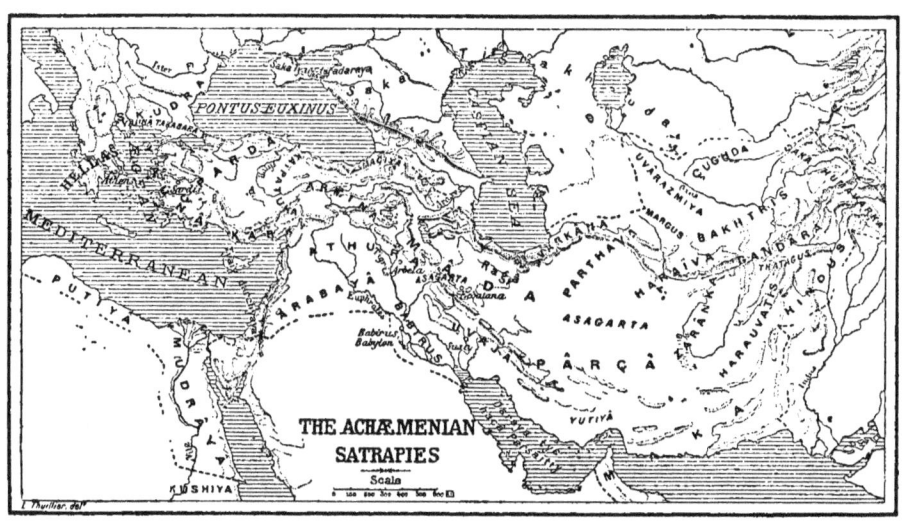

the couriers, caravans, and armies which passed through their territory. Native magistrates and kings still bore

[1] Herodotus cites among the commanders of the Persian fleet three Carian dynasts, Histiæus, Pigres, and Damasithymus, besides the famous Artemisia of Halicarnassus.

[2] In Herodotus where a dynast named Kyberniskos, son of Sika, is mentioned among the commanders of the fleet. The received text of Herodotus needs correction, and we should read Kybernis, son of Kossika, some of whose coins are still in existence.

[3] The Cilician contingent in the fleet of Xerxes at Salamis was commanded by Syennesis himself, and Cilicia never had a satrap until the time of Cyrus the younger.

sway in Phœnicia[1] and Cyprus, and the shêkhs of the desert preserved their authority over the marauding and semi-nomadic tribes of Idumæa, Nabatæa, Moab, and Ammon, and the wandering Bedâwin on the Euphrates and the Khabur. Egypt, under Darius, remained what she had been under the Saitic and Ethiopian dynasties, a feudal state governed by a Pharaoh, who, though a foreigner, was yet reputed to be of the solar race; the land continued to be divided unequally into diverse principalities, Thebes still preserving its character as a theocracy under the guidance of the pallacide of Amon and her priestly counsellors, while the other districts subsisted under military chieftains. Our information concerning the organisation of the central and eastern provinces is incomplete, but it is certain that here also the same system prevailed. In the years of peace which succeeded the troubled opening of his reign, that is, from 519 to 515 B.C.,[2] Darius divided the whole empire into satrapies, whose number varied at different periods of his reign from twenty to twenty-three, and even twenty-eight.[3]

---

[1] Three kings, viz. the kings of Sidon, Tyre, and Arvad, bore commands in the Phœnician fleet of Xerxes.

[2] Herodotus states that this dividing of the empire into provinces took place immediately after the accession of Darius, and this mistake is explained by the fact that he ignores almost entirely the civil wars which filled the earliest years of the reign. His enumeration of twenty satrapies comprises India and omits Thrace, which enables us to refer the drawing up of his list to a period before the Scythian campaign, viz. before 514 B.C. Herodotus very probably copied it from the work of Hecatæus of Miletus, and consequently it reproduces a document contemporary with Darius himself.

[3] The number twenty is, as has been remarked, that given by Herodotus, and probably by Hecatæus of Miletus. The great Behistun Inscription

Persia proper was not included among these, for she had been the cradle of the reigning house, and the instrument of conquest.[1] The Iranian table-land, and the parts of India or regions beyond the Oxus which bordered on it, formed twelve important vice-royalties—Media, Hyrcania, Parthia, Zaranka, Aria, Khorasmia, Bactriana, Sogdiana, Gandaria, and the country of the Sakæ—reaching from the plains of Tartary almost to the borders of China, the country of the Thatagus in the upper basin of the Elmend, Arachosia, and the land of Maka on the shores of the Indian Ocean. Ten satrapies were reckoned in the west—Uvayâ, Elam, in which lay Susa, one of the favourite residences of Darius; Babirus (Babylon) and Chaldæa; Athurâ, the ancient kingdom of Assyria; Arabayâ, stretching from the Khabur to the Litany, the Jordan, and the Orontes; Egypt, the peoples of the sea, among whom were reckoned the Phœnicians, Cilicians, and Cypriots, and the islanders of the Ægean; Yaunâ, which comprised Lycia, Caria, and the Greek colonies along the coast; Sparda, with Phrygia and Mysia; Armenia; and lastly, Katpatuka or Cappadocia, which lay on both sides of the Halys from the Taurus to the Black Sea. If each of these provinces had been governed, as formerly, by a single individual, who thus became king in all but name and descent, the empire would have run great

enumerates twenty-three countries, and the Inscription of Nakhsh-î-Rustem gives twenty-eight.

[1] In the great Behistun Inscription Darius mentions Persia first of all the countries in his possession. In the Inscription E of Persepolis he omits it entirely, and in that of Nakhsh-î-Rustem he does not include it in the general catalogue.

risk of a speedy dissolution. Darius therefore avoided concentrating the civil and military powers in the same hands. In each province he installed three officials independent of each other, but each in direct communication with himself—a satrap, a general, and a secretary of state. The satraps were chosen from any class in the nation, from among the poor as well as from among the wealthy, from foreigners as well as from Persians;[1] but the most important satrapies were bestowed only on persons allied by birth[2] or marriage with the Achæmenids,[3] and, by preference, on the legitimate descendants of the six noble houses. They were not appointed for any prescribed period, but continued in office during the king's pleasure. They exercised absolute authority in all civil matters, and maintained a court, a body-guard,[4] palaces and extensive parks, or *paradises*, where they indulged in the pleasures of the chase; they controlled the incidence of taxation,[5] administered justice, and possessed the power

---

[1] Herodotus mentions a satrap chosen from among the Lydians, Pactyas, and another satrap of Greek extraction, Xenagoras of Halicarnassus.

[2] The most characteristic instance is that of Hystaspes, who was satrap of Persia under Cambyses, and of Parthia and Hyrcania under his own son. One of the brothers of Darius, Artaphernes, was satrap of Sardes, and three of the king's sons, Achemenes, Ariaʋignes, and Masistes, were satraps of Egypt, Ionia, and Bactriana respectively.

[3] To understand how well established was the custom of bestowing satrapies on those only who were allied by marriage to the royal house, it is sufficient to recall the fact that, later on, under Xerxes I., when Pausanias, King of Sparta, had thoughts of obtaining the position of satrap in Greece, he asked for the hand of an Achæmenian princess.

[4] We know, for example, that Orœtes, satrap of Sardes under Cyrus, Cambyses, and Darius, had a body-guard of 1000 Persians.

[5] Thus, Artaphernes, satrap of Sardes, had a cadastral survey made

of life and death. Attached to each satrap was a secretary of state, who ostensibly acted as his chancellor, but whose real function was to exercise a secret supervision over his conduct and report upon it to the imperial ministers.[1] The Persian troops, native militia and auxiliary forces quartered in the province, were placed under the orders, moreover, of a general, who was usually hostile to the satrap and the secretary.[2] These three officials counterbalanced each other, and held each other mutually in check, so that a revolt was rendered very difficult, if not impossible. All three were kept in constant communication with the court by relays of regular couriers, who carried their despatches on horseback or on camels, from one end of Asia to the other, in the space of a few weeks.[3] The most celebrated of the post-roads was that which ran from Sardes to Susa through Lydia and Phrygia, crossing the Halys, traversing Cappadocia and Cilicia, and passing through Armenia and across the Euphrates, until at length, after passing through Matiênê and the country of the Cossæans, it reached Elam. This main route was divided

of the territory of the Ionians, and by the results of this survey he regulated the imposition of taxes, "which from that time up to the present day are exacted according to his ordinance."

[1] The rôle played by the secretary is clearly indicated by the history of Orœtes, satrap of Sardes.

[2] While Darius appoints his brother Artaphernes satrap of Lydia, he entrusts the command of the army and the fleet to Otanes, son of Sisamnes. Similarly several generals are met with at the side of Artaphernes in the Ionic revolt.

[3] Xenophon compares their speed in travelling to the flight of birds. A good example of the use of the camel for the postal service is cited by Strabo, on the occasion of the death of Philotas and the execution of Parmenion under Alexander.

into one hundred and eleven stages, which were performed by couriers on horseback and partly in ferry-boats, in eighty-four days. Other routes, of which we have no particular information, led to Egypt, Media, Bactria, and India,[1] and by their means the imperial officials in the capital were kept fully informed of all that took place in the most distant parts of the empire. As an extra precaution, the king sent out annually certain officers, called his "eyes" or his "ears,"[2] who appeared on the scene when they were least expected, and investigated the financial or political situation, reformed abuses in the administration, and reprimanded or even suspended the government officials; they were accompanied by a body of troops to support their decisions, whose presence invested their counsels with the strongest sanction.[3] An unfavourable report, a slight irregularity, a mere suspicion, even, was sufficient to disqualify a satrap. Sometimes he was deposed, often secretly condemned to death without a trial, and the execution of the judgment was committed even to his own servants. A messenger would arrive unexpectedly, and remit to the guards an order charging them to put their chief to death—an order which was promptly executed at the mere sight of the royal decree.

[1] Ctesias at the end of his work describes the route leading from Ephesus to Bactriana and India. It is probable that the route described by Isidorus of Charax in his *Stathma Parthica* already existed in the times of the Achæmenids, and was traversed by their postal couriers.

[2] Mention of the *Eye of the king* occurs in Herodotus, in Æschylus, and in Plutarch, of the *Ear* in Xenophon; cf. the Persian proverb, according to which "The king has many eyes and many ears."

[3] Xenophon affirms that these inspections were still held in his day.

THE FINANCIAL SYSTEM—THE DARIC

This reform in the method of government was displeasing to the Persian nobles, whose liberty of action it was designed to curtail, and they took their revenge in sneering at the obedience they could not refuse to render. Cyrus, they said, had been a father, Cambyses a master, but Darius was only a pedler greedy of gain. The chief reason for this division of the empire into provinces was, indeed, fiscal rather than political: to arrange the incidence of taxation in his province, to collect the revenue in due time and forward the total amount to the imperial treasury, formed the fundamental duty of a satrap, to which all others had to yield. Persia proper was exempt from the payment of any fixed sum, its inhabitants being merely required to offer presents to the king whenever he passed through their districts. These semi-compulsory gifts were proportioned to the fortunes of the individual contributors; they might consist merely of an ox or a sheep, a little milk or cheese, some dates, a handful of flour, or some vegetables. The other provinces, after being subjected to a careful survey, were assessed partly in money, partly in kind, according to their natural capacity or wealth. The smallest amount of revenue raised in any province amounted to 170 talents of silver—the sum, for instance, collected from Arachosia with its dependencies Gedrosia and Gandara; while Egypt yielded a revenue of 700 talents, and the amount furnished by Babylon, the wealthiest province of all, amounted to 1000 talents. The total revenue of the empire reached the enormous sum of £3,311,997, estimated by weight of silver, which is equivalent to over £26,000,000 of modern English money, if the greater value of silver in antiquity is taken into consideration. In order to facilitate the collection of the revenue, Darius issued the gold and silver coins which are named after him. On the obverse side these darics are stamped with a figure of the sovereign, armed with the bow or javelin. They were coined on the scale of 3000 gold darics to one talent, each daric weighing normally ·2788 oz. troy, and being worth exactly 20 silver drachmæ or Medic shekels; so that the relative value of the two metals was approximately 1 to $13\frac{1}{2}$. The most ancient type of daric was thick and irregular in shape, and rudely stamped, but of remarkable fineness, the amount of alloy being never more than three per cent. The use of this coinage was nowhere obligatory, and it only became general in the countries bordering on the Mediterranean, where it met the requirements of international traffic and political relations, and in the payment of the army and the navy. In the interior, the medium of exchange used in wholesale and retail commercial transactions continued to be metals estimated by weight, and the kings of Persia themselves preferred to store their revenues in the shape of bullion; as the metal was received at the royal treasury it was melted and poured into clay moulds, and was minted into money only gradually, according to the whim or necessity of the moment.[2] Taxes

DARIC OF DARIUS, SON OF HYSTASPES.[1]

[1] Drawn by Faucher-Gudin, from a specimen in the Bibliothèque Nationale.
[2] Arrian relates that Alexander found 50,000 talents' weight of silver in

in kind were levied even more largely than in money, but the exact form they assumed in the different regions of the empire has not yet been ascertained. The whole empire was divided into districts, which were charged with the victualling of the army and the court, and Babylon alone bore a third of the charges under this head. We learn elsewhere that Egypt was bound to furnish corn for the 120,000 men of the army of occupation, and that the fisheries of the Fayum yielded the king a yearly revenue of 240 talents. The Medes furnished similarly 100,000 sheep, 4000 mules, and 3000 horses; the Armenians, 30,000 foals; the Cilicians, 365 white horses, one for each day in the year; the Babylonians, 500 youthful eunuchs; and any city or town which produced or manufactured any valuable commodity was bound to furnish a regular supply to the sovereign. Thus, Chalybon provided wine; Libya and the Oases, salt; India, dogs, with whose support four large villages in Babylonia were charged; the Æolian Assos, cheese; and other places, in like manner, wool, wines, dyes, medicines, and chemicals. These imperial taxes, though they seem to us somewhat heavy, were not excessive, but taken by themselves they give us no idea of the burdens which each province had to resign itself to bear. The state provided no income for the satraps; their maintenance and that of their suite were charged on the province, and they made ample exactions on the natives. The province of Babylon was required to furnish its satrap daily with an *ardeb* of silver; Egypt, India,

the treasury at Susa; other hoards quite as rich were contained in the palaces of Persepolis and Pasargadæ.

Media, and Syria each provided a no less generous allowance for its governor, and the poorest provinces were not less heavily burdened. The satraps required almost as much to satisfy their requirements as did the king; but for the most part they fairly earned their income, and saved more to their subjects than they extorted from them. They repressed brigandage, piracy, competition between the various cities, and local wars; while quarrels, which formerly would have been settled by an appeal to arms, were now composed before their judgment-seats, and in case of need the rival factions were forcibly compelled to submit to their decisions. They kept up the roads, and afforded complete security to travellers by night and day; they protected industries and agriculture, and, in accordance with the precepts of their religious code, they accounted it an honourable task to break up waste land or replant deserted sites. Darius himself did not disdain to send congratulations to a satrap who had planted trees in Asia Minor, and laid out one of those wooded parks in which the king delighted to refresh himself after the fatigues of government, by the exercise of walking or in the pleasures of the chase. In spite of its defects, the system of government inaugurated by Darius secured real prosperity to his subjects, and to himself a power far greater than that enjoyed by any of his predecessors. It rendered revolts on the part of the provincial governors extremely difficult, and enabled the court to draw up a regular budget and provide for its expenses without any undue pressure on its subjects; in one point only was it defective, but that point was a cardinal one, namely, in the military organisation. Darius himself maintained, for his personal protection, a bodyguard recruited from the Persians and the Medes. It was divided into three corps, consisting respectively of 2000 cavalry, 2000 infantry of noble birth, armed with lances whose shafts were ornamented below with apples of gold or silver—whence their name of *mêlophori*—and under them the 10,000 "immortals," in ten battalions, the first of which had its lances ornamented with golden pomegranates. This guard formed the nucleus of the standing army, which could be reinforced by the first and second grades of Persian and Median feudal nobility at the first summons. Forces of varying strength garrisoned the most important fortresses of the empire, such as Sardes, Memphis, Elephantinê, Daphnæ, Babylon, and many others, to hold the restless natives in check. These were, indeed, the only regular troops on which the king could always rely. Whenever a war broke out which demanded no special effort, the satraps of the provinces directly involved summoned the military contingents of the cities and vassal states under their control, and by concerted action endeavoured to bring the affair to a successful issue without the necessity of an appeal to the central authority. If, on the contrary, troubles arose which threatened the welfare of the whole empire, and the sovereign felt called upon to conduct the campaign in person, he would mobilise his guard, and summon the reserves from several provinces or even from all of them. Veritable hordes of recruits then poured in, but these masses of troops, differing from each other in their equipment and methods of fighting, in disposition and in language, formed a herd of men rather than an army. They had no cohesion or confidence in themselves, and their leaders, unaccustomed to command such enormous numbers, suffered themselves to be led rather than exercise authority as guides. Any good qualities the troops may have possessed were neutralised by lack of unity in their methods of action, and their actual faults exaggerated this defect, so that, in spite of their splendid powers of endurance and their courage under every ordeal, they ran the risk of finding themselves in a state of hopeless inferiority when called upon to meet armies very much smaller, but composed of homogenous elements, all animated with the same spirit and drilled in the same school.

By continual conquests, the Persians were now reduced to only two outlets for their energies, in two opposite directions—in the east towards India, in the west towards Greece. Everywhere else their advance was arrested by the sea or other obstacles almost as impassable to their heavily armed battalions: to the north the empire was bounded by the Black Sea, the Caucasus, the Caspian Sea, and the Siberian steppes; to the south, by the Indian Ocean, the sandy table-land of Arabia, and the African deserts. At one moment, about 512 B.C., it is possible that they pushed forward towards the east.[1] From the Iranian plateau they beheld from afar the immense plain

[1] India is not referred to in the Behistun Inscription, but is mentioned in one of the Inscriptions of Persepolis, and in that of Nakhsh-î-Rustem. The campaign in which it was subjugated must be placed about 512 B.C.

FUNERAL OFFERINGS.

of the Hapta Hindu (or the Punjab). Darius invaded this territory, and made himself master of extensive districts which he formed into a new satrapy, that of India, but subsequently, renouncing all idea of pushing eastward as far as the Ganges, he turned his steps towards the southeast. A fleet, constructed at Peukêla and placed under the command of a Greek admiral, Scylax of Caryanda, descended the Indus by order of the king;[1] subjugating the tribes who dwelt along the banks as he advanced, Scylax at length reached the ocean, on which he ventured forth, undismayed by the tides, and proceeded in a westerly direction, exploring, in less than thirty months, the shores of Gedrosia and Arabia. Once on the threshold of India, the Persians saw open before them a brilliant and lucrative career: the circumstances which prevented them from following up this preliminary success are unknown— perhaps the first developments of nascent Buddhism deterred them—but certain it is that they arrested their steps when they had touched merely the outskirts of the basin of the Indus, and retreated at once towards the west. The conquest of Lydia, and subsequently of the Greek cities and islands along the coast of the Ægean, had doubtless enriched the empire by the acquisition of active subject populations, whose extraordinary aptitude in the arts of peace as well as of war might offer incalculable resources to a sovereign who should know

---

[1] Scylax published an account of his voyage which was still extant in the time of Aristotle. Hugo Berger questions the authenticity of the circumnavigation of Arabia, as that of the circumnavigation of Africa under Necho.

how to render them tractable and rule them wisely. Not only did they possess the elements of a navy as enterprising and efficacious as that of the Phœnicians, but the perfection of their equipment and their discipline on land rendered them always superior to any Asiatic army, in whatever circumstances, unless they were crushed by overwhelming numbers. Inquisitive, bold, and restless, greedy of gain, and inured to the fatigues and dangers of travel, the Greeks were to be encountered everywhere— in Asia Minor, Egypt, Syria, Babylon, and even Persia itself; and it was a Greek, we must remember, whom the great king commissioned to navigate the course of the Indus and the waters of the Indian Ocean. At the same time, the very ardour of their temperament, and their consequent pride, their impatience of all regular control, their habitual proneness to civic strife, and to sanguinary quarrels with the inhabitants of the neighbouring cities, rendered them the most dangerous subjects imaginable to govern, and their loyalty very uncertain. Moreover, their admission as vassals of the Persian empire had not altered their relations with European Greece, and commercial transactions between the opposite shores of the Ægean, inter-marriages, the travels of voyagers, movements of mercenaries, and political combinations, went on as freely and frequently under the satraps of Sardes as under the Mermnadæ. It was to Corinth, Sparta, and Athens that the families banished by Cyrus after his conquest fled for refuge, and every time a change of party raised a new tyrant to power in one of the Æolian, Ionian, or Doric communities, the adherents of the deposed ruler

CONQUEST OF INDIA AND RELATIONS WITH GREECE 195

rushed in similar manner to seek shelter among their friends across the sea, sure to repay their hospitality should occasion ever require it. Plots and counterplots were formed between the two shores, without any one paying much heed to the imperial authority of Persia, and the constant support which the subject Greeks found among their free brethren was bound before long to rouse the anger of the court at Susa. When Polycrates, foreseeing the fall of Amasis, placed himself under the suzerainty of Cambyses, the Corinthians and Spartans came to besiege him in Samos without manifesting any respect for the great king. They failed in this particular enterprise,[1] but later on, after Orœtes had been seized and put to death, it was to the Spartans that the successor of Polycrates, Mæandrios, applied for help to assert his claim to the possession of the tyranny against Syloson, brother of Polycrates and a personal friend of Darius.[2] This constant intervention of the foreigner was in evident contradiction to the spirit which had inspired the reorganisation of the empire. Just when efforts were being made to strengthen the imperial power and ensure more effective obedience from the provincials by the institution of satrapies, it was impossible to put up with acts of unwarrantable interference, which would endanger the prestige of the sovereign and the authority of his officers. Conquest presented the

[1] The date of the death of Polycrates must be placed between that of the conquest of Egypt and that of the revolt of Gaumâta, either in 524 or 523 B.C.

[2] The reinstatement of Syloson may be placed in 516 B.C., about the time when Darius was completing the reorganisation of the empire and preparing to attack Greece.

one and only natural means of escape from the difficulties of the present situation and of preventing their recurrence; when satraps should rule over the European as well as over the Asiatic coasts of the Ægean, all these turbulent Greeks would be forced to live at peace with one another and in awe of the sovereign, as far as their fickle nature would allow. It was not then, as is still asserted, the mere caprice of a despot which brought upon the Greek world the scourge of the Persian wars, but the imperious necessity of security, which obliges well-organised empires to subjugate in turn all the tribes and cities which cause constant trouble on its frontiers. Darius, who was already ruler of a good third of the Hellenic world, from Trebizond to Barca, saw no other means of keeping what he already possessed, and of putting a stop to the incessant fomentation of rebellion in his own territories, than to conquer the mother-country as he had conquered the colonies, and to reduce to subjection the whole of European Hellas.

THE LAST DAYS OF THE OLD EASTERN WORLD

THE MEDIAN WARS—THE LAST NATIVE DYNASTIES OF EGYPT—THE EASTERN WORLD ON THE EVE OF THE MACEDONIAN CONQUEST.

The Persians in 512 B.C.—European Greece and the dangers which its independence presented to the safety of the empire—The preliminaries of the Median wars: the Scythian expedition, the conquest of Thrace and Macedonia— The Ionic revolt, the intervention of Athens and the taking of Sardes; the battle of Ladê—Mardonius in Thrace and in Macedonia.

The Median wars—The expedition of Datis and Artaphernes: the taking of Eretria, the battle of Marathon (490)—The revolt of Egypt under Khabbisha; the death of Darius and the accession of Xerxes I.—The revolt of Babylon under Shamasherib—The invasion of Greece: Artemision, Thermopylœ, the taking of Athens, Salamis—Platæa and the final retreat of the Persians: Mycalê—The war carried on by the Athenians and the league of Delos: Inaros, the campaigns in Cyprus and Egypt, the peace of Callias—The death of Xerxes.

Artaxerxes I. (465-424): the revolt of Megabyzos—The palaces of Pasargadœ. Persepolis, and Susa; Persian architecture and sculpture; court life, the king and his harem—Revolutions in the palace—Xerxes II., Sekudianos, Darius II.— Intervention in Greek affairs and the convention of Miletus; the end of the peace of Callias—Artaxerxes II. (404-359) and Cyrus the Younger: the battle of Kunaxa and the retreat of the ten thousand (401).

Troubles in Asia Minor, Syria, and Egypt—Amyrtœus and the XXVIIIth Saite dynasty—The XXIXth Sebennytic dynasty—Nephorites I., Hakoris, Psammutis, their alliances with Evagoras and with the states of Continental Greece—The XXXth Mendesian dynasty—Nectanebo I., Tachós and the invasion of Syria, the revolt of Nectanebo II.—The death of Artaxerxes II.—The accession of Ochus (359 B.C.), his unfortunate wars in the Delta, the conquest of Egypt (342) and the reconstitution of the empire.

The Eastern world: Elam, Urartu, the Syrian kingdoms, the ancient Semitic states decayed and decaying—Babylon in its decline—The Jewish state and its miseries—Nehemiah, Ezra—Egypt in the eyes of the Greeks: Sais, the Delta, the inhabitants of the marshes—Memphis, its monuments, its population—Travels in Upper Egypt: the Fayum, Khemmis, Thebes, Elephantiné—The apparent vigour and actual feebleness of Egypt.

Persia and its powerlessness to resist attack: the rise of Macedonia, Philippi —Arses (337) and Darius Codomannos (336)—Alexander the Great—The invasion of Asia—The battle of Granicus and the conquest of the Asianic peninsula—Issus, the siege of Tyre and of Gaza, the conquest of Egypt, the foundation of Alexandria—Arbela: the conquest of Babylon, Susa, and Ecbatana—The death of Darius and the last days of the old Eastern world.

A LION-HUNT, PERSIANS AND MACEDONIANS.[1]

CHAPTER II

THE LAST DAYS OF THE OLD EASTERN WORLD

The Median wars—The last native dynasties of Egypt—The Eastern world on the eve of the Macedonian conquest.

DARIUS appears to have formed this project of conquest immediately after his first victories, when his initial attempts to institute satrapies had taught him not only the condition and needs of Asia Minor, but of the

[1] Drawn by Boudier, from one of the sarcophagi of Sidon, now in the Museum of St. Irene. The vignette, which is by Faucher-Gudin, represents the sitting cynocephalus of Nectanebo I., now in the Egyptian Museum at the Vatican.

various other regions subject to his laws. Two roads lay open before him by which to achieve his end. One by sea, from the Ionian to the Attic coast, straight through the Cyclades; the other by land, with the exception of the narrow straits of the Bosphorus or of the Hellespont, through Thrace and Macedonia. The first was by far the shorter, but the more perilous. It required the possession of an immense fleet, for such a bold undertaking could not be carried out without a considerable force of men, and the largest vessels then built could transport only a small number of troops and horses in addition to their ordinary crew; it also incurred the risk of a naval engagement—an event always to be dreaded with vessels heavily laden with men and the material of war, when it was a question of encountering such experienced seamen as the Greeks of that period. Prudence, therefore, prompted its rejection, however great an economy of time and fatigue it promised, unless it were possible to avoid an encounter with the enemy's fleet, and on landing to be sure of meeting with partisans willing to throw open the gates of their towns, or at least facilitate the work of disembarkation. Attica was the point aimed at, for it was the key of the position, and the possession of it would have permitted Darius to adopt the sea-route without undue risk; but Athens was in the hands of the Pisistratidæ, and Hippias, although he was the vassal of Persia through holding the fief of Sigæum in the Troad, was not at all anxious to see Darius establish himself in the heart of Hellas. As long as Athens was hostile, the safest route, and, indeed, the only one practicable for the entire Persian army, was that bordering the north of the Ægean, debouching at the defiles of Thessaly. It was this road that the authorities at Susa finally selected, although its choice entailed a host of preliminary precautions which demanded time, men, and money; there were fresh Greek colonies to be subdued, and beyond them the warlike people of Thrace, while behind these lay the Scythian tribes. Even though a century had elapsed since the death of Madyes, the remembrance of the Scythians continued to alarm the whole of Asia; tales were still told among the Medes, in Lydia, in the sanctuary of Ascalon, on the frontier of Egypt, and in the sacred cities of Pteria, of their wild raids over mountain and valley, their path marked by cities given to the flames or razed to the ground, populations carried away as slaves, violated temples, and always, as a sequel to these chapters of horrors, the vengeance which the offended gods wreaked upon them for these acts of sacrilege. More recently the accounts given by the Greek colonists and the itinerant merchants of the northern shores of the Black Sea, without detracting from the report of their courage and ferocity, had added to it that of their wealth; gold-mines were said to be scattered over the regions occupied by them, guarded by griffins, and worked for the good of the inhabitants by harmless ants as large as foxes. Besides this, Darius was constantly coming into conflict with one or other of their hordes on his northern frontiers—on the Iaxartes, beyond Bactriana and Sogdiana, in the Caucasus, and latterly in Europe, on the Ister and the borders of Thrace. It is, therefore, not to be wondered at that, before attacking Greece, he desired to provide against all risks by teaching the Scythians such a lesson as would prevent them from bearing down upon his right flank during his march, or upon his rear while engaged in a crucial struggle in the Hellenic peninsula. On the other hand, the geographical information possessed by the Persians with regard to the Danubian regions was of so vague a character, that Darius must have believed the Scythians to have been nearer to his line of operations, and their country less desolate than was really the case.[1] A flotilla, commanded by Ariaramnes, satrap of Cappadocia, ventured across the Black Sea in 515,[2] landed a few thousand men upon the opposite shore, and brought back prisoners who furnished those in command with the information they required.[3] Darius, having learned what he could from these poor wretches, crossed the Bosphorus in 514, with a body of troops which tradition computed at 800,000, conquered the eastern coast of Thrace, and won his way in

[1] The motives imputed to Darius by the ancients for making this expedition are the desire of avenging the disasters of the Scythian invasion, or of performing an exploit which should render him as famous as his predecessors in the eyes of posterity.

[2] The reconnaissance of Ariaramnes is intimàtely connected with the expedition itself in Ctesias, and could have preceded it by a few months only. If we take for the date of the latter the year 514–513, the date given in the Table of the Capitol, that of the former cannot be earlier than 515. Ariaramnes was not satrap of Cappadocia, for Cappadocia belonged then to the satrapy of Daskylion.

[3] The supplementary paragraphs of the Inscription of Behistun speak of an expedition of Darius against the Sakæ, which is supposed to have had as its objective either the sea of Aral or the Tigris. Would it not be possible to suppose that the sea mentioned is the Pontus Euxinus, and to take the mutilated text of Behistun to be a description either of the campaign beyond the Danube, or rather of the preliminary *reconnaissance* of Ariaramnes a year before the expedition itself?

a series of conflicts as far as the Ister. The Ionian sailors built for him a bridge of boats, which he entrusted to their care, and he then started forward into the steppes in search of the enemy. The Scythians refused a pitched battle, but they burnt the pastures before him on every side, filled up the wells, carried off the cattle, and then slowly retreated into the interior, leaving Darius to face the vast extent of the steppes and the terrors of famine. Later tradition stated that he wandered for two months in these solitudes between the Ister and the Tanais; he had constructed on the banks of this latter river a series of earthworks, the remains of which were shown in the time of Herodotus, and had at length returned to his point of departure with merely the loss of a few sick men. The barbarians stole a march upon him, and advised the Greeks to destroy the bridge, retire within their cities, and abandon the Persians to their fate. The tyrant of the Chersonnesus, Miltiades the Athenian, was inclined to follow their advice; but Histiæus, the governor of Miletus, opposed it, and eventually carried his point. Darius reached the southern bank without difficulty, and returned to Asia.[1] The Greek towns of Thrace thought themselves rid of him, and rose in revolt; but he left 80,000 men in Europe who, at first

[1] Ctesias limits the campaign beyond the Danube to a fifteen days' march; and Strabo places the crossing of the Danube near the mouth of that river, at the island of Peukê, and makes the expedition stop at the Dniester. Neither the line of direction of the Persian advance nor their farthest point reached is known. The eight forts which they were said to have built, the ruins of which were shown on the banks of the Oaros as late as the time of Herodotus, were probably tumuli similar to those now met with on the Russian steppes, the origin of which is ascribed by the people to persons celebrated in their history or traditions.

under Megabyzos, and then under Otanes, reduced them to subjection one after another, and even obliged Amyntas I., the King of Macedonia, to become a tributary of the empire. The expedition had not only failed to secure the submission of the Scythians, but apparently provoked reprisals on their part, and several of their bands penetrated ere long into the Chersonnesus. It nevertheless was not without solid result, for it showed that Darius, even if he could not succeed in subjugating the savage Danubian tribes, had but little to fear from them; it also secured for him a fresh province, that of Thrace, and, by the possession of Macedonia, brought his frontier into contact with Northern Greece. The overland route, in any case the more satisfactory of the two, was now in the hands of the invader.

Revolutions at Athens prevented him from setting out on his expedition as soon as he had anticipated. Hippias had been overthrown in 510, and having taken refuge at Sigæum, was seeking on all sides for some one to avenge him against his fellow-citizens. The satrap of Sardes, Artaphernes, declined at first to listen to him, for he hoped that the Athenians themselves would appeal to him, without his being obliged to have recourse to their former tyrant. As a matter of fact, they sent him an embassy, and begged his help against the Spartans. He promised it on condition that they would yield the traditional homage of earth and water, and their delegates complied with his demand, though on their return to Athens they were disowned by the citizens (508). Artaphernes, disappointed in this direction, now entered into communications with Hippias, and such close relations soon existed between the two that the Athenians showed signs of uneasiness. Two years later they again despatched fresh deputies to Sardes to beg the satrap not to espouse the cause of their former ruler. For a reply the satrap summoned them to recall the exiles, and, on their refusing (506),[1] their city became thenceforward the ostensible objective of the Persian army and fleet. The partisans of Hippias within the town were both numerous and active; it was expected that they would rise and hand over the city as soon as their chief should land on a point of territory with a force sufficient to intimidate the opposing faction. Athens in the hands of Hippias, would mean Athens in the hands of the Persians, and Greece accessible to the Persian hordes at all times by the shortest route. Darius therefore prepared to make the attempt, and in order to guard against any mishap, he caused all the countries that he was about to attack to be explored beforehand. Spies attached to his service were sent to scour the coasts of the Peloponnesus and take note of all its features, the state of its ports, the position of the islands and the fortresses; and they penetrated as far as Italy, if we may believe the story subsequently told to Herodotus.[2] While he thus studied the territory from a distance, he did not neglect precautions nearer to hand, but ordered the Milesians to occupy in his name the principal stations of the Ægean between Ionia and Attica. Histiæus,

[1] Herodotus fixes the date at the time when the Athenians first ostracised the principal partisans of the Pisistratids, and amongst others Hipparchus, son of Charmes, *i.e.* in 507–6.

[2] Herodotus said that Darius sent spies with the physician Democedes of Crotona shortly before the Scythian expedition.

whose loyalty had stood Darius in such good stead at the bridge over the Danube, did not, however, appear to him equal to so delicate a task: the king summoned him to Susa on some slight pretext, loaded him with honours, and replaced him by his nephew Aristagoras. Aristagoras at once attempted to justify the confidence placed in him by taking possession of Naxos; but the surprise that he had prepared ended in failure, discontent crept in among his men, and after a fruitless siege of four months he was obliged to withdraw (499).[1] His failure changed the tide of affairs. He was afraid that the Persians would regard it as a crime, and this fear prompted him to risk everything to save his fortune and his life. He retired from his office as tyrant, exhorted the Milesians, who were henceforth free to do so, to make war on the barbarians, and seduced from their allegiance the crews of the vessels just returned from Naxos, and still lying in the mouths of the Mæander; the tyrants who commanded them were seized, some exiled, and some put to death. The Æolians soon made common cause with their neighbours the Ionians, and by the last days of autumn the whole of the Ægean littoral was under arms (499).[2] From the outset Aristagoras realised that they would be promptly overcome if Asiatic Hellas were not supported by Hellas in Europe. While the Lydian

[1] Herodotus attributes an unlikely act of treachery to Megabates the Persian, who was commanding the Iranian contingent attached to the Ionian troops.

[2] The Dorian cities took no part in the revolt—at least Herodotus never mentions them among the confederates. The three Ionian cities of Ephesus, Kolophon, and Lebedos also seem to have remained aloof, and we know that the Ephesians were not present at the battle of Ladê.

satrap was demanding reinforcements from his sovereign, Aristagoras therefore repaired to the Peloponnesus as a suppliant for help. Sparta, embroiled in one of her periodical quarrels with Argos, gave him an insolent refusal;[1] even Athens, where the revolution had for the moment relieved her from the fear of the Pisistratidæ and the terrors of a barbarian invasion, granted him merely twenty triremes—enough to draw down reprisals on her immediately after their defeat, without sensibly augmenting the rebels' chances of success; to the Athenian contingent Eretria added five vessels, and this comprised his whole force. The leaders of the movement did not hesitate to assume the offensive with these slender resources. As early as the spring of 498, before Artaphernes had received reinforcements, they marched suddenly on Sardes. They burnt the lower town, but, as on many previous occasions, the citadel held out; after having encamped for several days at the foot of its rock, they returned to Ephesus laden with the spoil.[2] This indeed was a check to their hostilities, and such an abortive attempt was calculated to convince them of their powerlessness against the foreign rule. None the less, however, when it was generally known that they

[1] Aristagoras had with him a map of the world engraved on a bronze plate, which was probably a copy of the chart drawn up by Hecatæus of Miletus.

[2] Herodotus says that the Ionians on their return suffered a serious reverse near Ephesus. The author seems to have adopted some Lydian or Persian tradition hostile to the Ionians, for Charon of Lampsacus, who lived nearer to the time of these events, mentions only the retreat, and hints at no defeat. If the expedition had really ended in this disaster, it is not at all likely that the revolt would have attained the dimensions it did immediately afterwards.

had burnt the capital of Asia Minor, and had with impunity made the representative of the great king feel in his palace the smoke of the conflagration, the impression was such as actual victory could have produced. The cities which had hitherto hesitated to join them, now espoused their cause— the ports of the Troad and the Hellespont, Lycia, the Carians, and Cyprus—and their triumph would possibly have been secured had Greece beyond the Ægean followed the general movement and joined the coalition. Sparta, however, persisted in her indifference, and Athens took the opportunity of withdrawing from the struggle. The Asiatic Greeks made as good a defence as they could, but their resources fell far short of those of the enemy, and they could do no more than delay the catastrophe and save their honour by their bravery. Cyprus was the first to yield during the winter of 498–497. Its vessels, in conjunction with those of the Ionians, dispersed the fleet of the Phœnicians off Salamis, but the troops of their princes, still imbued with the old system of military tactics, could not sustain the charge of the Persian battalions; they gave way under the walls of Salamis, and their chief, Onesilus, was killed in a final charge of his chariotry.[1] His death effected the ruin of the Ionian cause in Cyprus, which on the continent suffered at the same time no less serious reverses. The towns of the Hellespont and of Æolia succumbed one after another; Kymê and Clazomenæ next

---

[1] The movement in Cyprus must have begun in the winter of 499–498, for Onesilus was already in the field when Darius heard of the burning of Sardes ; and as it lasted for a year, it must have been quelled in the winter of 498–497.

opened their gates; the Carians were twice beaten, once near the White Columns, and again near Labranda, and their victory at Pedasos suspended merely for an instant the progress of the Persian arms, so that towards the close of 497 the struggle was almost entirely concentrated round Miletus. Aristagoras, seeing that his cause was now desperate, agreed with his partisans that they should expatriate themselves. He fell fighting against the Edonians of Thrace, attempting to force the important town of Enneahodoi, near the mouth of the Strymon (496);[1] but his defection had not discouraged any one, and Histiæus, who had been sent to Sardes by the great king to negotiate the submission of the rebels, failed in his errand.

A CYPRIOT CHARIOT.[2]

Even when blockaded on the land side, Miletus could defy an attack so long as communication with the sea was not cut off. Darius therefore brought up the Phœnician fleet, reinforced it with the Cypriot contingents, and despatched the united squadrons to the Archipelago during the summer

[1] In Herodotus the town is not named, but a passage in Thucydides shows that it was Enneahodoi, afterwards Amphipolis, and that the death of Aristagoras took place thirty-two years before the Athenian defeat at Drabeskos, *i.e.* probably in 496.

[2] Drawn by Faucher-Gudin, from the terra-cotta group in the New York Museum.

of 494. The confederates, even after the disasters of the preceding years, still possessed 353 vessels, most of them of 30 to 50 oars; they were, however, completely defeated near the small island of Ladê, in the latter part of the summer, and Miletus, from that moment cut off from the rest of the world, capitulated a few weeks later. A small proportion of its inhabitants continued to dwell in the ruined city, but the greater number were carried away to Ampê, at the mouth of the Tigris, in the marshes of the Nâr-Marratum.[1] Caria was reconquered during the winter of 494-493, and by the early part of 493, Chios, Lesbos, Tenedos, the cities of the Chersonnesus and of Propontis—in short, all which yet held out—were reduced to obedience. Artaphernes reorganised his vanquished states entirely in the interest of Persia. He did not interfere with the constitutions of the several republics, but he reinstated the tyrants. He regulated and augmented the various tributes, prohibited private wars, and gave to the satrap the right of disposing of all quarrels at his own tribunal. The measures which he adopted had long after his day the force of law among the Asiatic Greeks, and it was by them they regulated their relations with the representatives of the great king.

If Darius had ever entertained doubts as to the necessity for occupying European Greece to ensure the preservation of peace in her Asiatic sister-country, the revolt of Ionia must have completely dissipated them. It was a question

[1] The year 497, *i.e.* three years before the capture of the town, appears to be an unlikely date for the battle of Ladê: Miletus must have fallen in the autumn or winter months following the defeat.

whether the cities which had so obstinately defied him for six long years, would ever resign themselves to servitude as long as they saw the peoples of their race maintaining their independence on the opposite shores of the Ægean, and while the misdeeds of which the contingents of Eretria and Athens had been guilty during the rebellion remained unpunished. A tradition, which sprang up soon after the event, related that on hearing of the burning of Sardes, Darius had bent his bow and let fly an arrow towards the sky, praying Zeus to avenge him on the Athenians: and at the same time he had commanded one of his slaves to repeat three times a day before him, at every meal, "Sire, remember the Athenians!"[1] As a matter of fact, the intermeddling of these strangers between the sovereign and his subjects was at once a serious insult to the Achæmenids and a cause of anxiety to the empire; to leave it unpunished would have been an avowal of weakness or timidity, which would not fail to be quickly punished in Syria, Egypt, Babylon, and on the Scythian frontiers, and would ere long give rise to similar acts of revolt and interference. Darius, therefore, resumed his projects, but with greater activity than before, and with a resolute purpose to make a final reckoning with the Greeks, whatever it might cost him. The influence of his nephew Mardonius at first inclined him to adopt the overland route, and he sent him into Thrace with a force of men and a fleet of galleys sufficient

---

[1] The legend is clearly older than the time of Herodotus, for in the *Persæ* of Æschylus the shade of Darius, when coming out of his tomb, cries to the old men, "Remember Athens and Greece!"

to overcome all obstacles. Mardonius marched against the Greek colonies and native tribes which had throw off the yoke during the Ionian war, and reduced those who had still managed to preserve their independence. The Bryges opposed him with such determination, that summer was drawing to its close before he was able to continue his march. He succeeded, however, in laying hands on Macedonia, and obliged its king, Alexander, to submit to the conditions accepted by his father Amyntas; but at this juncture half of his fleet was destroyed by a tempest in the vicinity of Mount Athos, and the disaster, which took place just as winter was approaching, caused him to suspend his operations (492). He was recalled on account of his failure, and the command was transferred to Datis the Mede and to the Persian Artaphernes. Darius, however, while tentatively using the land routes through Greece for his expeditions, had left no stone unturned to secure for himself that much-coveted sea-way which would carry him straight into the heart of the enemy's position, and he had opened negotiations with the republics of Greece proper. Several of them had consented to tender him earth and water, among them being Ægina,[3]

ALEXANDER I. OF MACEDON.[1]

A PHŒNICIAN GALLEY.[2]

---

[1] Drawn by Faucher-Gudin, from a coin in the *Cabinet des Médailles*.

[2] Drawn by Fanoher-Gudin, from a coin of Byblos in the *Cabinet des Médailles*.

[3] Herodotus states that *all* the island-dwelling Greeks submitted to the

and besides this, the state of the various factions in Athens was such, that he had every reason to believe that he could count on the support of a large section of the population when the day came for him to disembark his force on the shores of Attica. He therefore decided to direct his next expedition against Athens itself, and he employed the year 491 in concentrating his troops and triremes in Cilicia, at a sufficient distance from the European coast to ensure their safety from any sudden attack. In the spring of 490 the army recruited from among the most warlike nations of the empire—the Persians, Medes, and Sakæ—went aboard the Phœnician fleet, while galleys built on a special model were used as transports for the cavalry. The entire convoy sailed safely out of the mouth of the Pyramos to the port of Samos, coasting the shores of Asia Minor, and then passing through the Cyclades, from Samos to Naxos, where they met with no opposition from the inhabitants, headed for Delos, where Datis offered a sacrifice to Apollo, whom he confounded with his god Mithra; finally they reached Eubœa, where Eretria and Carystos vainly endeavoured to hold their own against them. Eretria was reduced to ashes, as Sardes had been, and such of its citizens as had not fled into the mountains at the enemy's approach were sent into exile among the Kissians in the township of Arderikka. Hippias meanwhile had joined the Persians and had been taken into their confidence. While awaiting the result of the intrigues of his partisans

great king. But Herodotus himself says later on that the people of Naxos, at all events, proved refractory.

in Athens, he had advised Datis to land on the eastern coast of Attica, in the neighbourhood of Marathon, at the very place from whence his father Pisistratus had set out forty years before to return to his country after his first exile. The position was well chosen for the expected engagement. The bay and the strand which bordered it afforded an excellent station for the fleet, and the plain, in spite of its marshes and brushwood, was one of those rare spots where cavalry might be called into play without serious drawbacks.

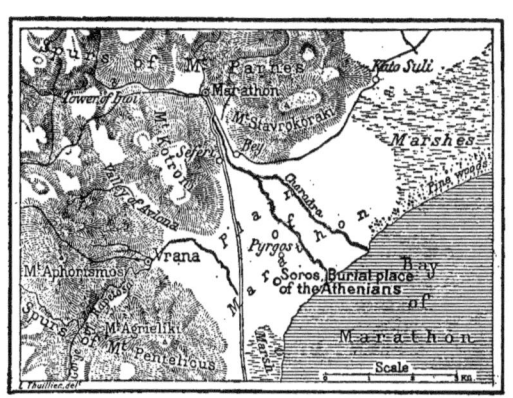

A few hours on foot would bring the bulk of the infantry up to the Acropolis by a fairly good road, while by the same time the fleet would be able to reach the roadstead of Phalerum. All had been arranged beforehand for concerted action when the expected rising should take place; but it never did take place, and instead of the friends whom the Persians expected, an armed force presented itself, commanded by the polemarch Callimachus and the ten strategi, among whom figured the famous Miltiades. At the first news of the disembarkation of the enemy, the republic had despatched the messenger Phidippides to Sparta to beg for immediate assistance, and in the mean time had sent forward all her able-bodied troops to meet the invaders. They comprised about 10,000 hoplites, accompanied, as was customary, by nearly as many more light infantry, who were shortly reinforced by 1000 Platæans. They encamped in the valley of Avlona, around a small temple of Heracles, in a position commanding the roads into the interior, and from whence they could watch the enemy without

THE BATTLE-FIELD OF MARATHON.[1]

exposing themselves to an unexpected attack. The two armies watched each other for a fortnight, Datis expecting a popular outbreak which would render an engagement unnecessary, Miltiades waiting patiently till the Lacedæmonians had come up, or till some false move on the part of his opponent gave him the opportunity of risking a decisive action. What took place at the end of this

[1] Drawn by Boudier, from a photograph by M. Amédée Hauvette.

time is uncertain. Whether Datis grew tired of inaction, or whether he suddenly resolved to send part of his forces by sea, so as to land on the neighbouring shore of Athens, and Miltiades fell upon his rear when only half his men had got on board the fleet, is not known. At any rate, Miltiades, with the Platæans on his left, set his battalions in movement without warning, and charged the enemy with a rush. The Persians and the Sakæ broke the centre of the line, but the two wings, after having dispersed the assailants on their front, wheeled round upon them and overcame them: 6000 barbarians were left dead upon the field as against some 200 Athenians and Platæans, but by dint of their valiant efforts the remainder managed to save the fleet with a loss of only seven galleys. Datis anchored that evening off the island of Ægilia, and at the same moment the victorious army perceived a signal hoisted on the heights of Pentelicus apparently to attract his attention; when he set sail the next morning and, instead of turning eastwards, proceeded to double Cape Sunion, Miltiades had no longer any doubt that treachery was at work, and returned to Athens by forced marches. Datis, on entering the roads of Phalerum, found the shore defended, and the army that he had left at Marathon encamped upon the Cynosargê. He cruised about for a few hours in sight of the shore, and finding no movement made to encourage him to land, he turned his vessels about and set sail for Ionia.

The material loss to the Persians was inconsiderable, for even the Cyclades remained under their authority; Miltiades, who endeavoured to retake them, met with a reverse before Paros, and the Athenians, disappointed by his unsuccessful attempt, made no further efforts to regain them. The moral effect of the victory on Greece and the empire was extraordinary. Up till then the Median soldiers had been believed to be the only invincible troops in the world; the sight of them alone excited dread in the bravest hearts, and their name was received everywhere with reverential awe. But now a handful of hoplites from one of the towns of the continent, and that not the most renowned for its prowess, without cavalry or bowmen, had rushed upon and overthrown the most terrible of all Oriental battalions, the Persians and the Sakæ. Darius could not put up with such an affront without incurring the risk of losing his prestige with the people of Asia and Europe, who up till then had believed him all-powerful, and of thus exposing himself to the possibility of revolutions in recently subdued countries, such as Egypt, which had always retained the memory of her past greatness. In the interest of his own power, as well as to soothe his wounded pride, a renewed attack was imperative, and this time it must be launched with such dash and vigour that all resistance would be at once swept before it. Events had shown him that the influence of the Pisistratidæ had not been strong enough to secure for him the opening of the gates of Athens, and that the sea route did not permit of his concentrating an adequate force of cavalry and infantry on the field of battle; he therefore reverted to the project of an expedition by the overland route, skirting the coasts of Thrace and Macedonia. During three years he collected arms, provisions, horses, men, and vessels, and was ready to commence hostilities in the spring of 487, when affairs in Egypt prevented him. This country had undeniably prospered under his suzerainty. It formed, with Cyrene and the coast of Libya, the sixth of his satrapies, to which were attached the neighbouring Nubian tribes of the southern frontier.[1] The Persian satrap, installed at the White Wall in the ancient palace of the Pharaohs, was supported by an army of 120,000 men, who occupied the three entrenched camps of the Saites—Daphnæ and Marea on the confines of the Delta, and Elephantinê in the south.[2] Outside these military stations, where the authority of the great king was exercised in a direct manner, the ancient feudal organisation existed intact. The temples retained their possessions and their vassals, and the nobles within their principalities were as independent and as inclined to insurrection as in past times. The annual tribute, the heaviest paid by any province with the exception of Chaldæa and Assyria, amounted only to 700 talents of silver. To this sum must be added the farming of the fishing in Lake Mœris, which, according to Herodotus,[3] brought in one talent a day during the six months of the high Nile, but, according to Diodorus,[4] during the whole

[1] The Nubian tribes, who are called Ethiopians by Herodotus and the cuneiform inscriptions, paid no regular tribute, but were obliged to send annually two *chœnikes* of pure gold, two hundred pieces of ebony, twenty elephants' tusks, and five young slaves, all under the name of a free gift.

[2] Herodotus states that in his own time the Persians, like the Saite Pharaohs, still had garrisons at Daphnæ and at Elephantinê.

[3] Herodotus says that the produce sank to the value of a third of a talent a day during the six other months.

[4] Diodorus Siculus says that the revenue produced by the fisheries in the Lakê had been handed over by Mœris to his wife for the expenses of her toilet.

year, as well as the 120,000 medimni of wheat required for the army of occupation, and the obligation to furnish the court of Susa with Libyan nitre and Nile water; the total of these impositions was far from constituting a burden disproportionate to the wealth of the Nile valley. Commerce brought in to it, in fact, at least as much money as the tribute took out of it. Incorporated with an empire which extended over three continents, Egypt had access to regions whither the products of her industry and her soil had never yet been carried. The produce of Ethiopia and the Sudan passed through her emporia on its way to attract customers in the markets of Tyre, Sidon, Babylon, and Susa, and the isthmus of Suez and Kosseir were the nearest ports through which Arabia and India could reach the Mediterranean. Darius therefore resumed the work of Necho, and beginning simultaneously at both extremities, he cut afresh the canal between the Nile and the Gulf of Suez. Trilingual stelæ in Egyptian, Persian, and Medic were placed at intervals along its banks, and set forth to all comers the method of procedure by which the sovereign had brought his work to a successful end. In a similar manner he utilised the Wadys which wind between Koptos and the Red Sea, and by their means placed the cities of the Saïd in communication with the "Ladders of Incense," Punt and the Sabæans.[2] He

DARIUS ON THE STELE OF THE ISTHMUS.[1]

---

[1] Drawn by Faucher-Gudin, from the *Description de l'Égypte*.

[2] Several of the inscriptions engraved on the rocks of the Wady Hammamât show to what an extent the route was frequented at certain

extended his favour equally to the commerce which they carried on with the interior of Africa; indeed, in order to ensure the safety of the caravans in the desert regions nearest to the Nile, he skilfully fortified the Great Oasis. He erected at Habît, Kushît, and other places, several of those rectangular citadels with massive walls of unburnt brick, which resisted every effort of the nomad tribes to break through them; and as the temple at Habît, raised

WALLS OF THE FORTRESS OF DUSH-EL-QALÂA.[1]

in former times by the Theban Pharaohs, had become ruinous, he rebuilt it from its foundations. He was generous in his gifts to the gods, and even towns as obscure as Edfu was then received from him grants of money and lands. The Egyptians at first were full of gratitude for the favours shown them, but the news of the

times during the reign. They bear the dates of the 26th, 27th, 28th, 30th, and 36th years of Darius. The country of Saba (Sheba) is mentioned on one of the stelæ of the isthmus.

[1] Drawn by Boudier, from the engraving by Cailliaud. Dush is the Kushît of the hieroglyphs, the Kysis of Græco-Roman times, and is situated on the southern border of the Great Oasis, about the latitude of Assuân.

defeat at Marathon, and the taxes with which the Susian court burdened them in order to make provision for the new war with Greece, aroused a deep-seated discontent, at all events amongst those who, living in the Delta, had had their patriotism or their interests most affected by the downfall of the Saite dynasty. It would appear that the

THE GREAT TEMPLE OF DARIUS AT HABÎT.[1]

priests of Buto, whose oracles exercised an indisputable influence alike over Greeks and natives, had energetically incited the people to revolt. The storm broke in 486, and a certain Khabbîsha, who perhaps belonged to the family of Psammetichus, proclaimed himself king both at Sais and Memphis.[2] Darius did not believe the revolt to be of

[1] Drawn by Boudier, from the engraving by Cailliaud.
[2] Herodotus does not give the name of the leader of the rebellion, but says that it took place in the fourth year after Marathon. A demotic

sufficient gravity to delay his plans for any length of time. He hastily assembled a second army, and was about to commence hostilities on the banks of the Nile simultaneously with those on the Hellespont, when he died in 485, in the thirty-sixth year of his reign. He was one of the great sovereigns of the ancient world—the greatest without exception of those who had ruled over Persia. Cyrus and Cambyses had been formidable warriors, and the kingdoms of the East had fallen before their arms, but they were purely military sovereigns, and if their successor had not possessed other abilities than theirs, their empire would have shared the fate of that of the Medes and the Chaldæans; it would have sunk to its former level as rapidly as it had risen, and the splendour of its opening years would have soon faded from remembrance. Darius was no less a general by instinct and training than they, as is proved by the campaigns which procured him his crown; but, after having conquered, he knew how to organise and build up a solid fabric out of the materials which his predecessors had left in a state of chaos; if Persia maintained her rule over the East for two entire centuries, it was due to him and to him alone.

The question of the succession, with its almost inevitable

contract in the Turin Museum bears the date of the third month of the second season of the thirty-fifth year of Darius I.: Khabbîsha's rebellion therefore broke out between June and September, 486. Stern makes this prince to have been of Libyan origin. From the form of his name, Révillout has supposed that he was an Arab, and Birch was inclined to think that he was a Persian satrap who made a similar attempt to that of Aryandes. But nothing is really known of him or of his family previous to his insurrection against Darius.

THE DEATH OF DARIUS

popular outbreaks, had at once to be dealt with. Darius had had several wives, and among them, the daughter of Gobryas, who had borne him three children : Artabazanes, the eldest, had long been regarded as the heir-presumptive, and had probably filled the office of regent during the expedition in Scythia. But Atossa, the daughter of Cyrus, who had already been queen under Cambyses and Gaumâta, was indignant at the thought of her sons bowing down before the child of a woman who was not of Achæmenian race, and at the moment when affairs in Egypt augured ill for the future, and when the old king, according to custom, had to appoint his successor, she intreated him to choose Khshayarsha, the eldest of her children, who had been borne to the purple, and in whose veins flowed the blood of Cyrus. Darius acceded to her request, and on his death, a few months after, Khshayarsha ascended the throne. His brothers offered no opposition, and the Persian nobles did homage to their new king. Khshayarsha, whom the Greeks called Xerxes, was at that time thirty-four years of age. He was tall, vigorous, of an imposing figure and noble countenance, and he had the reputation of being the handsomest man of his time, but neither his intelligence nor disposition corresponded to his outward appearance ; he was at once violent and feeble, indolent, narrow-minded, and sensual, and was easily swayed by his courtiers and mistresses. The idea of a war had no attractions for him, and he was inclined to shirk it. His uncle Artabanus exhorted him to follow his inclination for peace, and he lent a favourable ear to his advice until his cousin Mardonius remonstrated with

224 THE LAST DAYS OF THE OLD EASTERN WORLD

him, and begged him not to leave the disgrace of Marathon unpunished, or he would lower the respect attached to the name of Persia throughout the world. He wished, at all events, to bring Egyptian affairs to an issue before involving himself in a serious European war. Khabbîsha had done his best to prepare a stormy reception for him. During a period of two years Khabbîsha had worked at the extension of the entrenchments along the coast and at the mouths of the Nile, in order to repulse the attack that he foresaw would take place simultaneously with that on land, but his precautions proved fruitless when the decisive moment arrived, and he was completely crushed by the superior numbers of Xerxes. The nomes of the Delta which had taken a foremost part in the rising were ruthlessly raided, the priests heavily fined, and the oracle of Buto deprived of its possessions as a punishment for the encouragement freely given to the rebels. Khabbîsha disappeared, and his fate is unknown. Achæmenes, one of the king's brothers, was made satrap, but, as on previous occasions, the constitution of the country underwent no modification. The temples retained their inherited domains, and the nomes continued in the hands of their hereditary princes, without a suspicion crossing the mind of Xerxes that his tolerance of the priestly institutions and the local dynasties was responsible for the maintenance of a body of chiefs ever in readiness for future insurrection (483).[2] Order was once more restored, but

XERXES I.[1]

---

[1] Drawn by Faucher-Gudin, from a daric in the *Cabinet des Médailles*.

[2] The only detailed information on this revolt furnished by the Egyptian

he was not yet entirely at liberty to pursue his own plan of action. Classical tradition tells us, that on the occasion of his first visit to Babylon he had offended the religious prejudices of the Chaldæans by a sacrilegious curiosity. He had, in spite of the entreaties of the priests, forced an entrance into the ancient burial-place of Bel-Etana, and had beheld the body of the old hero preserved in oil in a glass sarcophagus, which, however, was not quite full of the liquid. A notice posted up beside it, threatened the king who should violate the secret of the tomb with a cruel fate, unless he filled the sarcophagus to the brim, and Xerxes had attempted to accomplish this mysterious injunction, but all his efforts had failed. The example set by Egypt and the change of sovereign are sufficient to account for the behaviour of the Babylonians; they believed that the accession of a comparatively young monarch, and the difficulties of the campaign on the banks of the Nile, afforded them a favourable occasion for throwing off the yoke. They elected as king a certain Shamasherib, whose antecedents are unknown; but their independence was of short duration,[1] for Megabyzos, son of Zopyrus, who governed the province by hereditary right, forced them to disarm after a siege of a few months. It

monuments is given in the Stele of Ptolemy, the son of Lagos. An Apis, whose sarcophagus still exists, was buried by Khabbîsha in the Serapæum in the second year of his reign, which proves that he was in possession of Memphis: the White Wall had perhaps been deprived of its garrison in order to reinforce the army prepared against Greece, and it was possibly thus that it fell into the hands of Khabbîsha.

[1] This Shamasherib is mentioned only on a contract dated from his accession, which is preserved in the British Museum.

would appear that Xerxes treated them with the greatest severity: he pillaged the treasury and temple of Bel, appropriated the golden statue which decorated the great inner hall of the ziggurât, and carried away many of the people into captivity (581). Babylon never recovered this final blow: the quarters of the town that had been pillaged remained uninhabited and fell into ruins; commerce dwindled and industry flagged. The counsellors of Xerxes had, no doubt, wished to give an object-lesson to the province by their treatment of Babylon, and thus prevent the possibility of a revolution taking place in Asia while its ruler was fully engaged in a struggle with the Greeks. Meanwhile all preparations were completed, and the contingents of the eastern and southern provinces concentrated at Kritalla, in Cappadocia, merely awaited the signal to set out. Xerxes gave the order to advance in the autumn of 481, crossed the Halys and took up his quarters at Sardes, while his fleet prepared to winter in the neighbouring ports of Phocæ and Kymê.[1] Gathered together in that little corner of the world, were forces such as no king had ever before united under his command; they comprised 1200 vessels of various build, and probably 120,000 combatants, besides the rabble of servants, hucksters, and women which followed all the armies of that period. The Greeks exaggerated the number of the force beyond all probability. They estimated it variously at 800,000, at 3,000,000, and at 5,283,220 men; 1,700,000 of whom were able-bodied foot-soldiers, and 80,000 of them

[1] Diodorus, who probably follows Ephorus, is the only writer who informs us of the place where the fleet was assembled.

horsemen.[1] The troops which they could bring up to oppose these hordes were, indeed, so slender in number, when reckoned severally, that all hope of success seemed impossible. Xerxes once more summoned the Greeks to submit, and most of the republics appeared inclined to comply; Athens and Sparta alone refused, but from different motives. Athens knew that, after the burning of Sardes and the victory of Marathon, they could hope for

A TRIREME IN MOTION.[2]

no pity, and she was well aware that Persia had decreed her complete destruction; the Athenians were familiar with the idea of a struggle in which their very existence was at stake, and they counted on the navy with which Themistocles had just provided them to enable them to emerge from the affair with honour. Sparta was not threatened with the same fate, but she was at that time the first military state in Greece, and the whole of the

[1] Herodotus records the epigram to the effect that 3,000,000 men attacked Thermopylæ. Ctesias and Ephorus adopt the same figures; Isocrates is contented with 700,000 combatants and 5,000,000 men in all.

[2] Drawn by Faucher-Gudin: the left portion is a free reproduction of a photograph of the bas-relief of the Acropolis; the right, of the picture of Pozzo. The two partly overlap one another, and give both together the idea of a trireme going at full speed.

Peloponnesus acknowledged her sway; in the event of her recognising the suzerainty of the barbarians, the latter would not fail to require of her the renunciation of her hegemony, and she would then be reduced to the same rank as her former rivals, Tegea and Argos. Athens and Sparta therefore united to repulse the common enemy, and the advantage that this alliance afforded them was so patent that none of the other states ventured to declare openly for the great king. Argos and Crete, the boldest of them, announced that they would observe neutrality; the remainder, Thessalians, Bœotians, and people of Corcyra, gave their support to the national cause. but did so unwillingly.

Xerxes crossed the Hellespont in the spring of 480, by two bridges of boats thrown across it between Abydos and Sestos; he then formed his force into three columns, and made his way slowly along the coast, protected on the left by the whole of his fleet from any possible attack by the squadrons of the enemy. The Greeks had three lines of defence which they could hold against him, the natural strength of which nearly compensated them for the inferiority of their forces; these were Mount Olympus, Mount Œta, and the isthmus of Corinth. The first, however, was untenable, owing to the ill will of the Thessalians; as a precautionary measure 10,000 hoplites were encamped upon it, but they evacuated the position as soon as the enemy's advance-guard came into sight. The natural barrier of Œta, less formidable than that of Olympus, was flanked by the Eubœan straits on the extreme right, but the range was of such extent that it did not require to be guarded with equal vigilance along its whole length. The Spartans did not at first occupy it, for they intended to accumulate all the Greek forces, both troops and vessels, around the isthmus. At that point the neck of land was so narrow, and the sea so shut in, that the numbers of the invading force proved a drawback to them, and the advantage almost of necessity lay with that of the two adversaries who should be best armed and best officered. This plan of the Spartans was a wise one, but Athens, which was thereby sacrificed to the general good, refused to adopt it, and as she alone furnished almost half the total number of vessels, her decision had to be deferred to. A body of about 10,000 hoplites was therefore posted in the pass of Thermopylæ under the command of Leonidas, while a squadron of 271 vessels disposed themselves near the promontory of Artemision, off the Euripus, and protected the right flank of the pass against a diversion from the fleet. Meanwhile Xerxes had been reinforced in the course of his march by the contingents from Macedonia, and had received the homage of the cities of Thessaly; having reached the defiles of the Œta and the Eubœa, he began by attacking the Greeks directly in front, both fleets and armies facing one another. Leonidas succeeded in withstanding the assault on two successive days, and then the inevitable took place. A detachment of Persians, guided by the natives of the country, emerged by a path which had been left unguarded, and bore down upon the Greeks in the rear; a certain number managed to escape, but the bulk of the force, along with the 300 Spartans and their king, succumbed after a desperate resistance. As for the fleet, it had borne itself bravely, and had retained the ascendency throughout, in spite of the superiority of the enemy's numbers; on hearing the news of the glorious death of Leonidas, they believed their task ended for the time being, and retired with the Athenians in their wake, ready to sustain the attack should they come again to close quarters. The victorious side had suffered considerable losses in men and vessels, but they had forced the passage, and Central Greece now lay at their mercy. Xerxes received the submission of the Thebans, the Phocæans, the Locrians, the Dorians, and of all who appealed to his clemency; then, having razed to the ground Platæa and Thespiæ, the only two towns which refused to come to terms with him, he penetrated into Attica by the gorges of the Cithæron. The population had taken refuge in Salamis, Ægina, and Trœzen. The few fanatics who refused to desist in their defence of the Acropolis, soon perished behind their ramparts; Xerxes destroyed the temple of Pallas by fire to avenge the burning of Sardes, and then entrenched his troops on the approaches to the isthmus, stationing his squadrons in the ports of Munychia, Phalerum, and the Piræus, and suspended all hostilities while waiting to see what policy the Greeks would pursue. It is possible that he hoped that a certain number of them would intreat for mercy, and others being encouraged by their example to submit, no further serious battle would have to be fought. When he found that no such request was proffered, he determined to take advantage of the superiority of his numbers, and, if possible, destroy at one blow the whole of the Greek naval reserve; he therefore gave orders to his admirals to assume the offensive. The Greek fleet lay at anchor across the bay of Salamis. The left squadron of the Persians, leaving Munychia in the middle of the night, made for the promontory of Cynosura, landing some troops as it passed on the island of Psyttalia, on which it was proposed to fall back in case of accident, while the right division, sailing close to the coast of Attica, closed the entrance to the straits in the direction of Eleusis; this double movement was all but completed, when the Greeks were informed by fugitives of what was taking place, and the engagement was inevitable. They ac‑

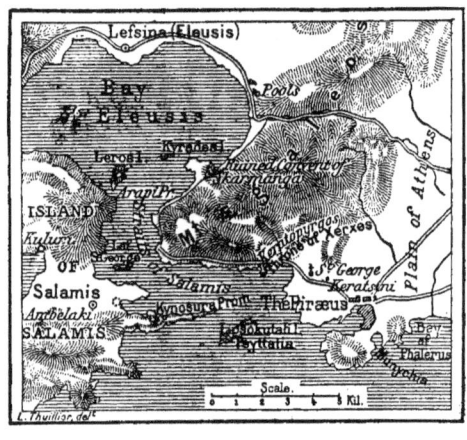

cepted it fearlessly. Xerxes, enthroned with his Immortals on the slopes of Ægialeos, could, from his exalted position, see the Athenians attack his left squadron: the rest of the allies followed them, and from afar these words were borne upon the breeze: "Go, sons of Greece, deliver your country, deliver your children, your wives, and the temples of the gods of your fathers and the tombs of your ancestors. A single battle will decide the fate of all you possess." The Persians fought with their accustomed bravery, "but before long their numberless vessels, packed closely together in a restricted space, begin to hamper each other's movements, and their rams of brass collide; whole rows of oars are broken." The Greek vessels, lighter and easier to manœuvre than those of the Phœnicians, surround the latter and disable them in detail. "The surface of the sea is hidden with floating wreckage and corpses; the shore and the rocks are covered with the dead." At length, towards evening, the energy of the barbarians beginning to flag, they slowly fell back upon the Piræus, closely followed by their adversaries, while Aristides bore down upon Psyttalia with a handful of Athenians. "Like tunnies, like fish just caught in a net, with blows from broken oars, with fragments of spars, they fall upon the Persians, they tear them to pieces. The sea resounds from afar with groans and cries of lamentation. Night at length unveils her sombre face" and separates the combatants.[1] The advantage lay that day with the Greeks, but hostilities might be resumed on the morrow, and the resources of the Persians were so considerable that their chances of victory were not yet exhausted. Xerxes at first showed signs of wishing to continue the struggle; he repaired the injured vessels and ordered a dyke to be constructed, which, by uniting Salamis to the mainland, would enable him to oust the Athenians from their last retreat. But he had never exhibited much zest for the war; the inevitable fatigues and dangers of a campaign were irksome to his indolent nature, and winter was approaching, which he would be obliged to spend far from Susa, in the midst of a country wasted and trampled

[1] Æschylus gives the only contemporaneous account of the battle, and the one which Herodotus and all the historians after him have paraphrased, while they also added to it oral traditions.

PART OF THE BATTLE-FIELD OF SALAMIS.
Drawn by Boudier, from a photograph by Monsieur Amédée Hauvette.

underfoot by two great armies. Mardonius, guessing what was passing in his sovereign's mind, advised him to take advantage of the fine autumn weather to return to Sardes; he proposed to take over from Xerxes the command of the army in Greece, and to set to work to complete the conquest of the Peloponnesus. He was probably glad to be rid of a sovereign whose luxurious habits were a hindrance to his movements. Xerxes accepted his proposal with evident satisfaction, and summarily despatching his vessels to the Hellespont to guard the bridges, he set out on his return journey by the overland route.

At the time of his departure the issue of the struggle was as yet unforeseen. Mardonius evacuated Attica, which was too poor and desolate a country to support so large an army, and occupied comfortable winter quarters in the rich plains of Thessaly, where he recruited his strength for a supreme effort in the spring. He had with him about 60,000 men, picked troops from all parts of Asia—Medes, Sakæ, Bactrians, and Indians, besides the regiment of the Immortals and the Egyptian veterans who had distinguished themselves by their bravery at Salamis; the heavy hoplites of Thebes and of the Bœotian towns, the Thessalian cavalry, and the battalions of Macedonia were also in readiness to join him as soon as called on. The whole of these troops, relieved from the presence of the useless multitude which had impeded its movements under Xerxes, and commanded by a bold and active general, were anxious to distinguish themselves, and the probabilities of their final success were great. The confederates were aware of the fact, and although resolved to persevere to the end, their manœuvres betrayed an unfortunate indecision. Their fleet followed the Persian squadron bound for the Hellespont for several days, but on realising that the enemy were not planning a diversion against the Peloponnesus, they put about and returned to their various ports. The winter was passed in preparations on both sides. Xerxes, on his return to Sardes, had got together a fleet of 200 triremes and an army of 60,000 men, and had stationed them at Cape Mycale, opposite Samos, to be ready in case of an Ionian revolt, or perhaps to bear down upon any given point in the Peloponnesus when Mardonius had gained some initial advantage. The Lacædemonians, on their part, seem to have endeavoured to assume the defensive both by land and sea; while their foot-soldiers were assembling in the neighbourhood of Corinth, their fleet sailed as far as Delos and there anchored, as reluctant to venture beyond as if it had been a question of proceeding to the Pillars of Hercules. Athens, which ran the risk of falling into the enemy's hands for the second time through these hesitations, evinced such marked displeasure that Mardonius momentarily attempted to take advantage of it. He submitted to the citizens, through Alexander, King of Macedon, certain conditions, the leniency of which gave uneasiness to the Spartans; the latter at once promised Athens all she wanted, and on the strength of their oaths she at once broke off the negotiations with the Persians. Mardonius immediately resolved on action: he left his quarters in Thessaly in the early days of May, reached

Attica by a few quick marches, and spread his troops over the country before the Peloponnesians were prepared to resist. The people again took refuge in Salamis; the Persians occupied Athens afresh, and once more had recourse to diplomacy. This time the Spartans were alarmed to good purpose; they set out to the help of their ally, and from that moment Mardonius showed no further consideration in his dealing with Athens. He devastated the surrounding country, razed the city walls to the ground, and demolished and burnt the remaining houses and temples; he then returned to Bœotia, the plains of which were more suited to the movements of his squadrons, and took up a position in an entrenched camp on the right bank of the Asopos. The Greek army, under the command of Pausanias, King of Sparta, subsequently followed him there, and at first stationed themselves on the lower slopes of Mount Cithæron. Their force was composed of about 25,000 hoplites, and about as many more light troops, and was scarcely inferior in numbers to the enemy, but it had no cavalry of any kind. Several days passed in skirmishing without definite results, Mardonius fearing to let his Asiatic troops attack the heights held by the heavy Greek infantry, and Pausanias alarmed lest his men should be crushed by the Thessalian and Persian horse if he ventured down into the plains. Want of water at length obliged the Greeks to move slightly westwards, their right wing descending as far as the spring of Gargaphia, and their left to the bank of the Asopos. But this position facing east, exposed them so seriously to the attacks of the light Asiatic horse, that after enduring it for ten days they raised their camp and fell back in the night on Platæa. Unaccustomed to manœuvre together, they were unable to preserve their distances; when day dawned, their lines, instead of presenting a continuous front, were distributed into three unequal bodies occupying various parts of the plain. Mardonius unhesitatingly seized his opportunity. He crossed the Asopos, ordered the Thebans to attack the Athenians, and with the bulk of his Asiatic troops charged the Spartan contingents. Here, as at Marathon, the superiority of equipment soon gave the Greeks the advantage: Mardonius was killed while leading the charge of the Persian guard, and, as is almost always

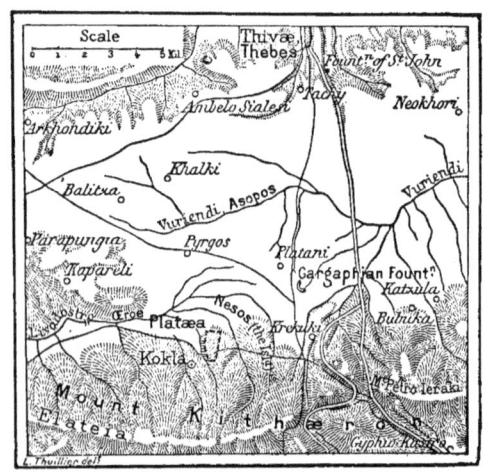

the case among Orientals, his death decided the issue of the battle. The Immortals were cut to pieces round his dead body, while the rest took flight and sought refuge in their camp. Almost simultaneously the Athenians succeeded in routing the Bœotians. They took the entrenchments by assault, gained possession of an immense quantity of spoil, and massacred many of the defenders, but they could not prevent Artabazus from retiring in perfect order with 40,000 of his best troops protected by his cavalry. He retired successively from Thessaly, Macedonia, and Thrace,

THE BATTLE-FIELD OF PLATÆA.
Drawn by Boudier, from photographs by Amédée Hauvette.

reached Asia after suffering severe losses, and European Greece was freed for ever from the presence of the barbarians. While her fate was being decided at Platæa, that of Asiatic Greece was being fought out on the coast of Ionia. The entreaties of the Samians had at length encouraged Leotychidas and Xanthippus to take the initiative. The Persian generals, who were not expecting this aggressive movement, had distributed the greater part of their vessels throughout the Ionian ports, and had merely a small squadron left at their disposal at Mycale. Surprised by the unexpected appearance of the enemy, they were compelled to land, were routed, and their vessels burnt (479). This constituted the signal for a general revolt: Samos, Chios, and Lesbos affiliated themselves to the Hellenic confederation, and the cities of the littoral, which Sparta would have been powerless to protect for want of a fleet, concluded an alliance with Athens, whose naval superiority had been demonstrated by recent events. The towns of the Hellespont threw off the yoke as soon as the triremes of the confederates appeared within their waters, and Sestos, the only one of them prevented by its Persian garrison from yielding to the Athenians, succumbed, after a long siege, during the winter of 479–478. The campaign of 478 completed the deliverance of the Greeks. A squadron commanded by Pausanias roused the islands of the Carian coast and Cyprus itself, without encountering any opposition, and then steering northwards drove the Persians from Byzantium. The following winter the conduct of operations passed out of the hands of Sparta into those of Athens—from the greatest military to the greatest naval power in Greece; and the latter, on assuming command, at once took steps to procure the means which would enable her to carry out her task thoroughly. She brought about the formation of a permanent league between the Asiatic Greeks and those of the islands. Each city joining it preserved a complete autonomy as far as its internal affairs were concerned, but pledged itself to abide by the advice of Athens in everything connected with the war against the Persian empire, and contributed a certain quota of vessels, men, and money, calculated according to its resources, for the furtherance of the national cause. The centre of the confederation was fixed at Delos; the treasure held in common was there deposited under the guardianship of the god, and the delegates from the confederate states met there every year at the solemn festivals, Athens to audit the accounts of her administration, and the allies to discuss the interests of the league and to decide on the measures to be taken against the common enemy.

Oriental empires maintain their existence only on condition of being always on the alert and always victorious. They can neither restrict themselves within definite limits nor remain upon the defensive, for from the day when they desist from extending their area their ruin becomes inevitable; they must maintain their career of conquest, or they must cease to exist. This very activity which saves them from downfall depends, like the control of affairs, entirely on the ruling sovereign; when he chances to be too indolent or too incapable of government, he retards progress by his inertness or misdirects it through his want of skill, and the fate of the people is made thus to depend entirely on the natural disposition of the prince, since none of his subjects possesses sufficient authority to correct the mistakes of his master. Having conquered Asia, the Persian race, finding itself hemmed in by insurmountable obstacles—the sea, the African and Arabian deserts, the mountains of Turkestan and the Caucasus, and the steppes of Siberia—had only two outlets for its energy, Greece and India. Darius had led his army against the Greeks, and, in spite of the resistance he had encountered from them, he had gained ground, and was on the point of striking a crucial blow, when death cut short his career. The impetus that he had given to the militant policy was so great that Xerxes was at first carried away by it; but he was naturally averse to war, without individual energy and destitute of military genius, so that he allowed himself to be beaten where, had he possessed anything of the instincts of a commander, he would have been able to crush his adversary with the sheer weight of his ships and battalions. Even after Salamis, even after Platæa and Mycale, the resources of Hellas, split up as it was into fifty different republics, could hardly bear comparison with those of all Asia concentrated in the hands of one man: Xerxes must have triumphed in the end had he persevered in his undertaking, and utilised the inexhaustible amount of fresh material with which his empire could have furnished him. But to do that he would have had to take a serious view of his duties as a sovereign, as Cyrus and Darius had done, whereas he appears to have made use of his power merely for the satisfaction of his luxurious tastes and his capricious affections. During the winter following his return, and while he was reposing at Sardes after the fatigues of his campaign in Greece, he fell in love with the wife of Masistes, one of his brothers, and as she refused to entertain his suit, he endeavoured to win her by marrying his son Darius to her daughter Artayntas. He was still amusing himself with this ignoble intrigue during the year which witnessed the disasters of Platæa and Mycale, when he was vaguely entertaining the idea of personally conducting a fresh army beyond the Ægean: but the marriage of his son having taken place, he returned to Susa in the autumn, accompanied by the entire court, and from thenceforward he remained shut up in the heart of his empire. After his departure the war lost its general character, and deteriorated into a series of local skirmishes between the satraps in the vicinity of the Mediterranean and the members of the league of Delos. The Phœnician fleet played the principal part in the naval operations, but the central and eastern Asiatics—Bactrians, Indians, Parthians, Arians, Arachosians, Armenians, and the people from Susa and Babylon—scarcely took any part in the struggle. The Athenians at the outset assumed the offensive under the intelligent direction of Cimon. They expelled the Persian garrisons from Eion and Thrace in 476. They placed successively under their own hegemony all the Greek communities of the Asianic littoral. Towards 466, they destroyed a fleet anchored within the Gulf of Pamphylia, close to the mouth of the Eurymedon, and, as at Mycale, they landed and dispersed the force destined to act in concert with the squadron. Sailing from thence to Cyprus, they destroyed a second Phœnician fleet of eighty vessels, and returned to the Piræus laden with booty. Such exploits were not devoid of glory and profit for the time being, but they had no permanent results. All these naval expeditions were indeed successful, and the islands and towns of the Ægean, and even those of the Black Sea and the southern coasts of Asia Minor, succeeded without difficulty in freeing themselves from the Persian yoke under the protection of the Athenian triremes; but their influence did not penetrate further inland than a few miles from the shore, beyond which distance they ran the risk of being cut off from their vessels, and the barbarians of the interior— Lydians, Phrygians, Mysians, Pamphylians, and even most of the Lycians and Carians—remained subject to the rule of the satraps. The territory thus liberated formed but a narrow border along the coast of the peninsula; a border rent and interrupted at intervals, constantly in peril of seizure by the enemy, and demanding considerable efforts every year for its defence. Athens was in danger of exhausting her resources in the performance of this ungrateful task, unless she could succeed in fomenting some revolution in the vast possessions of her adversary which should endanger the existence of his empire, or which, at any rate, should occupy the Persian soldiery in constantly recurring hostilities against the rebellious provinces. If none of the countries in the centre of Asia Minor would respond to their call, and if the interests of their commercial rivals, the Phœnicians, were so far opposed to their own as to compel them to maintain the conflict to the very end, Egypt, at any rate, always proud of her past glory and impatient of servitude, was ever seeking to rid herself of the foreign yoke and recover her independent existence under the authority of her Pharaohs. It was not easy to come to terms with her and give her efficient help from Athens itself; but Cyprus, with its semi-Greek population hostile to the Achæmenids, could, if they were to take possession of it, form an admirable base of operations in that corner of the Mediterranean. The Athenians were aware of this from the outset, and, after their victory at the mouth of the Eurymedon, a year never elapsed without their despatching a more or less numerous fleet into Cypriot waters; by so doing they protected the Ægean from the piracy of the Phœnicians, and at the same time, in the event of any movement arising on the banks of the Nile, they were close enough to the Delta to be promptly informed of it, and to interfere to their own advantage before any repressive measures could be taken.

The field of hostilities having shifted, and Greece having now set herself to attempt the dismemberment of the Persian empire, we may well ask what has become of Xerxes. The little energy and intelligence he had possessed at the outset were absorbed by a life of luxury and debauchery. Weary of his hopeless pursuit of the wife of Masistes, he transferred his attentions to the Artayntas whom he had given in marriage to his son Darius, and succeeded in seducing her. The vanity of this unfortunate woman at length excited the jealously of the queen. Amestris believed herself threatened by the ascendency of this mistress; she therefore sent for the girl's mother, whom she believed guilty of instigating the intrigue, and, having cut off her breasts, ears, nose, lips, and torn out her tongue, she sent her back, thus mutilated, to her family. Masistes, wishing to avenge her, set out for Bactriana, of which district he was satrap: he could easily have incited the province to rebel, for its losses in troops during the wars in Europe had been severe, and a secret discontent was widespread; but Xerxes, warned in time, despatched horsemen in pursuit, who overtook and killed him. The incapacity of the king, and the slackness with which he held the reins of government, were soon so apparent as to produce intrigues at court: Artabanus, the chief captain of the guards, was emboldened by the state of affairs to attempt to substitute his own rule for that of the Achæmenids, and one night he assassinated Xerxes. His method of procedure was never exactly known, and several accounts of it were soon afterwards current. One of them related that he had as his accomplice the eunuch Aspamithres. Having committed the crime, both of them rushed to the chamber of Artaxerxes,[2] one of the sons of the sovereign, but still a child; they accused Darius, the heir to the throne, of the murder, and having obtained an order to seize him, they dragged him before his brother and stabbed him, while he loudly protested his innocence. Other tales

ARTAXERXES I.[1]

---

[1] Drawn by Faucher-Gudin, from a daric in the *Cabinet des Médailles*.

[2] Artaxerxes is the form commonly adopted by the Greek historians and by the moderns who follow them, but Ctesias and others after him prefer Artoxerxes. The original form of the Persian name was Artakhshathra.

related that Artabanus had taken advantage of the free access to the palace which his position allowed him, to conceal himself one night within it, in company with his seven sons. Having murdered Xerxes, he convinced Artaxerxes of the guilt of his brother, and conducting him to the latter's chamber, where he was found asleep, Artabanus stabbed him on the spot, on the pretence that he was only feigning slumber.[1] The murderer at first became the virtual sovereign, and he exercised his authority so openly that later chronographers inserted his name in the list of the Achæmenids, between that of his victim and his *protégé*; but at the end of six months, when he was planning the murder of the young prince, he was betrayed by Megabyzos and slain, together with his accomplices. His sons, fearing a similar fate, escaped into the country with some of the troops. They perished in a skirmish, sword in hand; but their prompt defeat, though it helped to establish the new king upon his throne, did not ensure peace, for the most turbulent provinces at the two extremes of the empire, Bactriana on the northeast and Egypt in the south-west, at once rose in arms. The Bactrians were led by Hystaspes, one of the sons of Xerxes, who, being older than Artaxerxes, claimed the throne; his pretensions were not supported by the neighbouring provinces, and two bloody battles soon sealed his

---

[1] Of the two principal accounts, the first is as old as Ctesias, who was followed in general outline by Ephorus, of whose account Diodorus Siculus preserves a summary compilation; the second was circulated by Dinon, and has come down to us through the abbreviation of Pompeius Trogus. The remains of a third account are met with in Aristotle. Ælian knew a fourth in which the murder was ascribed to the son of Xerxes himself.

fate (462).[1] The chastisement of Egypt proved a harder task. Since the downfall of the Saites, the eastern nomes of the Delta had always constituted a single fief, which the Greeks called the kingdom of Libya. Lords of Marea and of the fertile districts extending between the Canopic arm of the Nile, the mountains, and the sea, its princes probably exercised suzerainty over several of the Libyan tribes of Marmarica. Inaros, son of Psammetichus,[2] who was then the ruling sovereign, defied the Persians openly. The inhabitants of the Delta, oppressed by the tax-gatherers of Achæmenes,[3] welcomed him with open arms, and he took possession of the country between the two branches of the Nile, probably aided by the Cyrenians; the Nile valley itself and Memphis, closely guarded by the Persian garrisons, did not, however, range themselves on his side. Meanwhile the satrap, fearing that the troops at his disposal were insufficient, had gone to beg assistance of his nephew. Artaxerxes had assembled an army and a fleet, and, in the first moment of enthusiasm, had intended to assume the command in person; but, by the advice of his counsellors, he was with little difficulty dissuaded from carrying this

[1] The date 462 is approximate, and is inferred from the fact that the war in Bactriana is mentioned in Ctesias between the war against the sons of Artabanus which must have occupied a part of 463, and the Egyptian rebellion which broke out about 462, as Diodorus Siculus points out, doubtless following Ephorus.

[2] The name of the father of Inaros is given us by the contemporary testimony of Thucydides.

[3] Achæmenes is the form given by Herodotus and by Diodorus Siculus, who make him the son of Darius I., appointed governor of Egypt after the repression of the revolt of Khabbîsha. Ctesias calls him Achæmenides, and says that he was the son of Xerxes.

whim into effect, and he delegated the conduct of affairs to Achæmenes. The latter at first repulsed the Libyans (460), and would probably have soon driven them back into their deserts, had not the Athenians interfered in the fray. They gave orders to their fleet at Cyprus to support the insurgents by every means in their power, and their appearance on the scene about the autumn of 469 changed the course of affairs. Achæmenes was overcome at Papremis, and his army almost completely exterminated. Inaros struck him down with his own hand in the struggle; but the same evening he caused the body to be recovered, and sent it to the court of Susa, though whether out of bravado, or from respect to the Achæmenian race, it is impossible to say.[1] His good fortune did not yet forsake him. Some days afterwards, the Athenian squadron of Charitimides came up by chance with the Phœnician fleet, which was sailing to the help of the Persians, and had not yet received the news of the disaster which had befallen them at Papremis. The Greeks sunk thirty of the enemy's vessels and took twenty more, and, after this success, the allies believed that they had merely to show themselves to bring about a general rising of the fellahîn, and effect the expulsion of the Persians from the whole of Egypt. They sailed up the river and forced Memphis after a few days' siege; but the garrison of the White Wall refused to surrender, and the allies were obliged to lay siege to

[1] Diodorus Siculus says in so many words that the Athenians took part in the battle of Papremis; Thucydides and Herodotus do not speak of their being there, and several modern historians take this silence as a proof that their squadron arrived after the battle had been fought.

it in the ordinary manner (459) :[1] in the issue this proved their ruin. Artaxerxes raised a fresh force in Cilicia, and while completing his preparations, attempted to bring about a diversion in Greece. The strength of Pharaoh did not so much depend on his Libyan and Egyptian hordes, as on the little body of hoplites and the crews of the Athenian squadron; and if the withdrawal of the latter could be effected, the repulse of the others would be a certainty. Persian agents were therefore employed to beg the Spartans to invade Attica; but the remembrance of Salamis and Platæa was as yet too fresh to permit of the Lacedæmonians allying themselves with the common enemy, and their virtue on this occasion was proof against the darics of the Orientals.[2] The Egyptian army was placed in the field early in the year 456, under the leadership of Megabyzos, the satrap of Syria: it numbered, so it was said, some 300,000 men, and it was supported by 300 Phœnician vessels commanded by Artabazos.[3] The allies raised the blockade of the White Wall as soon as he entered the Delta, and hastened to attack him; but they had lost their opportunity. Defeated in a desperate encounter, in which Charitimides was killed and Inaros

[1] The date of 459-8 for the arrival of the Athenians is concluded from the passage of Thucydides, who gives an account of the end of the war after the cruise of Tolmides in 455, in the sixth year of its course.

[2] Megabyzos opened these negotiations, and his presence at Sparta during the winter of 457-6 is noticed.

[3] Ctesias here introduces the Persian admiral Horiscos, but Diodorus places Artabazos and Megabyzos side by side, as was the case later on in the war in Cyprus, one at the head of the fleet, the other of the army; it is probable that the historian from whom Diodorus copied, viz. Ephorus, recognised the same division of leadership in the Egyptian campaign.

wounded in the thigh, they barricaded themselves within the large island of Prosopitis, about the first fortnight in January of the year 455, and there sustained a regular siege for the space of eighteen months. At the end of that time Megabyzos succeeded in turning an arm of the river, which left their fleet high and dry, and, rather than allow it to fall into his hands, they burned their vessels, whereupon he gave orders to make the final assault. The bulk of the Athenian auxiliaries perished in that day's attack, the remainder withdrew with Inaros into the fortified town of Byblos, where Megabyzos, unwilling to prolong a struggle with a desperate enemy, permitted them to capitulate on honourable terms. Some of them escaped and returned to Cyrene, from whence they took ship to their own country; but the main body, to the number of 6000, were carried away to Susa by Megabyzos in order to receive the confirmation of the treaty which he had concluded. As a crowning stroke of misfortune, a reinforcement of fifty Athenian triremes, which at this juncture entered the Mendesian mouth of the Nile, was surrounded by the Phœnician fleet, and more than half of them destroyed. The fall of Prosopitis brought the rebellion to an end.[1] The nomes of the Delta were restored to order, and, as was often customary in Oriental kingdoms,

[1] The accounts of these events given by Ctesias and Thucydides are complementary, and, in spite of their brevity, together form a whole which must be sufficiently near the truth. That of Ephorus, preserved in Diodorus, is derived from an author who shows partiality to the Athenians, and who passes by everything not to their honour, while he seeks to throw the blame for the final disaster on the cowardice of the Egyptians. The summary of Aristodemus comes directly from that of Thucydides.

the vanquished petty princes or their children were reinvested in their hereditary fiefs; even Libya was not taken from the family of Inaros, but was given to his son Thannyras and a certain Psammetichus. A few bands of fugitives, however, took refuge in the marshes of the littoral, in the place where the Saites in former times had sought a safe retreat, and they there proclaimed king a certain Amyrtæus, who was possibly connected with the line of Amasis, and successfully defied the repeated attempts of the Persians to dislodge them.

The Greek league had risked the best of its forces in this rash undertaking, and had failed in its enterprise. It had cost the allies so dearly in men and galleys, that if the Persians had at once assumed the offensive, most of the Asiatic cities would have found themselves in a most critical situation; and Athens, then launched in a quarrel with the states of the Peloponnesus, would have experienced the greatest difficulty in succouring them. The feebleness of Artaxerxes, however, and possibly the intrigues at court and troubles in various other parts of the empire, prevented the satraps from pursuing their advantage, and when at length they meditated taking action, the opportunity had gone by. They nevertheless attempted to regain the ascendency over Cyprus; Artabazos with a Sidonian fleet cruised about the island, Megabyzos assembled troops in Cilicia, and the petty kings of Greek origin raised a cry of alarm. Athens, which had just concluded a truce with the Peloponnesians, at once sent two hundred vessels to their assistance under the command of Cimon (449). Cimon acted as though he were about to reopen the campaign in

Egypt, and despatched sixty of his triremes to King Amyrtæus, while he himself took Marion and blockaded Kition with the rest of his forces. The siege dragged on; he was perhaps about to abandon it, when he took to his bed and died. Those who succeeded him in the command were obliged to raise the blockade for want of provisions, but as they returned and were passing Salamis, they fell in with the Phœnician vessels which had just been landing the Cilician troops, and defeated them; they then disembarked, and, as at Mycale and Eurymedon, they gained a second victory in the open field, after which they joined the squadron which had been sent to Egypt, and sailed for Athens with the dead body of their chief. They had once more averted the danger of an attack on the Ægean, but that was all. The Athenian statesmen had for some time past realised that it was impossible for them to sustain a double conflict, and fight the battles of Greece against the common enemy, while half of the cities whose safety was secured by their heroic devotion were harassing them on the continent, but the influence of Cimon had up till now encouraged them to persist; on the death of Cimon, they gave up the attempt, and Callias, one of their leaders, repaired in state to Susa for the purpose of opening negotiations. The peace which was concluded on the occasion of this embassy might at first sight appear advantageous to their side. The Persian king, without actually admitting his reverses, accepted their immediate consequences. He recognised the independence of the Asiatic Greeks, of those at least who belonged to the league of Delos, and he promised that his armies on land should never advance further than three days' march from the Ægean littoral. On the seas, he forbade his squadrons to enter Hellenic waters from the Chelidonian to the Cyanæan rocks—that is, from the eastern point of Lycia to the opening of the Black Sea : this prohibition did not apply to the merchant vessels of the contracting parties, and they received permission to traffic freely in each other's waters— the Phœnicians in Greece, and the Greeks in Phœnicia, Cilicia, and Egypt. And yet, when we consider the matter, Athens and Hellas were, of the two, the greater losers by this convention, which appeared to imply their superiority. Not only did they acknowledge indirectly that they felt themselves unequal to the task of overthrowing the empire, but they laid down their arms before they had accomplished the comparatively restricted task which they had set themselves to perform, that of freeing all the Greeks from the Iranian yoke : their Egyptian compatriots still remained Persian tributaries, in company with the cities of Cyrenaïca, Pamphylia, and Cilicia, and, above all, that island of Cyprus in which they had gained some of their most signal triumphs. The Persians, relieved from a war which for a quarter of a century had consumed their battalions and squadrons, drained their finances, and excited their subjects to revolt, were now free to regain their former wealth and perhaps their vigour, could they only find generals to command their troops and guide their politics. Artaxerxes was incapable of directing this revival, and his inveterate weakness exposed him perpetually to the plotting of his satraps or to the intrigues of the women of his harem. The example of Artabanus, followed by that of Hystaspes, had shown how easy it was for an ambitious man to get rid secretly of a monarch or a prince and seriously endanger the crown. The members of the families who had placed Darius on the throne, possessed by hereditary right, or something little short of it, the wealthiest and most populous provinces—Babylonia, Syria, Lydia, Phrygia, and the countries of the Halys—and they were practically kings in all but name, in spite of the *surveillance* which the general and the secretary were supposed to exercise over their actions. Besides this, the indifference and incapacity of the ruling sovereigns had already tended to destroy the order of the administrative system so ably devised by Darius: the satrap had, as a rule, absorbed the functions of a general within his own province, and the secretary was too insignificant a personage to retain authority and independence unless he received the constant support of the sovereign. The latter, a tool in the hands of women and eunuchs, usually felt himself powerless to deal with his great vassals. His toleration went to all lengths if he could thereby avoid a revolt; when this was inevitable, and the rebels were vanquished, he still continued to conciliate them, and in most cases their fiefs and rights were preserved or restored to them, the monarch knowing that he could rid himself of them treacherously by poison or the dagger in the case of their proving themselves too troublesome. Megabyzos by his turbulence was a thorn in the side of Artaxerxes during the half of his reign. He had ended his campaign in Egypt by engaging to preserve the lives of Inaros and the 6000 Greeks who had capitulated at Byblos, and, in spite of the anger of the king, he succeeded in keeping his word for five years, but at the end of that time the demands of Amestris prevailed. She succeeded in obtaining from him some fifty Greeks whom she beheaded, besides Inarcs himself, whom she impaled to avenge Achæmenes. Megabyzos, who had not recovered from the losses he had sustained in his last campaign against Cimon, at first concealed his anger, but he asked permission to visit his Syrian province, and no sooner did he reach it, than he resorted to hostilities. He defeated in succession Usiris and Menostates, the two generals despatched against him, and when force failed to overcome his obstinate resistance, the government condescended to treat with him, and swore to forget the past if he would consent to lay down arms. To this he agreed, and reappeared at court; but once there, his confidence nearly proved fatal to him. Having been invited to take part in a hunt, he pierced with his javelin a lion which threatened to attack the king: Artaxerxes called to mind an ancient law which punished by death any intervention of that kind, and he ordered that the culprit should be beheaded. Megabyzos with difficulty escaped this punishment through the entreaties of Amestris and of his wife Amytis; but he was deprived of his fiefs, and sent to Kyrta, on the shores of the Persian Gulf. After five years this exile became unbearable; he therefore spread the report that he was attacked by leprosy, and he returned home without any one venturing to hinder him, from fear of defiling themselves by contact with his person. Amestris and Amytis brought about his reconciliation with his sovereign; and thenceforward he regulated his conduct so successfully that the past was completely forgotten, and when he died, at the age of seventy-six years, Artaxerxes deeply regretted his loss.¹

Peace having been signed with Athens, and the revolt of Megabyzos being at an end, Artaxerxes was free to enjoy himself without further care for the future, and to pass his time between his various capitals and palaces.

VIEW OF THE ACHÆMENIAN RUINS OF ISTAKHR.²

His choice lay between Susa and Persepolis, between Ecbatana and Babylon, according as the heat of the summer or the cold of the winter induced him to pass from the plains to the mountains, or from the latter to

¹ These events are known to us only through Ctesias. Their date is uncertain, but there is no doubt that they occurred after Cimon's campaign in Cyprus and the conclusion of the peace of Callias.

² Drawn by Boudier, from the engraving of Flandin and Coste.

the plains. During his visits to Babylon he occupied one of the old Chaldæan palaces, but at Ecbatana he possessed merely the ancient residence of the Median kings, and the seraglio built or restored by Xerxes in the fashion of the times: at Susa and in Persia proper, the royal buildings were entirely the work of the Achæmenids, mostly that of Darius and Xerxes. The memory of Cyrus and of the kings to whom primitive Persia owed her organisation in the obscure century preceding her career of conquest, was piously preserved in the rude buildings of Pasargadæ, which was regarded as a sacred city, whither the sovereigns repaired for coronation as soon as their predecessors had expired. But its lonely position and simple appointments no longer suited their luxurious and effeminate habits, and Darius had in consequence fixed his residence a few miles to the south of it, near to the village, which after its development became the immense royal city of Persepolis. He there erected buildings more suited to the splendour of his court, and found the place so much to his taste during his lifetime, that he was unwilling to leave it after death. He therefore caused his tomb to be cut in the steep limestone cliff which borders the plain about half a mile to the north-west of the town. It is an opening in the form of a Greek cross, the upper part of which contains a bas-relief in which the king, standing in front of the altar, implores the help of Ahura-mazdâ poised with extended wings above him; the platform on which the king stands is supported by two rows of caryatides in low relief, whose features and dress are characteristic of

Persian vassals, while other personages, in groups of three on either side, are shown in the attitude of prayer. Below, in the transverse arms of the cross, is carved a flat portico with four columns, in the centre of which is the entrance

THE TOMB OF DARIUS.[1]

to the funeral vault. Within the latter, in receptacles hollowed out of the rock, Darius and eight of his family were successively laid. Xerxes caused a tomb in every way similar to be cut for himself near that of Darius,

[1] Drawn by Faucher-Gudin, from the heliogravure by Marcel Dieulafoy.

THE TOMBS OF THE ACHÆMENIAN KINGS 261

and in the course of years others were added close by.[1] Both the tombs and the palace are built in that eclectic style which characterises the Achæmenian period of Iranian art. The main features are borrowed from the architecture of those nations which were vassals or neighbours of the

THE HILL OF THE ROYAL ACHÆMENIAN TOMBS AT NAKHSH-Î-RUSTEM.[2]

empire—Babylonia, Egypt, and Greece; but these various elements have been combined and modified in such a manner as to form a rich and harmonious whole. The core of the walls was of burnt bricks, similar to those employed in the Euphrates valley, but these were covered with a

---

[1] The tomb of Darius alone bears an inscription. Darius III. was also buried there by command of Alexander.

[2] Drawn by Boudier, from the engraving of Flandin and Coste.

facing of enamelled tiles, disposed as a skirting or a frieze, on which figured those wonderful processions of archers, and the lions which now adorn the Louvre, while the pilasters at the angles, the columns, pillars, window-frames,

ONE OF THE CAPITALS FROM SUSA.[1]

and staircases were of fine white limestone or of hard bluish-grey marble. The doorways are high and narrow; the moulding which frames them is formed of three Ionic fillets, each projecting beyond the other, surmounted by

[1] Drawn by Boudier, from a photograph taken in the Louvre by Faucher-Gudin.

GENERAL VIEW OF THE RUINS OF PERSEPOLIS.

Drawn by Boudier, from FLANDIN and COSTE, *La Perse Antique*, pl. 66.

a coved Egyptian lintel springing from a row of alternate eggs and disks. The framing of the doors is bare, but the embrasures are covered with bas-reliefs representing various scenes in which the king is portrayed fulfilling his royal functions—engaged in struggles with evil genii which have the form of lions or fabulous animals, occupied in hunting, granting audiences, or making an entrance in state, shaded by an umbrella which is borne by a eunuch behind him. The columns employed in this style of architecture constitute its most original feature. The base of them usually consists of two mouldings, resting either on a square pedestal or on a cylindrical drum, widening out below into a bell-like curve, and sometimes ornamented with several rows of inverted leaves. The shafts, which have forty-eight perpendicular ribs cut on their outer surface, are perhaps rather tall in proportion to their thickness. They terminate in a group of large leaves, an evident imitation of the Egyptian palm-leaf capital, from which spring a sort of rectangular fluted die or abacus, flanked on either side with four rows of volutes curved in opposite directions, generally two at the base and two at the summit. The heads and shoulders of two bulls, placed back to back, project above the volutes, and take the place of the usual abacus of the capital. The dimensions of these columns, their gracefulness, and the distance at which they were placed from one another, prove that they supported not a stone architrave, but enormous beams of wood, which were inserted between the napes of the bulls' necks, and upon which the joists of the roof were superimposed. The palace of Persepolis, built by Darius after he had crushed the revolts which took place at the outset of his reign, was situated at the foot of a chain of rugged mountains which skirt the plain on its eastern side, and was raised on an irregularly shaped platform or terrace, which was terminated by a wall of enormous polygonal blocks of masonry. The terrace was reached by a double flight of steps, the lateral walls of which are covered with bas-reliefs, representing processions of satellites, slaves, and tributaries, hunting scenes, fantastic episodes of battle, and lions fighting with and devouring bulls. The area of the raised platform was not of uniform level, and was laid out in gardens, in the midst of which rose the pavilions that served as dwelling-places. The reception-rooms were placed near the top of the flight of steps, and the more important of them had been built under the two preceding kings. Those nearest to the edge of the platform were the propylæa of Xerxes—gigantic entrances whose gateways were guarded on either side by winged bulls of Assyrian type; beyond these was the *apadana*, or hall of honour, where the sovereign presided in state at the ordinary court ceremonies. To the east of the *apadana*, and almost in the centre of the raised terrace, rose the Hall of a Hundred Columns, erected by Darius, and used only on special occasions. Artaxerxes I. seems to have had a particular affection for Susa. It had found favour with his predecessors, and they had so frequently resided there, even after the building of Persepolis, that it had continued to be regarded as the real capital of the empire by other nations, whereas the Persian sovereigns themselves had sought to make it rather an impregnable retreat than a luxurious residence. Artaxerxes built there an *apadana* on a vaster scale than any hitherto designed. It comprised three colonnades,

THE PROPYLÆA OF XERXES I. AT PERSEPOLIS.[1]

which, taken together, formed a rectangle measuring 300 feet by 250 feet on the two sides, the area being approximately that of the courtyard of the Louvre. The central

[1] Drawn by Boudier, from the heliogravure of Marcel Dieulafoy.

268 THE LAST DAYS OF THE OLD EASTERN WORLD

colonnade, which was the largest of the three, was enclosed by walls on three sides, but was open to the south. Immense festoons of drapery hung from the wooden entablature, and curtains, suspended from rods between the first row of columns, afforded protection from the sun and

BAS-RELIEF ON THE STAIRCASE LEADING TO THE APADANA OF XERXES I.[1]

from the curiosity of the vulgar. At the hour appointed for the ceremonies, the great king took his seat in solitary grandeur on the gilded throne of the Achæmenids; at the extreme end of the colonnade his eunuchs, nobles, and guards ranged themselves in silence on either side, each in the place which etiquette assigned to him. Meanwhile the foreign ambassadors who had been honoured

[1] Drawn by Faucher-Gudin, from Marcel Dieulafoy.

THE ETIQUETTE OF THE PERSIAN COURT

by an invitation to the audience—Greeks from Thebes, Sparta, or Athens; Sakæ from the regions of the north; Indians, Arabs, nomad chiefs from mysterious Ethiopia—ascended in procession the flights of steps which led from the town to the palace, bearing the presents destined for its royal master. Having reached the terrace, the curtains of the *apadana* were suddenly parted, and in the distance, through a vista of columns, they perceived a motionless figure, resplendent with gold and purple, before whom they fell prostrate with their faces to the earth. The heralds were the bearers of their greetings, and brought back to them a gracious or haughty reply, as the case may be. When they rose from the ground, the curtains had closed, the kingly vision was eclipsed, and the escort which had accompanied them into the palace conducted them back to the town, dazzled with the momentary glimpse of the spectacle vouchsafed to them.

THE KING ON HIS THRONE.[1]

The Achæmenian monarchs were not regarded as gods or as sons of gods, like the Egyptian Pharaohs, and the Persian religion forbade their ever becoming so, but the person of the king was hedged round with such ceremonial

[1] Drawn by Faucher-Gudin, from Flandin and Coste.

respect as in other Oriental nations was paid only to the gods: this was but natural, for was he not a despot, who with a word or gesture could abase the noblest of his subjects, and determine the well-being or misery of his people? His dress differed from that of his nobles only by the purple dye of its material and the richness of the gold embroideries with which it was adorned, but he was

A VIEW OF THE APADANA OF SUSA, RESTORED.[1]

distinguished from all others by the peculiar felt cap, or *kidaris*, which he wore, and the blue-and-white band which encircled it like a crown; the king is never represented without his long sceptre with pommelled handle, whether he be sitting or standing, and wherever he went he was attended by his umbrella- and fan-bearers. The prescriptions of court etiquette were such as to convince his subjects and persuade himself that he was sprung from a

[1] Drawn by Boudier, from the restoration by Marcel Dieulafoy.

nobler race than that of any of his magnates, and that he was outside the pale of ordinary humanity. The greater part of his time was passed in privacy, where he was attended only by the eunuchs appointed to receive his orders; and these orders, once issued, were irrevocable, as was also the king's word, however much he might desire to recall a promise once made. His meals were, as a rule, served to him alone; he might not walk on foot beyond the precincts of the palace, and he never showed himself in public except on horseback or in his chariot, surrounded by his servants and his guards. The male members of the royal family and those belonging to the six noble houses enjoyed the privilege of approaching the king at any hour of the day or night, provided he was not in the company of one of his wives. These privileged persons formed his council, which he convoked on important occasions, but all ordinary business was transacted by means of the scribes and inferior officials, on whom devolved the charge of the various departments of the government. A vigorous ruler, such as Darius had proved himself, certainly trusted no one but himself to read the reports sent in by the satraps, the secretaries, and the generals, or to dictate the answers required by each; but Xerxes and Artaxerxes delegated the heaviest part of such business to their ministers, and they themselves only fulfilled such state functions as it was impossible to shirk—the public administration of justice, receptions of ambassadors or victorious generals, distributions of awards, annual sacrifices, and state banquets: they were even obliged, in accordance with an ancient and inviolable tradition, once a year to set aside their usual sober habits and drink to excess on the day of the feast of Mithra. Occasionally they would break through their normal routine of life to conduct in person some expedition of small importance, directed against one of the semi-independent tribes of Iran, such as the Cadusians, but their most glorious and frequent exploits were confined to the chase. They delighted to hunt the bull, the wild boar, the deer, the wild ass, and the hare, as the Pharaohs or Assyrian kings of old had done; and they would track the lion to his lair and engage him single-handed; in fact, they held a strict monopoly in such conflicts, a law which punished with death any huntsman who had the impertinence to interpose between the monarch and his prey being only abolished by Artaxerxes. A crowd of menials, slaves, great nobles, and priests filled the palace; grooms, stool-bearers, umbrella- and fan-carriers, *kavasses*, " Immortals," bakers, perfumers, soldiers, and artisans formed a retinue so numerous as to require a thousand bullocks, asses, and stags to be butchered every day for its maintenance; and when the king made a journey in full state, this enormous train looked like an army on the march. The women of the royal harem lived in seclusion in a separate wing of the palace, or in isolated buildings erected in the centre of the gardens. The legitimate wives of the sovereign were selected from the ladies of the royal house, the sisters or cousins of the king, and from the six princely Persian families; but their number were never very large, usually three or four at most.[1] The concubines, on the other hand,

[1] Cambyses had had three wives, including his two sisters Atossa and

THE ACHÆMENIAN KING AND HIS HAREM 273

were chosen from all classes of society, and were counted by hundreds. They sang or played on musical instruments at the state banquets of the court, they accompanied their master to the battle-field or the chase, and probably performed the various inferior domestic duties in the interior of the harem, such as spinning, weaving, making perfumes, and attending to the confectionery and cooking. Each of the king's wives had her own separate suite of

PROCESSIONAL DISPLAY OF TRIBUTE BROUGHT TO THE KING OF PERSIA.[1]

apartments and special attendants, and occupied a much higher position than a mere concubine; but only one was actually queen and had the right to wear the crown, and this position belonged of right to a princess of Achæmenian race. Thus Atossa, daughter of Cyrus, was queen successively to Cambyses, Gaumâta, and Darius; Amestris to Xerxes; and Damaspia to Artaxerxes. Besides the influence naturally exerted by the queen

Roxana. Darius had four wives—two daughters of Cyrus, Atossa and Artystônê, Parmys daughter of Smerdis, and a daughter of Otanes.
[1] Drawn by Faucher-Gudin, from plates in Flandin and Coste.

over the mind of her husband, she often acquired boundless authority in the empire, in spite of her secluded life.[1] Her power was still further increased when she became a widow, if the new king happened to be one of her own sons. In such circumstances she retained the external attributes of royalty, sitting at the royal table whenever the king deigned to dine in the women's apartments, and everywhere taking precedence of the young queen; she was attended by her own body of eunuchs, of whom, as well as of her private revenues, she had absolute control. Those whom the queen-mother took under her protection escaped punishment, even though they richly deserved it, but the object of her hatred was doomed to perish in the end, either by poison treacherously administered, or by some horrible form of torture, being impaled, suffocated in ashes, tortured in the trough, or flayed alive. Artaxerxes reigned for forty-two years, spending his time between the pleasures of the chase and the harem; no serious trouble disturbed his repose after his suppression of the revolt under Megabyzos, but on his death in 424 B.C. there was a renewal of the intrigues and ambitious passions which had stained with bloodshed the opening years of his reign. The legitimate heir, Xerxes II., was assassinated, after a reign of forty-five days, by Secudianus (Sogdianus), one of his illegitimate brothers, and the *cortège* which was escorting the bodies of his parents conveyed his also to the royal burying-place at Persepolis. Meanwhile Secudianus became suspicious of another of his brothers, named Oohus, whom Artaxerxes had caused to marry Parysatis, one of the daughters of

[1] Thus Atossa induced Darius to designate Xerxes as his heir-apparent.

Xerxes, and whom he had set over the important province of Hyrcania. Ochus received repeated summonses to appear in his brother's presence to pay him homage, and at last obeyed the mandate, but arrived at the head of an army. The Persian nobility rose at his approach, and one by one the chief persons of the state declared themselves in his favour: first Arbarius, commander of the cavalry; then Arxanes, the satrap of Egypt; and lastly, the eunuch Artoxares, the ruler of Armenia. These three all combined in urging Ochus to assume the *kidaris* publicly, which he, with feigned reluctance, consented to do, and proceeded, at the suggestion of Parysatis, to open negotiations with Secudianus, offering to divide the regal power with him. Secudianus accepted the offer, against the advice of his minister Menostanes, and gave himself up into the hands of the rebels. He was immediately seized and cast into the ashes, where he perished miserably, after a reign of six months and fifteen days.

On ascending the throne, Ochus assumed the name of Darius. His confidential advisers were three eunuchs, who ruled the empire in his name—Artoxares, who had taken such a prominent part in the campaign which won him the crown, Artibarzanes, and Athôos; but the guiding spirit of his government was, in reality, his wife, the detestable Parysatis. She had already borne him two children before she became queen; a daughter, Amestris, and a son, Arsaces, who afterwards became king under the name of Artaxerxes. Soon after the accession of her husband, she bore him a second son, whom she named Cyrus, in memory of the founder of the empire, and a daughter, Artostê; several other children were born subsequently, making thirteen in all, but these all died in childhood, except one named Oxendras. Violent, false, jealous, and passionately fond of the exercise of power, Parysatis hesitated at no crime to rid herself of those who thwarted her schemes, even though they might be members of her own family; and, not content with putting them out of the way, she delighted in making them taste

DARIUS II.[1]

her hatred to the full, by subjecting them to the most skilfully graduated refinements of torture; she deservedly left behind her the reputation of being one of the most cruel of all the cruel queens, whose memory was a terror not only to the harems of Persia, but to the whole of the Eastern world. The numerous revolts which broke out soon after her husband's accession, furnished occasions for the revelation of her perfidious cleverness. All the malcontents of the reign of Artaxerxes, those who had been implicated in the murder of Xerxes II., or who had sided with Secudianus, had rallied round a younger brother of Darius, named Arsites, and one of them, Artyphios, son of Megabyzos, took the field in Asia Minor. Being supported by a large contingent of Greek mercenaries, he won two successive victories at the opening of the campaign, but was subsequently defeated, though his forces still remained formidable. But Persian gold accomplished what Persian bravery had failed to achieve, and prevailed over the mercenaries so successfully that all

[1] Drawn by Faucher-Gudin, from one of the coins in the *Cabinet des Médailles*.

deserted him with the exception of three Milesians. Artyphios and Arsites, thus discouraged, committed the imprudence of capitulating on condition of receiving a promise that their lives should be spared, and that they should be well treated; but Parysatis persuaded her husband to break his plighted word, and they perished in the ashes. Their miserable fate did not discourage the satrap of Lydia, Pissuthnes, who was of Achæmenian race: he entered the lists in 418 B.C., with the help of the Athenians. The relations between the Persian empire and Greece had continued fairly satisfactory since the peace of 449 B.C., and the few outbreaks which had taken place had not led to any widespread disturbance. The Athenians, absorbed in their quarrel with Sparta, preferred to close their eyes to all side issues, lest the Persians should declare war against them, and the satraps of Asia Minor, fully alive to the situation, did not hesitate to take advantage of any pretext for recovering a part of the territory they coveted: it was thus that they had seized Colophon about 430 B.C., and so secured once more a port on the Ægean. Darius despatched to oppose Pissuthnes a man of noble birth, named Tissaphernes, giving him plenary power throughout the whole of the peninsula, and Tissaphernes endeavoured to obtain by treachery the success he would with difficulty have won on the field of battle: he corrupted by his darics Lycon, the commander of the Athenian contingent, and Pissuthnes, suddenly abandoned by his best auxiliaries, was forced to surrender at discretion. He also was suffocated in the ashes, and Darius bestowed his office on Tissaphernes.

But the punishment of Pissuthnes did not put an end to the troubles: his son Amorges roused Caria to revolt, and with the title of king maintained his independence for some years longer. While these incidents were taking place, the news of the disasters in Sicily reached the East: as soon as it was known in Susa that Athens had lost at Syracuse the best part of her fleet and the choicest of her citizens, the moment was deemed favourable to violate the treaty and regain control of the whole of Asia Minor. Two noteworthy men were at that time set over the western satrapies, Tissaphernes ruling at Sardes, and Tiribazus over Hellespontine Phrygia. These satraps opened negotiations with Sparta at the begining of 412 B.C., and concluded a treaty with her at Miletus itself, by the terms of which the Peloponnesians recognised the suzerainty of Darius over all the territory once held by his ancestors in Asia, including the cities since incorporated into the Athenian league. They hoped shortly to be strong enough to snatch from him what they now ceded, and to set free once more the Greeks whom they thus condemned to servitude after half a century of independence, but their expectations were frustrated. The towns along the coast fell one after another into the power of Tissaphernes, Amorges was taken prisoner in Iassos, and at the beginning of 411 B.C. there remained to the Athenians in Ionia and Caria merely the two ports of Halicarnassus and Notium, and the three islands of Cos, Samos, and Lesbos: from that time the power of the great king increased from year to year, and weighed heavily on the destinies of Greece. Meanwhile Darius II. was growing old, and intrigues with regard to

THE TREATY OF MILETUS—CYRUS THE YOUNGER 279

the succession were set on foot. Two of his sons put forward claims to the throne: Arsaces had seniority in his favour, but had been born when his father was still a mere satrap; Cyrus, on the contrary, had been born in the purple, and his mother Parysatis was passionately devoted to him.[1] Thanks to her manœuvres, he was practically created viceroy of Asia Minor in 407 B.C., with such abundant resources of men and money at his disposal, that he was virtually an independent sovereign. While he was consolidating his power in the west, his mother endeavoured to secure his accession to the throne by intriguing at the court of the aged king; if her plans failed, Cyrus was prepared to risk everything by an appeal to arms. He realised that the Greeks would prove powerful auxiliaries in such a contingency; and as soon as he had set up his court at Sardes, he planned how best to conciliate their favour, or at least to win over those whose support was likely to be most valuable. Athens, as a maritime power, was not in a position to support him in an enterprise which especially required the co-operation of a considerable force of heavily armed infantry. He therefore deliberately espoused the cause of the Peloponnesians, and the support he gave them was not without its influence on the issue of the struggle: the terrible day of Ægos Potamos was a day

CYRUS THE YOUNGER.[2]

[1] Cyrus was certainly not more than seventeen years old in 407 B.C., evening admitting that he was born immediately after his father's accession in 424–3 B.C.

[2] Drawn by Faucher-Gudin, from one of the coins in the *Cabinet des Médailles*.

of triumph for him as much as for the Lacedæmonians (405 B.C.).

His intimacy with Lysander, however, his constant enlistments of mercenary troops, and his secret dealings with the neighbouring provinces, had already aroused suspicion, and the satraps placed under his orders, especially Tissaphernes, accused him to the king of treason. Darius summoned him to Susa to explain his conduct (405 B.C.), and he arrived just in time to be present at his father's death (404), but too late to obtain his designation as heir to the throne through the intervention of his mother, Parysatis; Arsaces inherited the crown, and assumed the name of Artaxerxes. Cyrus entered the temple of Pasargadæ surreptitiously during the coronation ceremony, with the intention of killing his brother at the foot of the altar; but Tissaphernes, warned by one of the priests, denounced him, and he would have been put to death on the spot, had not his mother thrown her arms around him and prevented the executioner from fulfilling his office. Having with difficulty obtained pardon and been sent back to his province, he collected thirty thousand Greeks and a hundred thousand native troops, and, hastily leaving Sardes (401 B.C.), he crossed Asia Minor, Northern Syria, and Mesopotamia, encountered the royal army at Cunaxa, to the north of

ARTAXERXES MNEMON.[1]

[1] Drawn by Faucher-Gudin, from a coin in the *Cabinet des Médailles*. This coin, which was struck at Mallos, in Cilicia, bears as a counter-mark the figure of a bull and the name of the city of Issus.

DEATH OF CYRUS

Babylon, and rashly met his end at the very moment of victory. He was a brave, active, and generous prince, endowed with all the virtues requisite to make a good Oriental monarch, and he had, moreover, learnt, through contact with the Greeks, to recognise the weak points of his own nation, and was fully determined to remedy them: his death, perhaps, was an irreparable misfortune for his country. Had he survived and supplanted the feeble Artaxerxes, it is quite possible that he might have confirmed and strengthened the power of Persia, or, at least, temporarily have arrested its decline. Having lost their leader, his Asiatic followers at once dispersed; but the mercenaries did not lose heart, and, crossing Asia and Armenia, gained at length the shores of the Black Sea. Up to that time the Greeks had looked upon Persia as a compact state, which they were sufficiently powerful to conquer by sea and hold in check by land, but which they could not, without imprudence, venture to attack within its own frontiers. The experience of the Ten Thousand was a proof to them that a handful of men, deprived of their proper generals, without guides, money, or provisions, might successfully oppose the overwhelming forces of the great king, and escape from his clutches without any serious difficulty. National discords prevented them from at once utilising the experience they thus acquired, but the lesson was not lost upon the court of Susa. The success of Lysander had been ensured by Persian subsidies, and now Sparta hesitated to fulfil the conditions of the treaty of Miletus; the Lacedæmonians demanded liberty once more for the former allies of Athens, fostered the war in Asia in order to enforce their claims, and their king Agesilaus, penetrating to the very heart of Phrygia, would have pressed still further forward in the tracks of the Ten Thousand, had not an opportune diversion been created in his rear by the bribery of the Persians. Athens once more flew to arms: her fleet, in conjunction with the Phœnicians, took possession of Cythera; the Long Walls were rebuilt at the expense of the great king, and Sparta, recalled by these reverses to a realisation of her position, wisely abandoned her inclination for distant enterprises. Asia Minor was reconquered, and Persia passed from the position of a national enemy to that of the friend and arbiter of Greece; but she did so by force of circumstances only, and not from having merited in any way the supremacy she attained. Her military energy, indeed, was far from being exhausted; but poor Artaxerxes, bewildered by the rivalries between his mother and his wives, did not know how to make the most of the immense resources still at his disposal, and he met with repeated checks as soon as he came face to face with a nation and leaders who refused to stoop to treachery. He had no sooner recovered possession of the Ægean littoral than Egypt was snatched from his grasp by a new Pharaoh who had arisen in the Nile valley. The peace had not been seriously disturbed in Egypt during the forty years which had elapsed since the defeat of Inarus. Satrap had peaceably succeeded satrap in the fortress of Memphis; the exhaustion of Libya had prevented any movement on the part of Thannyras; the aged Amyrtæus had passed from the scene, and his son,

Pausiris, bent his neck submissively to the Persian yoke. More than once, however, unexpected outbursts had shown that the fires of rebellion were still smouldering. A Psammetichus, who reigned about 445 B.C. in a corner of the Delta, had dared to send corn and presents to the Athenians, then at war with Artaxerxes I., and the second year of Darius II. had been troubled by a sanguinary sedition, which, however, was easily suppressed by the governor then in power; finally, about 410 B.C., a king of Egypt had, not without some show of evidence, laid himself open to the charge of sending a piratical expedition into Phœnician waters, an Arab king having contributed to the enterprise.[1] It was easy to see, moreover, from periodical revolts—such as that of Megabyzos in Syria, those of Artyphios and Arsites, of Pissuthnes and Amorges in Asia Minor—with what impunity the wrath of the great king could be defied: it was not to be wondered at, therefore, that, about 405 B.C., an enemy should appear in the heart of the Delta in the person of a grandson and namesake of Amyrtæus. He did not at first rouse the whole country to revolt, for Egyptian troops were still numbered in the army of Artaxerxes at the battle of Cunaxa in 401 B.C.; but he succeeded in establishing a regular native government, and struggled so resolutely against the foreign domination that the historians of the sacred colleges inscribed his name on the list of the Pharaohs. He is there made to represent a whole dynasty, the XXVIIIth,

---

[1] The revolt mentioned by Ctesias has nothing to do with the insurrection of the satrap of Egypt which is here referred to, the date of which is furnished by the Syncellus.

which lasted six years, coincident with the six years of his reign. It was due to a Mendesian dynasty, however, whose founder was Nephorites, that Egypt obtained its entire freedom, and was raised once more to the rank of a nation. This dynasty from the very outset adopted the policy which had proved so successful in the case of the Saites three centuries previously, and employed it with similar success. Egypt had always been in the position of a besieged fortress, which needed, for its complete security, that its first lines of defence should be well in advance of its citadel: she must either possess Syria or win her as an ally, if she desired to be protected against all chance of sudden invasion. Nephorites and his successors, therefore, formed alliances beyond the isthmus, and even on the other side of the Mediterranean, with Cyprus, Caria, and Greece, in one case to purchase support, and in another to re-establish the ancient supremacy exercised by the Theban Pharaohs.[1] Every revolt against the Persians, every quarrel among the satraps, helped forward their cause, since they compelled the great king to suspend his attacks against Egypt altogether or to prosecute them at wide intervals: the Egyptians therefore fomented such quarrels, or even, at need, provoked them, and played their game so well that for a long time they had to oppose only a fraction of the Persian forces. Like the Saite Pharaohs before them, they were aware how little reliance could be placed on

---

[1] This is, at any rate, the idea given of him by Egyptian tradition in the time of the Ptolemies, as results from a passage in the *Demotic Rhapsody*, where his reign is mentioned.

native troops, and they recruited their armies at great expense from the European Greeks. This occurred at the time when mercenary forces were taking the place of native levies throughout Hellas, and war was developing into a lucrative trade for those who understood how to conduct it: adventurers, greedy for booty, flocked to the standards of the generals who enjoyed the best reputation for kindness or ability, and the generals themselves sold their services to the highest bidder. The Persian kings took large advantage of this arrangement to procure troops: the Pharaohs imitated their example, and in the years which followed, the most experienced captains, Iphicrates, Chabrias, and Timotheus, passed from one camp to another, as often against the will as with the consent of their fatherland. The power of Sparta was at her zenith when Nephorites ascended the throne, and she was just preparing for her expedition to Phrygia. The Pharaoh concluded an alliance with the Lacedæmonians, and in 396 B.C. sent to Agesilaus a fleet laden with arms, corn, and supplies, which, however, was intercepted by Conon, who was at that moment cruising in the direction of Rhodes in command of the Persian squadron. This misadventure and the abrupt retreat of the Spartans from Asia Minor cooled the good will of the Egyptian king towards his allies. Thinking that they had abandoned him, and that he was threatened with an imminent attack on the shore of the Delta, he assembled, probably at Pelusium, the forces he had apparently intended for a distant enterprise.

Matters took longer to come to a crisis than he had expected. The retreat of Agesilaus had not pacified the

Ægean satrapies; after the disturbance created by Cyrus the Younger, the greater number of the native tribes— Mysians, Pisidians, people of Pontus and Paphlagonia—had shaken off the Persian yoke, and it was a matter of no small difficulty to reduce them once more to subjection. Their incessant turbulence gave Egypt time to breathe and to organise new combinations. Cyprus entered readily into her designs. Since the subjugation of that island in 445 B.C., the Greek cities had suffered terrible oppression at the hands of the great king. Artaxerxes I., despairing of reducing them to obedience, depended exclusively for support on the Phœnician inhabitants of the island, who, through his favour, regained so much vigour that in the space of less than two generations they had recovered most of the ground lost during the preceding centuries: Semitic rulers replaced the Achæan tyrants at Salamis, and in most of the other cities, and Citium became what it had been before the rise of Salamis, the principal commercial centre in the island. Evagoras, a descendant of the ancient kings, endeavoured to retrieve the Grecian cause: after driving out of Salamis Abdemon, its Tyrian ruler, he took possession of all the other towns except Citium and Amathus. This is not the place to recount the brilliant part played by Evagoras, in conjunction with Conon, during the campaigns against the Spartans in the Peloponnesian war. The activity he then displayed and the ambitious designs he revealed soon drew upon him the dislike of the Persian governors and their sovereign; and from 391 B.C. he was at open war with Persia. He would have been unable, single-handed, to maintain the struggle for any

SUCCESSES OF HAKORIS

length of time, but Egypt and Greece were at his back, ready to support him with money or arms. Hakoris had succeeded Nephorites I. in 393 B.C.,[1] and had repulsed an attack of Artaxerxes between 390 and 386.[2] He was not unduly exalted by his success, and had immediately taken wise precautions in view of a second invasion. After safeguarding his western frontier by concluding a treaty with the Libyans of Barca, he entered into an alliance with Evagoras and the Athenians. He sent lavish gifts of corn to the Cypriots, as well as munitions of war, ships, and money, while Athens sent them several thousand men under the command of Chabrias; not only did an expedition despatched against them under Autophradates fail miserably, but Evagoras seized successively Citium and Amathus, and, actually venturing across the sea, took Tyre by assault and devastated Phœnicia and Cilicia. The princes of Asia Minor were already preparing for revolt, and one of them, Hecatomnus of Caria, had openly joined the allies, when Sparta suddenly opened negotiations with Persia : Antalcidas presented

HAKORIS.[3]

---

[1] The length of the reign of Nephorites I. is fixed at six years by the lists of Manetho; the last-known date of his reign is that of his fourth year, on a mummy-bandage preserved in the Louvre.

[2] This war is alluded to by several ancient authors in passages which have been brought together and explained by Judeich; but unfortunately the detailed history of the events is not known.

[3] Drawn by Faucher-Gudin, from Lepsius.

himself at Susa to pay homage before the throne of the great king. The treaty of Miletus had brought the efforts of Athens to naught, and sold the Asiatic Greeks to their oppressors: the peace obtained by Antalcidas effaced the results of Salamis and Platæa, and laid European Greece prostrate at the feet of her previously vanquished foes. An order issuing from the centre of Persia commanded the cities of Greece to suspend hostilities and respect each other's liberties; the issuing of such an order was equivalent to treating them as vassals whose quarrels it is the function of the suzerain to repress, but they nevertheless complied with the command (387 B.C.). Artaxerxes, relieved from anxiety for the moment, as to affairs on the Ægean, was now free to send his best generals into the rebel countries, and such was the course his ministers recommended. Evagoras was naturally the first to be attacked. Cyprus was, in fact, an outpost of Egypt; commanding as she did the approach by sea, she was in a position to cut the communications of any army, which, issuing from Palestine, should march upon the Delta. Artaxerxes assembled three hundred thousand foot-soldiers and three hundred triremes under the command of Tiribazus, and directed the whole force against the island. At first the Cypriot cruisers intercepted the convoys which were bringing provisions for this large force, and by so doing reduced the invaders to such straits that sedition broke out in their camp; but Evagoras was defeated at sea off the promontory of Citium, and his squadron destroyed. He was not in any way discouraged by this misfortune, but leaving his son, Pnytagoras, to hold the barbarian forces in check,

THE MENDESIAN DYNASTY

he hastened to implore the help of the Pharaoh (385 B.C.). But Hakoris was too much occupied with securing his own immediate safety to risk anything in so desperate an enterprise. Evagoras was able to bring back merely an insufficient subsidy; he shut himself up in Salamis, and there maintained the conflict for some years longer. Meanwhile Hakoris, realising that the submission of Cyprus would oppose his flank to attack, tried to effect a diversion in Asia Minor, and by entering into alliance with the Pisidians, then in open insurrection, he procured for it a respite, of which he himself took advantage to prepare for the decisive struggle. The peace effected by Antalcidas had left most of the mercenary soldiers of Greece without employment. Hakoris hired twenty thousand of them, and the Phœnician admirals, still occupied in blockading the ports of Cyprus, failed to intercept the vessels which brought him these reinforcements. It was fortunate for Egypt that they did so, for the Pharaoh died in 381 B.C., and his successors, Psamuthis II., Mutis, and Nephorites II., each occupied the throne for a very short time, and the whole country was in confusion for rather more than two years (381–379 B.C.) during the settlement of the succession.[1] The turbulent disposition of the great feudatory nobles,

[1] Hakoris reigned thirteen years, from 393 to 381 B.C. The reigns of the three succeeding kings occupied only two years and four months between them, from the end of 381 to the beginning of 378. Muthes or Mutis, who is not mentioned in all the lists of Manetho, seems to have his counterpart in the *Demotic Rhapsody*. Wiedemann has inverted the order usually adopted, and proposed the following series: Nephorites I., Muthes, Psamuthis, Hakoris, Nephorites II. The discovery at Karnak of a small temple where Psamuthis mentions Hakoris as his predecessor shows that on this point at least Manetho was well informed.

which had so frequently brought trouble upon previous Pharaohs during the Assyrian wars, was no less dangerous in this last century of Egyptian independence; it caused the fall of the Mendesian dynasty in the very face of the enemy, and the prince of Sebennytos, Nakht-har-habit, Nectanebo I., was raised to the throne by the military faction. According to a tradition current in Ptolemaic times, this sovereign was a son of Nephorites I., who had been kept out of his heritage by the jealousy of the gods; whatever his origin, the people had no cause to repent of having accepted him as their king. He began his reign by suppressing the slender subsidies which Evagoras had continued to receive from his predecessors, and this measure, if not generous, was at least politic. For Cyprus was now virtually in the power of the Persians, and the blockade of a few thousand men in Salamis did not draught away a sufficiently large proportion of their effective force to be of any service to Egypt: the money which had hitherto been devoted to the Cypriots was henceforth reserved for the direct defence of the Nile valley. Evagoras obtained unexpectedly favourable conditions: Artaxerxes conceded to him his title of king and the possession of his city (383 B.C.), and turned his whole attention to Nectanebo, the last of his enemies who still held out.

Nectanebo had spared no pains in preparing effectively to receive his foe. He chose as his coadjutor the Athenian Chabrias, whose capacity as a general had been manifested by recent events, and the latter accepted this office although he had received no instructions from his government to do so, and had transformed the Delta into an entrenched camp. He had fortified the most vulnerable points along the coast, had built towers at each of the mouths of the river to guard the entrance, and had selected the sites for his garrison fortresses so judiciously that they were kept up long after his time to protect the country. Two of them are mentioned by name : one, situated below Pelusium, called the Castle of Chabrias; the other, not far from Lake Mareotis, which was known as his township.[1] The Persian generals endeavoured to make their means of attack proportionate to the defences of the enemy. Acre was the only port in Southern Syria large enough to form the rendezvous for a fleet, where it might be secure from storms and surprises of the enemy. This was chosen as the Persian headquarters, and formed the base of their operations. During three years they there accumulated supplies of food and military stores, Phœnician and Greek vessels, and both foreign and native troops. The rivalries between the military commanders, Tithraustes, Datames, and Abrocomas, and the intrigues of the court, had on several occasions threatened the ruin of the enterprise, but Pharnabazus, who from the outset had held supreme command, succeeded in ridding himself of his rivals, and in the spring of 374 B.C. was at length ready for the advance. The expedition consisted of two hundred

PHARNABAZUS.[2]

[1] Both are mentioned by Strabo; the exact sites of these two places are not yet identified. Diodorus Siculus, describing the defensive preparations of Egypt, does not state expressly that they were the work of Chabrias, but this fact seems to result from a general consideration of the context.

[2] Drawn by Faucher-Gudin, from a coin in the *Cabinet des Médailles*.

thousand Asiatic troops, and twenty thousand Greeks, three hundred triremes, two hundred galleys of thirty oars, and numerous transports. Superiority of numbers was on the side of the Persians, and that just at the moment when Nectanebo lost his most experienced general. Artaxerxes had remonstrated with the Athenians for permitting one of their generals to serve in Egypt, in spite of their professed friendship for himself, and, besides insisting on his recall, had requested for himself the services of the celebrated Iphicrates. The Athenians complied with his demand, and while summoning Chabrias to return to Athens, despatched Iphicrates to Syria, where he was placed in command of the mercenary troops. Pharnabazus ordered a general advance in May, 374 B.C.,[1] but when he arrived before Pelusium, he perceived that he was not in a position to take the town by storm; not only had the fortifications been doubled, but the banks of the canals had been cut and the approaches inundated. Iphicrates advised him not to persevere in attempting a regular siege: he contended that it would be more profitable to detach an expeditionary force towards some less well-protected point on the coast, and there to make a breach in the system of defence which protected the enemies' front. Three thousand men were despatched with all secrecy to the mouth of the Mendesian branch of the Nile, and there disembarked unexpectedly before the forts which guarded

[1] As Kenrick justly observes, "the Persian and Athenian generals committed the same mistake which led to the defeat of Saint Louis and the capture of his army in 1249 A.D., and which Bonaparte avoided in his campaign of 1798." Anyhow, it seems that the fault must be laid on Pharnabazus alone, and that Iphicrates was entirely blameless.

THE PERSIAN INVASION

the entrance. The garrison, having imprudently made a sortie in face of the enemy, was put to rout, and pursued so hotly that victors and vanquished entered pell-mell within the walls. After this success victory was certain, if the Persians pursued their advantage promptly and pushed forward straight into the heart of the Delta; the moment was the more propitious for such a movement, since Nectanebo had drained Memphis of troops to protect his frontier. Iphicrates, having obtained this information from one of the prisoners, advised Pharnabazus to proceed up the Nile with the fleet, and take the capital by storm before the enemy should have time to garrison it afresh; the Persian general, however,

ARTAXERXES II.[1]

considered the plan too hazardous, and preferred to wait until the entire army should have joined him. Iphicrates offered to risk the adventure with his body of auxiliary troops only, but was suspected of harbouring some ambitious design, and was refused permission to advance. Meanwhile these delays had given the Egyptians time to recover from their first alarm; they boldly took the offensive, surrounded the position held by Pharnabazus, and were victorious in several skirmishes. Summer advanced, the Nile rose more rapidly than usual, and soon the water encroached upon the land; the invaders were obliged to beat a retreat before it, and fall back towards Syria. Iphicrates, disgusted at

[1] Drawn by Faucher-Gudin, from a silver stater in the *Cabinet des Médailles*.

the ineptitude and suspicion of his Asiatic colleagues, returned secretly to Greece: the remains of the army were soon after disbanded, and Egypt once more breathed freely. The check received by the Persian arms, however, was not sufficiently notorious to shake that species of supremacy which Artaxerxes had exercised in Greece since the peace of 387. Sparta, Thebes, and Athens vied with each other in obtaining an alliance with him as keenly as if he had been successful before Pelusium. Antalcidas reappeared at Susa in 372 B.C. to procure a fresh act of intervention; Pelopidas and Ismenias, in 367, begged for a rescript similar to that of Antalcidas; and finally Athens sent a solemn embassy to entreat for a subsidy. It seemed as if the great king had become a kind of supreme arbiter for Greece, and that all the states hitherto leagued against him now came in turn to submit their mutual differences for his decision. But this arbiter who thus imposed his will on states beyond the borders of his empire was never fully master within his own domains. Of gentle nature and pliant disposition, inclined to clemency rather than to severity, and, moreover, so lacking in judgment as a general that he had almost succumbed to an attack by the Cadusians on the only occasion that he had, in a whim of the moment, undertaken the command of an army in person, Artaxerxes busied himself with greater zeal in religious reforms than in military projects. He introduced the rites of Mithra and Anâhita into the established religion of the state, but he had not the energy necessary to curb the ambitions of his provincial governors. Asia Minor, whose revolts followed closely on those of Egypt, rose in rebellion against him immediately after the campaign on the Nile, Ariobarzanes heading the rebellion in Phrygia, Datames and Aspis that in Cilicia and Cappadocia, and both defying his power for several years. When at length they succumbed through treachery, the satraps of the Mediterranean district, from the Hellespont to the isthmus of Suez, formed a coalition and simultaneously took the field: the break-up of the empire would have been complete had not Persian darics been lavishly employed once more in the affair. Meanwhile Nectanebo had died in 361,[1] and had been succeeded by Tachôs.[2] The new Pharaoh deemed the occasion opportune to make a diversion against Persia and to further secure his own safety: he therefore offered his support to the satraps, who sent Rheomitres as a delegate to discuss the terms of an offensive and defensive alliance. Having inherited from Nectanebo a large fleet and a full treasury, Tachôs entrusted to the ambassador 500 talents of silver, and gave him fifty ships, with which he cruised along the coast of Asia Minor towards Leukê. His accomplices were awaiting

[1] The lists of Manetho assign ten or eighteen years to his reign. A sarcophagus in Vienna bears the date of his fifteenth year, and the great inscription of Edfu speaks of gifts he made to the temple in this town in the eighteenth year of his reign. The reading eighteen is therefore preferable to the reading ten in the lists of Manetho; if the very obscure text of the *Demotic Rhapsody* really applies the number nine or ten to the length of the reign, this reckoning must be explained by some mystic calculations of the priests of the Ptolemaic epoch.

[2] The name of this king, written by the Greeks Teôs or Tachôs, in accordance with the pronunciation or different Egyptian dialects, has been discovered in hieroglyphic writing on the external wall of the temple of Khonsu at Karnak.

him there, rejoicing at the success of his mission, but he himself had no confidence in the final issue of the struggle, and merely sought how he might enter once more into favour with the Persian court; he therefore secured his safety by betraying his associates. He handed over the subsidies and the Egyptian squadron to Orontes, the satrap of Daskylium, and then seizing the insurgent chiefs sent them in chains to Susa. These acts of treachery changed the complexion of affairs; the league suddenly dissolved after the imprisonment of its leaders, and Artaxerxes re-established his authority over Asia Minor.

DATAMES III.[1]

Egypt became once more the principal object of attack, and by the irony of fate Pharaoh had himself contributed to enrich the coffers and reinforce the fleet of his foes. In spite of this mischance, however, circumstances were so much in his favour that he ventured to consider whether it would not be more advantageous to forestall the foe by attacking him, rather than passively to await an onslaught behind his own lines. He had sought the friendship of Athens,[2] and, though it had not been granted in explicit

---

[1] Drawn by Faucher-Gudin, from a coin in the *Cabinet des Médailles*.

[2] The memory of this embassy has been preserved for us by a decree of the Athenian assembly, unfortunately much mutilated, which has been assigned to various dates between 362 and 358 B.C. M. Paul Foucart has shown that the date of the decree must be referred to one of three archonships—the archonship of Callimedes, 360–59 ; that of Eucharistus, 359–8 ; or that of Cephisodotus, 358–7. Without entering into a discussion of the other evidence on the subject, it seems to me probable that the embassy may be most conveniently assigned to the archonship of Callimedes, towards the end of 360 B.C., at the moment when Chabrias had just arrived in Egypt,

terms, the republic had, nevertheless, permitted Chabrias to resume his former post at his side. Chabrias exhorted him to execute his project, and as he had not sufficient money to defray the expenses of a long campaign outside his own borders, the Athenian general instructed him how he might procure the necessary funds. He suggested to him that, as the Egyptian priests were wealthy, the sums of money annually assigned to them for the sacrifices and maintenance of the temples would be better employed in the service of the state, and counselled him to reduce or even to suppress most of the sacerdotal colleges. The priests secured their own safety by abandoning their personal property, and the king graciously deigned to accept their gifts, and then declared to them that in future, as long as the struggle against Persia continued, he should exact from them nine-tenths of their sacred revenues. This tax would have sufficed for all requirements if it had been possible to collect it in full, but there is no doubt that very soon the priests must have discovered means of avoiding part of the payment, for it was necessary to resort to other expedients. Chabrias advised that the poll and house taxes should be increased; that one obol should be exacted for each " ardeb " of corn sold, and a tithe levied on the produce of all ship-building yards, manufactories, and manual industries. Money now poured into the treasury, but a difficulty arose which demanded immediate solution. Egypt possessed very little specie, and the natives still employed barter in the ordinary transactions of life, while

and was certain to endeavour to secure the help of Athens for the king he served.

the foreign mercenaries refused to accept payment in kind or uncoined metal; they demanded good money as the price of their services. Orders were issued to the natives to hand over to the royal exchequer all the gold and silver in their possession, whether wrought or in ingots, the state guaranteeing gradual repayment through the nomarchs from the future product of the poll-tax, and the bullion so obtained was converted into specie for the payment of the auxiliary troops. These measures, though winning some unpopularity for Tachôs, enabled him to raise eighty thousand native troops and ten thousand Greeks, to equip a fleet of two hundred vessels, and to engage the best generals of the period. His eagerness to secure the latter, however, was injurious to his cause. Having already engaged Chabrias and obtained the good will of Athens, he desired also to gain the help of Agesilaus and the favourable opinion of the Lacedæmonians. Though now eighty years old, Agesilaus was still under the influence of cupidity and vanity; the promise of being placed in supreme command enticed him, and he set sail with one thousand hoplites. A disappointment awaited him at the moment of his disembarkation: Tachôs gave him command of the mercenary troops only, reserving for himself the general direction of operations, and placing the whole fleet under the orders of Chabrias. The aged hero, having vented his indignation by indulging a more than ordinary display of Spartan rudeness, allowed himself to be appeased by abundant presents, and assumed the post assigned to him. But soon after a more serious subject of disagreement arose between him and his ally; Agesilaus was disposed to

REVOLT OF NECTANEBO II.

think that Tachôs should remain quietly on the banks of the Nile, and leave to his generals the task of conducting the campaign. The ease with which mercenary leaders passed from one camp to the other, according to the fancy of the moment, was not calculated to inspire the Egyptian Pharaoh with confidence: he refused to comply with the wishes of Agesilaus, and, entrusting the regency to one of his relatives, proceeded to invade Syria. He found the Persians unprepared: they shut themselves up in their strongholds, and the Pharaoh confided to his cousin Nectanebo, son of the regent, the task of dislodging them. The war dragged on for some time; discontent crept in among the native levies, and brought treachery in its train. The fiscal measures which had been adopted had exasperated the priests and the common people; complaints, at first only muttered in fear, found bold expression as soon as the expeditionary force had crossed the frontier.

NECTANEBO I.[1]

The regent secretly encouraged the malcontents, and wrote to his son warning him of what was going on, and advised him to seize the crown. Nectanebo could easily have won over the Egyptian troops to his cause, but their support would have proved useless as long as the Greeks did not pronounce in his favour, and Chabrias refused to break his oaths. Agesilaus, however, was not troubled by the same scruples. His vanity had been sorely wounded by the

[1] Drawn by Faucher-Gudin, from Lepsius.

Pharaoh: after being denied the position which was, he fancied, his by right, his short stature, his ill-health, and native coarseness had exposed him to the unseemly mockery of the courtiers. Tachôs, considering his ability had been over-estimated, applied to him, it is said, the fable of the mountain bringing forth a mouse; to which he had replied, " When opportunity offers, I will prove to him that I am the lion." When Tachôs requested him to bring the rebels to order, he answered ironically that he was there to help the Egyptians, not to attack them; and before giving his support to either of the rival claimants, he should consult the Ephors. The Ephors enjoined him to act in accordance with the welfare of his country, and he thereupon took the side of Nectanebo, despite the remonstrances of Chabrias. Tachôs, deserted by his veterans, fled to Sidon, and thence to Susa, where Artaxerxes received him hospitably and without reproaching him (359 B.C.); but the news of his fall was not received on the banks of the Nile with as much rejoicing as he had anticipated. The people had no faith in any revolution in which the Greeks whom they detested took the chief part, and the feudal lords refused to acknowledge a sovereign whom they had not themselves chosen; they elected one of their number—the prince of Mendes—to oppose Nectanebo. The latter was obliged to abandon the possessions won by his predecessor, and return with his army to Egypt: he there encountered the forces of his enemy, which, though as yet undisciplined, were both numerous and courageous. Agesilaus counselled an immediate attack before these troops had time to become experienced in tactics, but he no longer stood well at court; the prince of Mendes had endeavoured to corrupt him, and, though he had shown unexpected loyalty, many, nevertheless, suspected his good faith. Nectanebo set up his headquarters at Tanis, where he was shortly blockaded by his adversary. It is well known how skilfully the Egyptians handled the pick-axe, and how rapidly they could construct walls of great strength; the circle of entrenchments was already near completion, and provisions were beginning to fail, when Agesilaus received permission to attempt a sortie. He broke through the besieging lines under cover of the night, and some days later won a decisive victory (359 B.C.). Nectanebo would now have gladly kept the Spartan general at his side, for he was expecting a Persian attack; but Agesilaus, who had had enough of Egypt and its intrigues, deserted his cause, and shortly afterwards died of exhaustion on the coast near Cyrene. The anticipated Persian invasion followed shortly after, but it was conducted without energy or decision. Artaxerxes had entrusted the conduct of the expedition to Tachôs, doubtless promising to reinstate him in his former power as satrap or vassal king of Egypt, but Tachôs died before he could even assume his post,[1] and the discords which rent the family of the Persian king prevented the generals who replaced him from taking any effective action. The aged Artaxerxes had had, it was reported, one hundred and fifteen sons by the different women in his harem, but only three of those by his queen Statira were now living—Darius,

[1] Ælian narrates, probably following Dinon, that Tachôs died of dysentery due to over-indulgence at dinner.

Ariaspes, and Ochus. Darius, the eldest of the three, had been formally recognised as heir-apparent—perhaps at the time of the disastrous war against the Cadusians[1]—but the younger brother, Oohns, who secretly aspired to the throne, had managed to inspire him with anxiety with regard to the succession, and incited him to put the aged king out of the way. Contemporary historians, ill informed as to the intrigues in the palace, whose effects they noted without any attempt to explore their intricacies, invented several stories to account for the conduct of the young prince. Some assigned as the reason of his conspiracy a romantic love-affair. They said that Cyrus the Younger had had an Ionian mistress named Aspasia, who, after the fatal battle of Cunaxa, had been taken into the harem of the conqueror, and had captivated him by her beauty. Darius conceived a violent passion for this damsel, and his father was at first inclined to give her up to him, but afterwards, repenting of his complaisance, consecrated her to the service of Mithra, a cult which imposed on her the obligation of perpetual chastity. Darius, exasperated by this treatment, began to contemplate measures of vengeance, but, being betrayed by his brother Oohus, was put to death with his whole family.[2] By the removal of this first

[1] Pompeius Trogus asserts that such co-regencies were contrary to Persian law; we have seen above that, on the contrary, they were obligatory when the sovereign was setting out on a campaign.

[2] This is the version of the story given by Dinon and accepted by Pompeius Trogus. A chronological calculation easily demonstrates its unlikelihood. It follows from the evidence given by Justin himself that Artaxerxes died of grief soon after the execution of his son; but, on the other hand, that the battle of Cunaxa took place in 400 B.C.: Aspasia must then have been fifty or sixty years old when Darius fell in love with her.

obstacle the crafty prince found himself only one step nearer success, for his brother Ariaspes was acknowledged as heir-apparent: Ochus therefore persuaded him that their father, convinced of the complicity of Ariaspes in the plot imputed to Darius, intended to put him to an ignominious death, and so worked upon him that he committed suicide to escape the executioner. A bastard named Arsames, who might possibly have aspired to the crown, was assassinated by Ochus. This last blow was too much for Artaxerxes, and he died of grief after a reign of forty-six years (358 B.C.).[1]

Ochus, who immediately assumed the name of Artaxerxes, began his reign by the customary massacre: he put to death all the princes of the royal family,[2] and having thus rid himself of all the rival claimants to the supreme power, he hastened on preparations for the war with Egypt which had been interrupted by his father's death and his own accession. The necessity for restoring Persian dominion on the banks of the Nile was then more urgent than at any previous time. During the half-century which had elapsed since the recovery of her independence, Egypt had been a perpetual source of serious embarrassment to the great king. The contemporaries of Amyrtæus, whether Greeks or

[1] This is the length attributed by Plutarch to this reign, and which is generally accepted. It was narrated in after-days that the king kept the fact of his father's death hidden for ten months, but it is impossible to tell how much truth there is in this statement, which was accepted by Dinon.

[2] According to the author followed by Pompeius Trogus, the princesses themselves were involved in this massacre. This is certainly an exaggeration, for we shall shortly see that Darius III., the last king of Persia, was accounted to be the grandson of Darius II.; the massacre can only have involved the direct heirs of Artaxerxes.

barbarians, had at first thought that his revolt was nothing more than a local rising, like many a previous one which had lasted but a short time and had been promptly suppressed. But when it was perceived that the native dynasties had taken a hold upon the country, and had carried on a successful contest with Persia, in spite of the immense disproportion in their respective resources; when not only the bravest soldiers of Asia, but the best generals of Greece, had miserably failed in their attacks on the frontier of the Delta, Phœnicia and Syria began to think whether what was possible in Africa might not also be possible in Asia. From that time forward, whenever a satrap or vassal prince meditated revolt, it was to Egypt that he turned as a natural ally, and from Egypt he sought the means to carry out his project; however needy the Pharaoh of that day might be, he was always able to procure for such a suitor sufficient money, munitions of war, ships, and men to enable him to make war against the empire. The attempt made by Ochus failed, as all previous attempts had done: the two adventurers who commanded the forces of Nectanebo, the Athenian Diophantes and Lamius of Sparta, inflicted a disastrous defeat on the imperial troops, and forced them to beat a hasty retreat. This defeat was all the more serious in its consequences because of the magnitude of the efforts which had been made: the king himself was in command of the troops, and had been obliged to turn his back precipitately on the foe. The Syrian provinces, which had been in an unsettled condition ever since the invasion under Tachôs, flew to arms; nine petty kings of Cyprus, including Evagoras II., nephew of the famous prince of that name, refused to pay tribute, and Artabazus roused Asia Minor to rebellion. The Phœnicians still hesitated; but the insolence of their satrap, the rapacity of the generals who had been repulsed from Egypt, and the lack of discipline in the Persian army forced them to a decision. In a convention summoned at Tripoli, the representatives of the Phœnician cities conferred on Tennes, King of Sidon, the perilous honour of conducting the operations of the confederate army, and his first act was to destroy the royal villa in the Lebanon, and his next to burn the provisions which had been accumulated in various ports in view of the Egyptian war (351-350 B.C.). Ochus imagined at the outset that his generals would soon suppress these rebellions, and, in fact, Idrieus, tyrant of Caria, supported by eight thousand mercenaries under the Athenian Phocion, overcame the petty tyrants of Cyprus without much difficulty; but in Asia Minor, Artabazus, supported by Athens and Thebes, held at bay the generals sent to oppose him, and Tennes won a signal victory in Syria. He turned for support to Egypt, and Nectanebo, as might be expected, put Greek troops at his disposal to the number of four thousand, commanded by one of his best generals, Mentor of Rhodes: Belesys, the satrap of Syria, and Mazæus, satrap of Cilicia, suffered a total defeat. Ochus, exasperated at their want of success, called out every available soldier, three hundred thousand Asiatics and ten thousand Greeks; the Sidonians, on their

EVAGORAS II. OF SALAMIS.[1]

---

[1] Drawn by Faucher-Gudin, from a coin in the *Cabinet des Médailles*.

side, dug a triple trench round their city, raised their ramparts, and set fire to their ships, to demonstrate their intention of holding out to the end. Unfortunately, their king, Tennes, was not a man of firm resolution. Hitherto he had lived a life of self-indulgence, surrounded by the women of his harem, whom he had purchased at great cost in Ionia and Greece, and had made it the chief object of his ambition to surpass in magnificence the most ostentatious princes of Cyprus, especially Nicocles of Salamis, son of Evagoras. The approach of Ochus confused his scanty wits; he endeavoured to wipe out his treachery towards his suzerain by the betrayal of his own subjects. He secretly despatched his confidential minister, a certain Thessalion, to the Persian camp, promising to betray Sidon to the Persian king, and to act as his guide into Egypt on condition of having his life preserved and his royal rank guaranteed to him. Ochus had already agreed to these conditions, when an impulse of vanity on his part nearly ruined the whole arrangement. Thessalion, not unreasonably doubting the king's good faith, had demanded that he should swear by his right hand to fulfil to the letter all the clauses of the treaty; whereupon Ochus, whose dignity was offended by this insistence, gave orders for the execution of the ambassador. But as the latter was being dragged away, he cried out that the king could do as he liked, but that if he disdained the help of Tennes, he would fail in his attacks both upon Phœnicia and Egypt. These words produced a sudden reaction, and Thessalion obtained all that he demanded. When the Persians had arrived within a few days' march of Sidon, Tennes proclaimed that a general assembly of the Phœnician deputies was to be held, and under pretext of escorting the hundred leading men of his city to the appointed place of meeting, led them into the enemy's camp, where they were promptly despatched by the javelins of the soldiery. The Sidonians, deserted by their king, were determined to carry on the struggle, in the expectation of receiving succour from Egypt; but the Persian darics had already found their way into the hands of the mercenary troops, and the general whom Nectanebo had lent them, declared that his men considered the position desperate, and that he should surrender the city at the first summons. The Sidonians thereupon found themselves reduced to the necessity of imploring the mercy of the conqueror, and five hundred of them set out to meet him as suppliants, carrying olive branches in their hands. But Ochus was the most cruel monarch who had ever reigned in Persia—the only one, perhaps, who was really bloodthirsty by nature; he refused to listen to the entreaties of the suppliants, and, like the preceding hundred delegates, they were all slain. The remaining citizens, perceiving that they could not hope for pardon, barricaded themselves in their houses, to which they set fire with their own hands; forty thousand persons perished in the flames, and so great was the luxury in the appointments of the private houses, that large sums were paid for the right to dig for the gold and silver ornaments buried in the ruins. The destruction of the city was almost as complete as in the days of Esarhaddon. When Sidon had thus met her fate, the Persians had no further reason for sparing its king, Tennes, and he was delivered to the executioner; whereupon the other Phœnician kings, terrified by his fate, opened their gates without a struggle.

Once more the treachery of a few traitors had disconcerted the plans of the Pharaoh, and delivered the outposts of Egypt into the hands of the enemy: but Ochus renewed his preparations with marvellous tenacity, and resolved to neglect nothing which might contribute to his final success. His victories had confirmed the cities of the empire in their loyalty, and they vied with one another in endeavouring to win oblivion for their former hesitation by their present zeal: "What city, or what nation of Asia did not send embassies to the sovereign? what wealth did they not lavish on him, whether the natural products of the soil, or the rare and precious productions of art? Did he not receive a quantity of tapestry and woven hangings, some of purple, some of diverse colours, others of pure white? many gilded pavilions, completely furnished, and containing an abundant supply of linen and sumptuous beds? chased silver, wrought gold, cups and bowls, enriched with precious stones, or valuable for the perfection and richness of their work? He also received untold supplies of barbarian and Grecian weapons, and still larger numbers of draught cattle and of sacrificial victims, bushels of preserved fruits, bales and sacks full of parchments or books, and all kinds of useful articles? So great was the quantity of salted meats which poured in from all sides, that from a distance the piles might readily be mistaken for rows of hillocks or high mounds." The land-force was divided into three corps, each under a barbarian and a Greek general. It advanced along the sea coast, following the ancient route pursued by the armies of the Pharaohs, and as it skirted the marshes of Sirbonis, some detachments, having imprudently ventured over the treacherous soil, perished to a man. When the main force arrived in safety before Pelusium, it found Nectanebo awaiting it behind his ramparts and marshes. He had fewer men than his adversary, his force numbering only six thousand Egyptians, twenty thousand Libyans, and the same number of Greeks; but the remembrance of the successes won by himself and his predecessors with inferior numbers inspired him with confidence in the issue of the struggle. His fleet could not have ventured to meet in battle the combined squadrons of Cyprus and Phœnicia, but, on the other hand, he had a sufficient number of flat-bottomed boats to prevent any adversary from entering the mouths of the Nile. The weak points along his Mediterranean seaboard and eastern frontier were covered by strongholds, fortifications, and entrenched camps: in short, his plans were sufficiently well laid to ensure success in a defensive war, if the rash ardour of his Greek mercenaries had not defeated his plans. Five thousand of these troops were in occupation of Pelusium, under command of Philophrôn. Some companies of Thebans, who were serving under Lacrates in the Persian army, crossed a deep canal which separated them from the city, and provoked the garrison to risk an encounter in the open field. Philophrôn, instead of treating their challenge with indifference, accepted it, and engaged in a combat which lasted till nightfall. On the following day, Lacrates, having drawn off the waters of the canal and thrown a dyke across it, led his entire force up to the glacis of the fortifications, dug some trenches, and brought up a line of battering-rams. He would soon have effected a breach, but the Egyptians understood how to use the spade as well as the lance, and while the outer wall was crumbling, they improvised behind it a second wall, crowned with wooden turrets. Nectanebo, who had come up with thirty thousand native, five thousand Greek troops, and half the Libyan contingent, observed the vicissitudes of the siege from a short distance, and by his presence alone opposed the advance of the bulk of the Persian army. Weeks passed by, the time of the inundation was approaching, and it seemed as if this policy of delay would have its accustomed success, when an unforeseen incident decided in a moment the fate of Egypt. Among the officers of Cchus was a certain Nicostratus of Argos, who on account of his prodigious strength was often compared to Heracles, and who out of vanity dressed himself up in the traditional costume of that hero, the lion's skin and the club. Having imbibed, doubtless, the ideas formerly propounded by Iphicrates, Nicostratus forced some peasants, whose wives and children he had seized as hostages, to act as his guides, and made his way up one of the canals which traverse the marshes of Menzaleh: there he disembarked his men in the rear of Nectanebo, and took up a very strong position on the border of the cultivated land. This enterprise, undertaken with a very insufficient force, was an extremely rash one; if the Egyptian generals had contented themselves with harassing Nicostratus without venturing on engaging him in a pitched battle, they would speedily have forced him to re-embark or to lay down his arms. Unfortunately, however, five thousand mercenaries, who formed the garrison of one of the neighbouring towns, hastened to attack him under the command of Clinias of Cos, and suffered a severe defeat. As a result, the gates of the town were thrown open to the enemy, and if the Persians, encouraged by the success of this forlorn hope, had followed it up boldly, Nectanebo would have run the risk of being cut off from his troops which were around Pelusium, and of being subsequently crushed. He thought it wiser to retreat towards the apex of the Delta, but this very act of prudence exposed him to one of those accidental misfortunes which are wont to occur in armies formed of very diverse elements. While he was concentrating his reserves at Memphis, the troops of the first line thought that, by leaving them exposed to the assaults of the great king, he was deliberately sacrificing them. Pelusium capitulated to Lacrates; Mentor of Rhodes pushed forward and seized Bubastis, and the other cities in the eastern portion of the Delta, fearing to bring upon themselves the fate of Sidon, opened their gates to the Persians after a mere show of resistance. The forces which had collected at Memphis thereupon disbanded, and Nectanebo, ruined by these successive disasters, collected his treasures and fled to Ethiopia. The successful issue of the rash enterprise of Nicostratus had overthrown the empire of the Pharaohs, and re-established the Persian empire in its integrity (342 B.C.).[1]

[1] The complete history of this war is related by Diodorus Siculus, who generally follows the narrative of Theopompus. The chronology is still

Egypt had prospered under the strong rule of its last native Pharaohs. Every one of them, from Amyrtæus down to Nectanebo, had done his best to efface all traces of the Persian invasions and restore to the country the appearance which it had presented before the days of its servitude; even kings like Psamutis and Tachôs, whose reign had been of the briefest, had, like those who ruled for longer periods, constructed or beautified the monuments of the country. The Thebaid was in this respect a special field of their labours. The island of Philæ, exposed to the ceaseless attacks of the Ethiopians, had been reduced to little more than a pile of ruins. Nectanebo II. erected a magnificent gate there, afterwards incorporated into the first pylon of the temple built by the Ptolemies, and one at least of the buildings that still remain, the charming rectangular kiosk, the pillars of which, with their

sufficiently uncertain to leave some doubt as to the exact date of each event; I have followed that arrangement which seems to accord best with the general history of the period. The following table may be drawn up of the last Egyptian dynasties as far as they can be restored at present:—

XXVII. (Persian) Dynasty.
I. Masutrî Kanbuti.
II. . . . [Gaumâta].
III. Satôuturî Ntaraiuasha.
IV. Sanentonen - sotpuniphtah Khabbîsha.
V. . . . . Khshayarsha.
VI. . . . . Artakhshayarsha.
VII. . . . . Khshayarsha.
VIII. . . . .
IX. Miamunrî Ntaraiuasha.
XXVIII. (Saite) Dynasty.
I. . . . .

XXIX. (Mendesian) Dynasty.
I. Bînri-Mînutîru Nefôrîti I.
II. Khnummarî - sotpunikhnumu Hakori.
III. Usiriphtahrî Psamutî.
IV. . . . .
V. . . . . . . Nefôrîti II.
XXX. (Sebennytic) Dynasty.
I. Snotmibrî-sotpunianhuri Nakhtharahbît - Mîanhuri- Siisît.
II. Irimaîtnirî Zadhu-Sotpunianhuri.
III. Khopirkerî Nakhtunabuf.

EGYPT UNDER ITS LAST NATIVE DYNASTY 313

Hathor capitals, rise above the southern extremity of the island and mark the spot at which the Ethiopian pilgrims first set foot on the sacred territory of the bountiful Isis. Nectanebo I. restored the sanctuaries of Nekhabît at El-Kab, and of Horus at Edfu, in which latter place he has

SMALL TEMPLE OF NECTANEBO, AT THE SOUTHERN EXTREMITY OF PHILÆ.[1]

left an admirable naos which delights the modern traveller by its severe proportions and simplicity of ornament, while Nectanebo II. repaired the ancient temple of Minu at Coptos; in short, without giving a detailed list of what was accomplished by each of these later Pharaohs, it may be said that there are few important sites in the valley of

[1] Drawn by Boudier, from a photograph by Beato.

314　THE LAST DAYS OF THE OLD EASTERN WORLD

the Nile where some striking evidence of their activity may not still be discovered even after the lapse of so many centuries. It will be sufficient to mention Thebes,

NAOS OF NECTANEBO IN THE TEMPLE AT EDFU.[1]

Memphis, Sebennytos, Bubastis, Pahabît, Patumu, and Tanis. Nor did the Theban oases, including that of Amon

[1] Drawn by Boudier, from a photograph by Beato.

himself, escape their zeal, for the few Europeans who have visited them in modern times have observed their cartouches there. Moreover, in spite of the brief space of

GREAT GATE OF NECTANEBO AT KARNAK.[1]

time within which they were carried out, the majority of these works betray no signs of haste or slipshod execution;

[1] Drawn by Boudier, from a photograph by Beato.

the craftsmen employed on them seem to have preserved in their full integrity all the artistic traditions of earlier times, and were capable of producing masterpieces which will bear comparison with those of the golden age. The Eastern gate, erected at Karnak in the time of Nectanebo II., is in no way inferior either in purity of proportion or in the beauty of its carvings to what remains of the gates of Amenôthes III. The sarcophagus of Nectanebo I. is carved and decorated with a perfection of skill which had never been surpassed in any age, and elsewhere, on all the monuments which bear the name of this monarch, the hieroglyphics have been designed and carved with as much care as though each one of them had been a precious cameo.² The basalt torso of Nectanebo · II., which attracts so much admiration in the Bibliothèque Nationale in Paris for accuracy of proportion and delicacy of modelling, deserves to rank with the finest statues of the ancient empire. The men's heads are veritable portraits, in which such details

FRAGMENT OF A NAOS OF THE TIME OF NECTANEBO II. IN THE BOLOGNA MUSEUM.¹

---

¹ Drawn by Boudier, from a photograph by Flinders Petrie.
² The sarcophagus was for a long time preserved near the mosque of Ibn-Tulun, and was credited with peculiar virtues by the superstitious inhabitants of Cairo.

as a peculiar conformation of the skull, prominent cheekbones, deep-set eyes, sunken cheeks, or the modelling of the chin, have all been observed and reproduced with a fidelity and keenness of observation which we fail to find in such works of the earlier artists as have come down to us. These later sculptors display the same regard for truth in their treatment of animals, and their dog-headed divinities; their dogs, lions, and sphinxes will safely bear comparison with the most lifelike presentments of these creatures to be found among the remains of the Memphite or Theban eras. Egypt was thus

ONE OF THE LIONS IN THE VATICAN.[1]

in the full tide of material prosperity when it again fell under the Persian yoke, and might have become a source of inexhaustible wealth to Ochus had he known how to secure acceptance of his rule, as Darius, son of Hystaspes, had done in the days of Amasis. The violence of his temperament, however, impelled him to a course of pitiless oppression, and his favourite minister, the eunuch Bagoas, seems to have done his best to stimulate his master's natural cruelty. In the days when they felt themselves securely protected from his anger by their Libyan and Greek troops, the fellahin had freely indulged in lampoons at the expense of their Persian suzerain; they had compared him to Typhon

[1] Drawn by Faucher-Gudin, from a photograph by Flinders Petrie.

on account of his barbarity, and had nicknamed him "the Ass," this animal being in their eyes a type of everything that is vile. On his arrival at Memphis, Ochus gave orders that an ass should be installed in the temple of Phtah, and have divine honours paid to it; he next had the bull Apis slaughtered and served up at a set banquet which he gave to his friends on taking possession of the White Wall. The sacred goat of Mendes suffered the same fate as the Apis, and doubtless none of the other sacred animals were spared. Bagoas looted the temples in the most systematic way, despatched the sacred books to Persia, razed the walls of the cities to the ground, and put every avowed partisan of the native dynasty to the sword. After these punitive measures had been carried out, Ochus disbanded his mercenaries and returned to Babylon, leaving Pherendates in charge of the reconquered province.[1] The downfall of Egypt struck terror into the rebellious satraps who were in arms elsewhere. Artabazus, who had kept Asia Minor in a ferment ever since the time of Artaxerxes II., gave up the struggle of his own accord and took refuge in Macedonia. The petty kings of the cities on the shores of the Hellespont and the Ægæan submitted themselves in order to regain favour, or if, like Hermias of Atarnæa, the friend of Aristotle, they still resisted, they were taken prisoners and condemned to death. The success of Ochus was a reality, but there was still much to be done before things were

---

[1] It seems that a part of the atrocities committed by Ochus and Bagoas soon came to be referred to the time of the "Impure" and to that of Cambyses.

restored to the footing they had occupied before the crisis. We know enough of the course of events in the western provinces to realise the pitch of weakness to which the imbecility of Darius II. and his son Artaxerxes II. had reduced the empire of Darius and Xerxes, but it is quite certain that the disastrous effects of their misgovernment were not confined to the shores of the Mediterranean, but were felt no less acutely in the eastern and central regions of the empire. There, as on the Greek frontiers, the system built up at the cost of so much ingenuity by Darius was gradually being broken down with each year that passed, and the central government could no longer make its power felt at the extremities of the empire save at irregular intervals, when its mandates were not intercepted or nullified in transmission. The functions of the "Eyes" and "Ears" of the king had degenerated into a mere meaningless formality, and were, more often than not, dispensed with altogether. The line of demarcation between the military and civil power had been obliterated: not only had the originally independent offices of satrap, general, and secretary ceased to exist in each separate province, but, in many instances, the satrap, after usurping the functions of his two colleagues, contrived to extend his jurisdiction till it included several provinces, thus establishing himself as a kind of viceroy. Absorbed in disputes among themselves, or in conspiracies against the Achæmenian dynasty, these officials had no time to look after the well-being of the districts under their control, and the various tribes and cities took advantage of this to break the ties of vassalage. To take Asia Minor alone, some of the petty kings of Bithynia, Paphlagonia, and certain districts of Cappadocia or the mountainous parts of Phrygia still paid their tribute intermittently, and only when compelled to do so; others, however, such as the Pisidians, Lycaonians, a part of the Lycians, and some races of Mount Taurus, no longer dreamed of doing so. The three satrapies on the shores of the Caspian, which a hundred years before had wedged themselves in between that sea and the Euxine, were now dissolved, all trace of them being lost in a confused medley of kingdoms and small states, some of which were ready enough to acknowledge the supremacy of Persia, while others, such as the Gordiæans, Taochi, Chalybes, Colchi, Mosynœki, and Tibarenians, obeyed no rule but their own. All along the Caspian, the Cadusians and Amardians, on either side of the chain of mountains bordering the Iranian plateau, defied all the efforts made to subdue them.[1] India and the Sakæ had developed from the condition of subjects into that of friendly allies, and the savage hordes of Gedrosia and the Paropamisus refused to recognise any authority at all.[2] The whole empire needed to be reconquered and reorganised bit by bit if it was to exercise that influence in the world to which its immense size entitled it, and the

[1] They appear in the history of every epoch as the irreconcilable foes of the great king, enemies against whom even the most peacefully disposed sovereigns were compelled to take the field in person.

[2] The Sakæ fought at Arbela, but only as allies of the Persians. The Indians who are mentioned with them came from the neighbourhood of Cabul; most of the races who had formerly figured in Darius' satrapy of India had become independent by the time Alexander penetrated into the basin of the Indus.

question arose whether the elements of which it consisted would lend themselves to any permanent reorganisation or readjustment.

The races of the ancient Eastern world, or, at any rate, that portion of them which helped to make its history, either existed no longer or had sunk into their dotage. They had worn each other out in the centuries of their prime, Chaldæans and Assyrians fighting against Cossæans or Elamites, Egyptians against Ethiopians and against Hittites, Urartians, Armæans, the peoples of Lebanon and of Damascus, the Phœnicians, Canaanites and Jews, until at last, with impoverished blood and flagging energies, they were thrown into conflict with younger and more vigorous nations. The Medes had swept away all that still remained of Assyria and Urartu; the Persians had overthrown the Medes, the Lydians, and the Chaldæans, till Egypt alone remained and was struck down by them in her turn. What had become of these conquered nations during the period of nearly two hundred years that the Achæmenians had ruled over them? First, as regards Elam, one of the oldest and formerly the most powerful of them all. She had been rent into two halves, each of them destined to have a different fate. In the mountains, the Uxians, Mardians, Elymæans, and Cossæans—tribes who had formerly been the backbone of the nation—had relapsed into a semi-barbarous condition, or rather, while the rest of the world had progressed in civilization and refinement, they had remained in a state of stagnation, adhering obstinately to the customs of their palmy days: just as they had harried the Chaldæans or Assyrians in the olden times, so now they harried the

Persians; then, taking refuge in their rocky fastnesses, they lived on the proceeds of their forays, successfully resisting all attempts made to dislodge them. The people of the plains, on the other hand, kept in check from the outset by the presence of the court at Susa, not only promptly resigned themselves to their fate, but even took pleasure in it, and came to look upon themselves as in some sort the masters of Asia. Was it not to their country, to the very spot occupied by the palace of their king, that, for nearly two hundred years, satraps, vassal kings, the legates of foreign races, ambassadors of Greek republics—in a word, all the great ones of this world—came every year to render homage, and had not the treasures which these visitors brought with them been expended, in part at any rate, on their country? The memory of their former prosperity paled before the splendours of their new destiny, and the glory of their ancestors suffered eclipse. The names of the national kings, the story of their Chaldæan and Syrian conquests, the trophies of their victories over the great generals of Nineveh, the horrors of their latest discords and of the final catastrophe were all forgotten; even the documents which might have helped to recall them lay buried in the heart of the mound which served as a foundation for the palace of the Achæmenides. Beyond the vague consciousness of a splendid past, the memory of the common people was a blank, and when questioned by strangers they could tell them nothing save legends of the gods or the exploits of mythical heroes; and from them the Greeks borrowed their Memnon, that son of Tithonus and Eôs who rushed to the aid of Priam with his band of

Ethiopians, and whose prowess had failed to retard by a single day the downfall of Troy. Further northwards, the Urartians and peoples of ancient Nairi, less favoured by fortune, lost ground with each successive generation, yielding to the steady pressure of the Armenians. In the time of Herodotus they were still in possession of the upper basins of the Euphrates and Araxus, and, in conjunction with the Matieni and Saspires, formed a satrapy—the eighteenth—the boundaries of which coincided pretty

COINS OF THE SATRAPS WITH ARAMÆAN INSCRIPTIONS.[1]

closely with those of the kingdom ruled over by the last kings of Van in the days of Assur-bani-pal; the Armenians, on their side, constituted the thirteenth satrapy, between Mount Taurus and the Lower Arsanias. The whole face of their country had undergone a profound change since that time: the Urartians, driven northwards, became intermingled with the tribes on the slopes of the Caucasus, while the Armenians, carried along towards the east, as though by some resistless current, were now scaling the mountainous bulwark of Ararat, and slowly but surely encroaching on the lower plains of the Araxes. These political changes had been almost completed by the time of Ochus, and Urartu had disappeared from the scene, but an

[1] Drawn by Faucher-Gudin, from coins in the *Cabinet des Médailles*.

Armenia now flourished in the very region where Urartu had once ruled, and its princes, who were related to the family of the Achæmenides, wielded an authority little short of regal under the modest name of satraps. Thanks to their influence, the religions and customs of Iran were introduced into the eastern borders of Asia Minor. They made their way into the valleys of the Iris and the Halys, into Cappadocia and the country round Mount Taurus, and thither they brought with them the official script of the empire, the Persian and Aramæan cuneiform which was employed in public documents, in inscriptions, and on coins. The centre of the peninsula remained very much the same as it had been in the period of the Phrygian supremacy, but further westward Hellenic influences gradually made themselves felt. The arts of Greece, its manners, religious ideals, and modes of thought, were slowly displacing civilisations of the Asianic type, and even in places like Lycia, where the language successfully withstood the Greek invasion, the life of the nations, and especially of their rulers, became so deeply impregnated with Hellenism as to differ but little from that in the cities on the Ionic,

A LYCIAN TOMB.[1]

[1] Drawn by Faucher-Gudin, from a woodcut in Benndorff.

THE ARTS OF GREECE

Æolian, or Doric seaboard. The Lycians still adhered to the ancient forms which characterised their funerary architecture, but it was to Greek sculptors, or pupils from the Grecian schools, that they entrusted the decoration of the sides of their sarcophagi and of their tombs. Their kings minted coins many of which are reckoned among the masterpieces of antique engraving; and if we pass from Lycia to the petty states of Caria, we come upon one of the greatest triumphs of Greek art—that huge mausoleum in which the inconsolable Artemisia enclosed the ashes and erected the statue of her husband. The Asia Minor of Egyptian times, with its old-world dynasties, its old-world names, and old-world races, had come to be nothing more than an historic memory; even that martial world, in which the Assyrian conquerors fought so many battles from the Euphrates to the Black Sea, was now no more, and its neighbours and enemies of former days had,

STATUE OF MAUSOLUS.[1]

COIN OF A LYCIAN KING.[2]

---

[1] Drawn by Faucher-Gudin, from a photograph of the original in the British Museum.

[2] Drawn by Faucher-Gudin, from a silver stater in the *Cabinet des Médailles*. The king in question was named Deneveles, and is only known by the coins bearing his superscription. He flourished about 395 B.C.

for the most part, disappeared from the land of the living. The Lotanu were gone, the Khâti were gone, and gone, too, were Carchemish, Arpad, and Qodshu, much of their domain having been swallowed up again by the desert for want of

LYCIAN SARCOPHAGUS DECORATED WITH GREEK CARVINGS.[1]

hands to water and till it; even Assyria itself seemed but a shadow half shrouded in the mists of oblivion. Sangara, Nisibis, Resaina, and Edessa still showed some signs of vigour, but on quitting the slopes of the Masios and proceeding southwards, piles of ruins alone marked the sites of

[1] Drawn by Faucher-Gudin, from a photogravure published by Hamdy-Beg and Th. Reinach.

those wealthy cities through which the Ninevite monarchs had passed in their journeyings towards Syria. Here wide tracts of arid and treeless country were now to be seen covered with aromatic herbage, where the Scenite Arabs were wont to pursue the lion, wild ass, ostrich, bustard, antelope, and gazelle; a few abandoned forts, such as Korsortê, Anatho, and Is (Hit) marked the halting-places of armies on the banks of the Euphrates. In the region of the Tigris, the descendants of Assyrian captives who, like the Jews, had been set free by Cyrus, had rebuilt Assur, and had there grown wealthy by husbandry and commerce,[1] but in the district of the Zab solitude reigned supreme.[2] Calah and Nineveh were alike deserted, and though their ruins still littered the sites where they had stood, their names were unknown in the neighbouring villages. Xenophon, relying on his guides, calls the former place Larissa, the second Mespila.[3] Already there were historians who took the ziggurât at Nineveh to be the burial-place of Sardanapalus. They declared that Cyrus had pulled it down in order to strengthen his camp during the siege of

[1] This seems to be indicated by a mutilated passage in the *Cylinder of Cyrus*, where Assur is mentioned in the list of towns and countries whose inhabitants were sent back to their homes by Cyrus after the capture of Babylon. Xenophon calls it Kænæ, this being, possibly, a translation of the name given to it by its inhabitants. Nothing could be more natural than for exiles to call the villages founded by them on their return "new." The town seems to have been a large and wealthy one.

[2] Xenophon calls this country Media, a desert region which the Ten Thousand took six days to cross.

[3] The name Larissa is, possibly, a corruption of some name similar to that of the city of Larsam in Chaldæa ; Mespila may be a generic term. [Mespila is Muspula, "the low ground" at the foot of Kouyunjik ; Larissa probably Al Resen or Res-eni, between Kouyunjik and Nebi Yunus.—ED.]

the town, and that formerly it had borne an epitaph afterwards put into verse by the poet Chœrilus of Iassus: "I reigned, and so long as I beheld the light of the sun, I ate, I drank, I loved, well knowing how brief is the life of man, and to how many vicissitudes it is liable." Many writers, remembering the Assyrian monument at Anchialê in Cilicia, were inclined to place the king's tomb there. It was surmounted by the statue of a man—according to one account, with his hands crossed upon his breast, according to another, in the act of snapping his fingers—and bore the following inscription in Chaldaic letters: "I, Sardanapalus, son of Anakyndaraxes, founded Anchialê and Tarsus in one day, but now am dead." Thus ten centuries of conquests and massacre had passed away like a vapour, leaving nothing but a meagre residue of old men's tales and moral axioms.

In one respect only does the civilisation of the Euphrates seem to have fairly held its own. Chaldæa, though it had lost its independence, had lost but little of its wealth; its former rebellions had done it no great injury, and its ancient cities were still left standing, though shorn of their early splendour. Uru, it is true, numbered but few citizens round its tottering sanctuaries, but Uruk maintained a school of theologians and astronomers no less famous throughout the East than those of Borsippa. The swamps, however, which surrounded it possessed few attractions, and Greek travellers rarely ventured thither. They generally stopped at Babylon, or if they ventured off the beaten track, it was only to visit the monuments of Nebuchadrezzar, or the tombs of the early kings in its immediate neighbourhood. Babylon was, indeed, one of the capitals of the empire—nay, for more than half a century, during the closing years of Artaxerxes I., in the reign of Darius II., and in the early days of Artaxerxes II., it had been the real capital; even under Ochus, the court spent the winter months there, and resorted thither in quest of those resources of industry and commerce which Susa lacked. The material benefits due to the presence of the sovereign seem to have reconciled the city to its subject condition; there had been no seditious movement there since the ill-starred rising of Shamasherîb, which Xerxes had quelled with ruthless severity. The Greek mercenaries or traders who visited it, though prepared for its huge size by general report, could not repress a feeling of astonishment as they approached it. First of all there was the triple wall of Nebuchadrezzar, with its moats, its rows of towers, and its colossal gateways. Unlike the Greek cities, it had been laid out according to a regular plan, and formed a perfect square, inside which the streets crossed one another at right angles, some parallel to the Euphrates, others at right angles to it; every one of the latter terminated in a brazen gate opening through the masonry of the quay, and giving access to the river. The passengers who crowded the streets included representatives of all the Asiatic races, the native Babylonians being recognisable by their graceful dress, consisting of a linen tunic falling to the feet, a fringed shawl, round cap, and heavy staff terminating in a knob. From this ever-changing background stood out many novel features calculated to stimulate Greek curiosity, such as the sick persons exposed at street-corners in order that they might beg the passers-by to prescribe for them, the prostitution of her votaries within the courts of the goddess Mylitta, and the disposal of marriageable girls by auction : Herodotus, however, regretted that this latter custom had fallen into abeyance. And yet to the attentive eye of a close observer even Babylon must have furnished many unmistakable symptoms of decay. The huge boundary wall enclosed too large an area for the population sheltered behind it; whole quarters were crumbling into heaps of ruins, and the flower and vegetable gardens were steadily encroaching on spaces formerly covered with houses. Public buildings had suffered quite as much as private dwellings from the Persian wars. Xerxes had despoiled the temples, and no restoration had been attempted since his time. The ziggurât of Bel lay half buried already beneath piles of rubbish; the golden statues which had once stood within its chambers had disappeared, and the priests no longer carried on their astronomical observations on its platform.[1] The palaces of the ancient kings were falling to pieces from lack of repairs, though the famous hanging gardens in the citadel were still shown to strangers. The guides, of course, gave them out to be a device of Semiramis, but the well-informed knew that they had been constructed by Nebuchadrezzar for one of his wives the daughter of

[1] Herodotus merely mentions that Xerxes had despoiled the temple; Strabo tells us that Alexander wished to restore it, but that it was in such a state of dilapidation that it would have taken ten thousand men two months merely to remove the rubbish.

Cyaxares, who pined for the verdure of her native mountains. " They were square in shape, each side being four hundred feet long; one approached them by steps leading to terraces placed one above the other, the arrangement of the whole resembling that of an amphitheatre. Each terrace rested on pillars which, gradually increasing in size, supported the weight of the soil and its produce. The loftiest pillar attained a height of fifty feet; it reached to the upper part of the garden, its capital being on a level with the balustrades of the boundary wall. The terraces were covered with a layer of soil of sufficient depth for the roots of the largest trees; plants of all kinds that delight the eye by their shape or beauty were grown there. One of the columns was hollowed from top to bottom; it contained hydraulic engines which pumped up quantities of water, no part of the mechanism being visible from the outside." Many travellers were content to note down only such marvels as they considered likely to make their narratives more amusing, but others took pains to collect information of a more solid character, and before they had carried their researches very far, were at once astounded and delighted with the glimpses they obtained of Chaldæan genius. No doubt, they exaggerated when they went so far as to maintain that all their learning came to them originally from Babylon, and that the most famous scholars of Greece, Pherecydes of Scyros, Democritus of Abdera, and Pythagoras,[1] owed the rudiments of philosophy,

---

[1] The story which asserts that Pythagoras served under Nergilos, King of Assyria, is probably based on some similarity of names: thus among the Greek kings of Cyprus, and in the time of Assur-bani-pal, we find one whose

mathematics, physics, and astrology to the school of the *Magi*. Yet it is not surprising that they should have believed this to be the case, when increasing familiarity with the priestly seminaries revealed to them the existence of those libraries of clay tablets in which, side by side with theoretic treatises dating from two thousand years back and more, were to be found examples of applied mechanics, observations, reckonings, and novel solutions of problems, which generations of scribes had accumulated in the course of centuries. The Greek astronomers took full advantage of these documents, but it was their astrologers and soothsayers who were specially indebted to them. The latter acknowledged their own inferiority the moment they came into contact with their Euphratean colleagues, and endeavoured to make good their deficiencies by taking lessons from the latter or persuading them to migrate to Greece. A hundred years later saw the Babylonian Berosus opening at Cos a public school of divination by the stars. From thenceforward "Chaldæan" came to be synonymous with "astrologer" or "sorcerer," and Chaldæan magic became supreme throughout the world at the very moment when Chaldæa itself was in its death-throes.

Nor was its unquestioned supremacy in the black art the sole legacy that Chaldæa bequeathed to the coming generations: its language survived, and reigned for centuries afterwards in the regions subjugated by its arms. The cultivated tongue employed by the scribes of Nineveh

name would recall that of Pythagoras, if the accuracy of the reading were beyond question.

and Babylon in the palmy days of their race, had long become a sort of literary dialect, used in writings of a lofty character and understood by a select few, but unintelligible to the common people. The populace in town or country talked an Aramaic jargon, clumsier and more prolix than Assyrian, but easier to understand. We know how successfully the Aramæans had managed to push their way along the Euphrates and into Syria towards the close of the Hittite supremacy: their successive encroachments had been favoured, first by the Assyrian, later by the Chaldæan conquests, and now they had become sole possessors of the ancient Naharaîna, the plains of Cilicia, the basin of the Orontes, and the country round Damascus; but the true home of the Aramæans was in Syria rather than in the districts of the Lower Euphrates. Even in the time of the Sargonids their alphabet had made so much headway that at Nineveh itself and at Calah it had come into everyday use; when Chaldæan supremacy gave way to that of the Persians, its triumph—in the western provinces, at any rate—was complete, and it became the recognised vehicle of the royal decrees: we come upon it in every direction, on the coins issued by the satraps of Asia Minor, on the seals of local governors or dynasts, on inscriptions or stelæ in Egypt, in the letters of the scribes, and in the rescripts of the great king. From Nisib to Raphia, between the Tigris and the Mediterranean, it gradually supplanted most of the other dialects—Semitic or otherwise—which had hitherto prevailed. Phœnician held its ground in the seaports, but Hebrew gave way before it, and ended by being restricted to religious purposes, as a literary and liturgical language. It was in the neighbourhood of Babylon itself that the Judæan exiles had, during the Captivity, adopted the Aramaic language, and their return to Canaan failed to restore either the purity of their own language or the dignity and independence of their religious life. Their colony at Jerusalem possessed few resources; the wealthier Hebrews had, for the most part, remained in Chaldæa, leaving the privilege of repopulating the holy city to those of their brethren who were less plenteously endowed with this world's goods. These latter soon learned to their cost that Zion was not the ideal city whose "gates shall be open continually; they shall not be shut day nor night; that men may bring unto thee the wealth of the nations;" far from "sucking the milk of nations and the breast of kings,"[1] their fields produced barely sufficient to satisfy the more pressing needs of daily life. "Ye have sown much, and bring in little," as Jahveh declared to them "ye eat, but ye have not enough; ye drink, but ye are not filled with drink; ye clothe you, but there is none warm; and he that earneth wages earneth wages to put it into a bag with holes."[2] They quickly relinquished the work of restoration, finding themselves forgotten by all—their Babylonian brethren included—in the midst of the great events which were then agitating the world, the preparations for the conquest of Egypt, the usurpation of the pseudo-Smerdis, the accession of Darius, the Babylonian and Median insurrections. Possibly they believed that the Achæmenides had had their day, and that a new Chaldæan empire, with a

---

[1] An anonymous prophet in *Isa.* lx. 11–16. [2] *Hagg.* i. 6.

second Nebuchadrezzar at its head, was about to regain the ascendency. It would seem that the downfall of Nadintavbel inspired them with new faith in the future and encouraged them to complete their task: in the second year of Darius, two prophets, Haggai and Zechariah, arose in their midst and lifted up their voices. Zerubbabel, a prince of the royal line, governed Judah in the Persian interest, and with him was associated the high priest Joshua, who looked after the spiritual interests of the community: the reproaches of the two prophets aroused the people from their inaction, and induced them to resume their interrupted building operations. Darius, duly informed of what was going on by the governor of Syria, gave orders that they were not to be interfered with, and four years later the building of the temple was completed.[2] For nearly a century after this the little Jewish republic remained quiescent. It had slowly developed until it had gradually won back a portion of the former territories of Benjamin and Judah, but its expansion southwards was checked by the Idumæans, to whom Nebuchadrezzar had years before handed over Hebron and Acrabattenê (Akrabbim) as a reward for the services they had rendered.

CHALDÆAN SEAL WITH ARAMAIC INSCRIPTION.[1]

---

[1] Drawn by Faucher-Gudin, from a photogravure published in Ménant.

[2] *Ezra* iv.-vi.; the account given by Josephus of the two expeditions of Zerubbabel seems to have been borrowed partly from the canonical book, partly from the Apocryphal writing known as the 1st *Book of Esdras*.

On the north its neighbours were the descendants of those Aramæan exiles whom Sargon, Sennacherib, and Esarhaddon, kings of Assyria, had, on various occasions, installed around Samaria in Mount Ephraim. At first these people paid no reverence to the "God of the land," so that Jahveh, in order to punish them, sent lions, which spread carnage in their ranks. Then the King of Assyria allotted them an Israelitish priest from among his prisoners, who taught them "the law" of Jahveh, and appointed other priests chosen from the people, and showed them how to offer up sacrifices on the ancient high places."[1] Thus another Israel began to rise up again, and, at first, the new Judah seems to have been on tolerably friendly terms with it: the two communities traded and intermarried with one another, the Samaritans took part in the religious ceremonies, and certain of their leaders occupied a court in the temple at Jerusalem. The alliance, however, proved dangerous to the purity of the faith, for the proselytes, while they adopted Jahveh and gave Him that supreme place in their devotions which was due to "the God of the land," had by no means entirely forsworn their national superstitions, and Adrammelek, Nergal, Tartak, Anammelek, and other deities still found worshippers among them. Judah, which in the days of its independence had so often turned aside after the gods of Canaan and Moab, was in danger of being led away by the

[1] 2 *Kings* xvii. 24–40. There do not seem to have been the continual disputes between the inhabitants of Judæa and Samaria before the return of Nehemiah, which the compilers of the Books of Ezra and Nehemiah seem to have believed.

idolatrous practices of its new neighbours; intermarriage with the daughters of Moab and Ammon, of Philistia and Samaria, was producing a gradual degeneracy: the national language was giving way before the Aramæan; unless some one could be found to stem the tide of decadence and help the people to remount the slope which they were descending, the fate of Judah was certain. A prophet—the last of those whose predictions have survived to our time—stood forth amid the general laxity and called the people to account for their transgressions, in the name of the Eternal, but his single voice, which seemed but a feeble echo of the great prophets of former ages, did not meet with a favourable hearing. Salvation came at length from the Jews outside Judah, the naturalised citizens of Babylon, a well-informed and wealthy body, occupying high places in the administration of the empire, and sometimes in the favour of the sovereign also, yet possessed by an ardent zeal for the religion of their fathers and a steadfast faith in the vitality of their race. One of these, a certain Nehemiah, was employed as cupbearer to Artaxerxes II. He was visited at Susa by some men of Judah whose business had brought them to that city and inquired of them how matters fared in Jerusalem. Hanani, one of his visitors, replied that "the remnant that are left of the captivity there in the province are in great affliction and reproach: the wall of Jerusalem also is broken down, and the gates thereof are burned with fire." Nehemiah took advantage of a moment when the king seemed in a jovial mood to describe the wretched state of his native land in moving terms: he obtained leave to quit Susa and authority to administer the city in which his fathers had dwelt.[1]

This took place in the twentieth year of Artaxerxes, about 385 B.C. Nehemiah at once made his way to Jerusalem with such escort as befitted his dignity, and the news of his mission, and, apparently, the sentiments of rigid orthodoxy professed by him from the beginning, provoked the resentment of the neighbouring potentates against him: Sanballat the Horonite, Tobiah the Ammonite, chief of the Samaritans, and Geshem the Bedâwin did their best to thwart him in the execution of his plans. He baffled their intrigues by his promptitude in rebuilding the walls, and when once he had rendered himself safe from any sudden attack, he proceeded with the reforms which he deemed urgent. His tenure of office lasted twelve years—from 384 to 373 B.C.—and during the whole of that time he refused to accept any of the dues to which he was entitled, and which his predecessors had received without scruple. Ever since their return from exile, the common people had been impoverished and paralysed by usury. The poor had been compelled to mortgage their fields and their vineyards in order to pay the king's taxes; then, when their land was gone, they had pledged their sons and their daughters; the moneyed classes of the new Israel thus absorbed the property of their poorer brethren, and reduced the latter to slavery. Nehemiah called the usurers before him and severely rebuking them for their covetousness, bade them surrender the interest and capital of existing debts, and

[1] *Nehemiah* i., ii.

restore the properties which had fallen into their hands owing to their shameful abuse of wealth, and release all those of their co-religionists whom they had enslaved in default of payment of their debts.[1] His high place in the royal favour doubtless had its effect on those whose cupidity suffered from his zeal, and prevented external enemies from too openly interfering in the affairs of the community: by the time he returned to the court, in 372 B.C., after an absence of twelve years,[2] Jerusalem and its environs had to some extent regained the material prosperity of former days. The part played by Nehemiah was, however, mainly political, and the religious problem remained in very much the same state as before. The high priests, who alone possessed the power of solving it, had fallen in with the current that was carrying away the people, and—latterly, at any rate—had become disqualified through intermarriage with aliens: what was wanted was a scribe deeply versed in sacred things to direct them in the right way, and such a man could be found only in Babylonia, the one country in which the study of the ancient traditions still flourished. A certain Ezra, son of Seraiah, presented himself in 369 B.C., and, as he was a man of some standing, Artaxerxes not only authorised him to go himself, but to take with him a whole company of priests and Levites and families formerly attached to the service of the temple. The books containing the Law of God and the history of His people

---

[1] *Neh.* v.

[2] *Neh.* xiii. 6: "in the two and thirtieth year of Artaxerxes, King of Babylon, I went unto the king."

had, since the beginning of the captivity, undergone alterations which had profoundly modified their text and changed their spirit. This work of revision, begun under the influence of Ezekiel, and perhaps by his own followers, had, since his time, been carried on without interruption, and by mingling the juridical texts with narratives of the early ages collected from different sources, a lengthy work had been produced, very similar in composition and wording to the five Books of Moses and the Book of Joshua as we now possess them.[1] It was this version of the Revelation of Jahveh that Ezra brought with him from Babylon in order to instruct the people of Judah, and the first impressions received by him at the end of his journey convinced him that his task would be no light one, for the number of mixed marriages had been so great as to demoralise not only the common people, but even the priests and leading nobles as well. Nevertheless, at a general assembly[2] of the people he succeeded in persuading them to consent to the repudiation of alien wives. But this preliminary success would have led to nothing unless he could secure formal recognition of the rigorous code of which he had constituted himself the champion, and protracted negotiations were necessary before he could claim a victory on this point as well

---

[1] This is the priestly revision presupposed by recent critics; here again, in order to keep within the prescribed limits of space, I have been compelled to omit much that I should have liked to add in regard to the nature of this work and the spirit in which it was carried out.

[2] *E*zra. vii.–xi., where the dates given do not form part of the work as written by Ezra, but have been introduced later by the editor of the book as it now stands.

as on the other. At length, about 367 B.C., more than a year after his arrival, he gained his point, and the covenant between Jahveh and His people was sealed with ceremonies modelled on those which had attended the promulgation of Deuteronomy in the time of Josiah. On the first day of the seventh month, a little before the autumn festival, the people assembled at Jerusalem in "the broad place which was before the water gate." Ezra mounted a wooden pulpit, and the chief among the priests sat beside him. He "opened the book in the sight of all the people ... and ... all the people stood up: and Ezra blessed the Lord, the great God. And all the people answered 'Amen, amen!' with the lifting up of their hands; and they bowed their heads and worshipped the Lord with their faces to the ground." Then began the reading of the sacred text. As each clause was read, the Levites stationed here and there among the people interpreted and explained its provisions in the vulgar tongue, so as to make their meaning clear to all. The prolix enumeration of sins and their expiation, and threats expressed in certain chapters, produced among the crowd the same effect of nervous terror as had once before been called forth by the precepts and maledictions of Deuteronomy. The people burst into tears, and so vehement were their manifestations of despair, that all the efforts of Ezra and his colleagues were needed to calm them. Ezra took advantage of this state of fervour to demand the immediate application of the divine ordinances. And first of all, it was "found written in the law, how that the Lord had commanded by Moses that the children of Israel should dwell in booths." For seven days Jerusalem was decked with leaves; tabernacles of olive, myrtle, and palm branches rose up on all sides, on the roofs of houses, in courtyards, in the courts of the temple, at the gates of the city. Then, on the 27th day of the same month, the people put on mourning in order to confess their own sins and the sins of their fathers. Finally, to crown the whole, Ezra and his followers required the assembly to swear a solemn oath that they would respect "the law of Moses," and regulate their conduct by it.[1] After the first enthusiasm was passed, a reaction speedily set in. Many even among the priests thought that Ezra had gone too far in forbidding marriage with strangers, and that the increase of the tithes and sacrifices would lay too heavy a burden on the nation. The Gentile women reappeared, the Sabbath was no longer observed either by the Israelites or aliens; Eliashib, son of the high priest Joiakim, did not even deprive Tobiah the Ammonite of the chamber in the temple which he had formerly prepared for him, and things were almost imperceptibly drifting back into the same state as before the reformation, when Nehemiah returned from Susa towards the close of the reign of Artaxerxes. He lost no time in re-establishing respect for the law, and from henceforward opposition, if it did not entirely die out, ceased to manifest itself in Jerusalem.[2]

[1] *Neh.* viii., ix., with an interpolation in ver. 9 of chap. viii., inserted in order to identify Nehemiah with the representative of the Persian government.
[2] *Neh.* xiii.

Elsewhere, however, among the Samaritans, Indumæans, and Philistines, it continued as keen as ever, and the Jews themselves were imprudent enough to take part in the political revolutions that were happening around them in their corner of the empire. Their traditions tell how they were mixed up in the rising of the Phœnician cities against Ochus, and suffered the penalty; when Sidon capitulated, they were punished with the other rebels, the more recalcitrant among them being deported into Hyrcania.

Assyria was nothing more than a name, Babylon and Phœnicia were growing weaker every day; the Jews, absorbed in questions of religious ethics, were deficient in material power, and had not as yet attained sufficient moral authority to exercise an influence over the eastern world: the Egypt indestructible had alone escaped the general shipwreck, and seemed fated to survive her rivals for a long time. Of all these ancient nations it was she who appealed most strongly to the imagination of the Greeks: Greek traders, mercenaries, scholars, and even tourists wandered freely within her borders, and accounts of the strange and marvellous things to be found there were published far and wide in the writings of Hecatæus of Miletus, Herodotus of Halicarnassus, and Hellanicus of Lesbos. As a rule, they entered the country from the west, as European tourists and merchants still do; but Rakôtis, the first port at which they touched, was a mere village, and its rocky Pharos had no claim to distinction beyond the fact that it had been mentioned by Homer. From hence they followed the channel of the

Canopic arm, and as they gradually ascended, they had pointed out to them Anthylla, Arkandrupolis, and Gynæcopolis, townships dependent on Naucratis, lying along the banks, or situated some distance off on one of the minor canals; then Naucratis itself, still a flourishing place, in spite of the rebellions in the Delta and the suppressive measures of the Persians. All this region seemed to them to be merely an extension of Greece under the African sky: to their minds the real Egypt began at Sais, a few miles further eastwards. Sais was full in memories of the XXVIth dynasty; there they had pointed out to them the tombs of the Pharaohs in the enclosure of Nît, the audience hall in which Psammetichus II. received the deputation of the Eleians, the prison where the unfortunate Apries had languished after his defeat. The gateways of the temple of Nit seemed colossal to eyes accustomed to the modest dimensions of most Greek sanctuaries; these were, moreover, the first great monuments that the strangers had seen since they landed, and the novelty of their appearance had a good deal to do with the keenness of the impression produced. The goddess showed herself in hospitable guise to the visitors; she welcomed them all, Greek or Persian, at her festivals, and initiated them into several of her minor rites, without demanding from them anything beyond tolerance on certain points of doctrine. Her dual attributes as wielder of the bow and shuttle had inspired the Greeks with the belief that she was identical with that one of their own goddesses who most nearly combined in her person this complex mingling of war and industry: in her they

worshipped the prototype of their own Pallas. On the evening of the 17th day of Thoth, Herodotus saw the natives, rich and poor, placing on the fronts of their dwellings large flat lamps filled with a mixture of salt and oil which they kept alight all night in honour of Osiris and of the dead.[1] He made his way into the dwelling of the ineffable god, and there, unobserved among the crowd, he witnessed scenes from the divine life represented by the priests on the lake by the light of torches, episodes of his passion, mourning, and resurrection. The priests did not disclose their subtler mysteries before barbarian eyes, nor did they teach the inner meaning of their dogmas, but the little they did allow him to discern filled the traveller with respect and wonder, recalling sometimes by their resemblance to them the mysteries in which he was accustomed to take part in his own country. Then, as now, but little attention was paid to the towns in the centre and east of the Delta; travellers endeavoured to visit one or two of them as types, and collected as much information as they could about the remainder. Herodotus and his rivals attached little importance to those details of landscape which possess so much attraction for the modern tourist. They bestowed no more than a careless glance on the chapels scattered up and down the country like the Mohammedan shrines at the present day, and the waters extending on all

[1] In my opinion it is not the festivals of Athyr that are here referred to, but those of the month of Thoth, when, as the inscriptions show, it was the practice to *light the new fire*, according to the ritual, after first extinguishing the fire of the previous year, not only in the temple of the god, but in all the houses of the city.

348 THE LAST DAYS OF THE OLD EASTERN WORLD

sides beneath the acacias and palm trees during the inundation, or the fellahin trotting along on their little asses beside the pools, did not strike them as being of sufficient interest to deserve passing mention in an account of their travels. They passed by the most picturesque villages with indifference, and it was only when they reached some great city, or came upon some exceptionally fine temple or eccentric deity, that their curiosity was aroused. Mendes worshipped its patron god in the form of a live ram,[1] and bestowed on all members of the same species some share of the veneration it lavished on the divine animal. The inhabitants of Atarbêkhis,[2] on the island of Prosopitis, gave themselves up to the worship of the bull. When one of these animals died in the neigh-

MODERN MOHAMMEDAN SHÊKHS' TOMBS.[3]

---

[1] Herodotus says that both the goats and the god were named Mendes in Egyptian, but he is here confusing ordinary goats with the special goat which was supposed to contain the soul of Osiris. It was the latter that the Egyptians named after the god himself, Baînibdîduît, i.e. *the soul of the master of the city of Diduît.*

[2] The old explanation of this name as the *City of Hathor* has been rightly rejected as inconsistent with one of the elementary rules of hieroglyphic grammar. The name, when properly divided into its three constituent parts, means literally *the Castle of Horus the Sparrow-hawk,* or *Hat-har-baki.*

[3] Drawn by Boudier, from a photograph by Gautier.

bourhood they buried it, leaving one horn above the earth in order to mark the spot, and once every year the boats of Atarbêkhis made a tour round the island to collect the skeletons or decaying bodies, in order that they might be interred in a common burying-place. The people of Busiris patronised a savage type of religion. During the festival of Isis they gave themselves up to fierce conflicts, their fanatical fury even infecting strangers who chanced to be present. The Carians also had hit upon a means of outdoing the extravagance of the natives themselves: like the Shiite Mohammedans of the present day at the festival of the Hassanên, they slashed their faces

PART OF THE INUNDATION IN A PALM GROVE.[1]

with knives amidst shrieks and yells. At Paprêmis a pitched battle formed part of the religious observances: it took place, however, under certain special conditions. On the evening of the festival of Anhurît, as the sun went down, a number of priests performed a hasty sacrifice in the temple, while the remainder of the local priesthood stationed themselves at the gate armed with heavy cudgels. When the ceremony was over, the celebrants placed the statue of the god on a four-wheeled car, as though about to take it away to some other locality, but their colleagues at the gate opposed its departure

[1] Drawn by Boudier, from a photograph by Gautier.

and barred the way. It was at this juncture that the faithful intervened; they burst in the door and set upon the priests with staves, the latter offering a stout resistance. The cudgels were heavy, the arms that wielded them lusty, and the fight lasted a long time, yet no one was ever killed in the fray—at least, so the priests averred —and I am at a loss to understand why Herodotus, who was not a native of Paprêmis, should have been so unkind as to doubt their testimony.[1]

EPHEMERAL HOVELS OF CLAY OR DRIED BRICKS.[2]

It is nearly always in connection with some temple or religious festival that he refers to the towns of the Delta, and, indeed, in most of the minor cities of Egypt, just as in those of modern Italy there is little to interest visitors except the religious monuments or ceremonies. Herodotus went to Tanis or Mendes as we go to Orvieto or Loretto, to admire the buildings or pay our devotions at a famous shrine. More often than not the place was nothing in itself, consisting merely of a fortified enclosure, a few commonplace houses occupied by the wealthy inhabitants

[1] The god whom the Greeks identified with their Ares was Anhurit, as is proved by one of the Leyden Papyri. So, too, in modern times at Cairo, it used to be affirmed that no Mohammedan who submitted to the *dôseh* was ever seriously injured by the hoofs of the horse which trampled over the bodies extended on the ground.

[2] Drawn by Boudier, from a photograph by Haussoullier.

or by government officials, and on mounds of ancient *débris*, the accumulation of centuries, a number of ephemeral hovels built of clay or dried bricks, divided into irregular blocks by winding alleys. The whole local interest was centred in the sanctuary and its inmates, human and divine. The traveller made his way in as best he could, went into ecstasies over the objects that were shown to him, and as soon as he had duly gone the rounds, set out for the next place on his list, deeming himself lucky if he happened to arrive during one of the annual fairs, such as that of Bubastis, for instance. Bands of pilgrims flocked in from all parts of Egypt; the river craft were overflowing with men and women, who converted the journey into one long carnival. Every time the vessel put in to land, the women rushed on shore, amid the din of castanets and flutes, and ran hither and thither challenging the women of the place with abuse to dance against them with uplifted garments. To the foreigners there was little to distinguish the festival of Bastît from many other Egyptian ceremonies of the kind; it consisted of a solemn procession, accompanied by the singing of hymns and playing of harps, dancing and sacrifices, but for weeks before and after it the town was transformed into one vast pleasure-ground. The people of Bubastis took a certain pride in declaring that more wine was drunk in it during a single day than during the rest of the whole year. Butô enjoyed exceptional popularity among the Greeks in Egypt. Its patron goddess, the Isis who took refuge amid the pools in a moving thicket of reeds and lotus, in order that she might protect her son Horus from the jealousy of Typhon, reminded them of the story of Latona and the cycle of the Delian legends; they visited her in crowds, and her oracle became to most of them what that of Delos was to their brethren in Europe. At Butô they found a great temple, similar to all Egyptian temples, a shrine in which the statues of the goddess continued her mysterious existence, and, in the midst of the sacred lake, the little island of Khemmis, which was said to float hither and thither upon the waters. Herodotus did not venture to deny this absolutely, but states that he had never seen it change its position or even stir: perhaps his incredulity may have been quickened by the fact that this miracle had already been inquired into by Hecatæus of Miletus, an author who was his pet aversion. The priests of Butô declared that their prophets had foretold everything that had happened for a long time past, and for each event they had a version which redounded to the credit of their goddess: she had shown Pheron how he might recover his sight, had foretold how long the reign of Mykerinos would last, had informed Psammetichus that he would be saved by men of brass rising out of the sea, and had revealed to Cambyses that he should die in a town named Ecbatana. Her priests had taken an active part in the revolt of Khabbîsha against Darius, and had lost a goodly portion of their treasure and endowments for their pains. They still retained their prestige, however, in spite of the underhand rivalry of the oracle of Zeus Ammon. The notaries of the Libyan deity could bring forward miracles even more marvellous than those credited to the Egyptian Latona, and in the case of many of the revolutions which had taken place on the banks of the Nile, a version of the legend in his honour was circulated side by side with the legends of Butô. The latter city lay on the very outskirts of one of those regions which excited the greatest curiosity among travellers, the almost inaccessible Bucolicum, where, it was said, no rebel ever failed to find a safe refuge from his alien pursuers. The Egyptians of the marshes were a very courageous race, but savage, poor, and ill fed. They drank nothing but beer, and obtained their oil not from the olive, but from the castor-oil plant,[1] and having no corn, lived on the seeds or roots of the lotus, or even on the stalks of the papyrus, which they roasted or boiled. Fish was their staple article of food, and this they obtained in considerable quantity from Lake Menzaleh, the lagoons along the coast, and the canals or pools left by the inundation. But little was known of their villages or monuments, and probably they were not worth the trouble of a visit after those of the cities of the plain: endless stories were told of feats of brigandage and of the mysterious hiding-places which these localities offered to every outlaw, one of the most celebrated being the isle of Elbô, where the blind Anysis defied the power of Ethiopia for thirty years, and in which the first Amyrtæus found refuge. With the exception of a few merchants or adventurers who visited them with an eye to gain, most travellers coming from or returning to Asia avoided their territory, and followed the military road along the Pelusiac

[1] It seems, moreover, that this custom was not confined to the Delta; Herodotus, in contrasting the custom of Bucolicum with that of the rest of Egypt, was evidently thinking of Sais, Memphis, and other great cities in which he had resided, where foreign olive oil obtained from Greece or Syria was generally used.

arm of the Nile from Pelusium to Daphnæ or Zalu, and from Daphnæ or Zalu to Bubastis. A little below Kerkasoron, near the apex of the Delta, the pyramids stood out on the horizon, looking insignificant at first, but afterwards so lofty that, during the period of inundation, when the whole valley, from the mountains of Arabia to those of Libya, was nothing but one vast river, a vessel seemed to sail in their shadow for a long time before it reached their base. The traveller passed Heliopolis on his left with its temple of the Sun, next the supposed sources of the Northern Nile, the quarries of the Red Mountain, and then entering at length the Nile itself, after a journey of some hours, came to anchor by the quays of Memphis.

To the Greeks of that time, Memphis was very much what Cairo is to us, viz. the typical Oriental city, the quintessence and chief representative of ancient Egypt. In spite of the disasters which had overwhelmed it during the last few centuries, it was still a very beautiful city, ranking with Babylon as one of the largest in the world. Its religious festivals, especially those in honour of Apis, attracted numberless pilgrims to it at certain seasons of the year, and hosts of foreigners, recruited from every imaginable race of the old continent, resorted to it for purposes of trade. Most of the nationalities who frequented it had a special quarter, which was named after them; the Phœnicians occupied the *Tyrian Camp*, the Greeks and Carians the *Hellenic Wall* and *Carian Wall*, and there were Caromemphites or Hellenomemphites side by side with the native inhabitants. A Persian garrison was stationed within the White Wall, ready to execute the satrap's orders in the event of rebellion, and could have held out for a long time even after the rest of the country had fallen into the hands of the insurgents. Animals which one would scarcely have expected to find in the streets of a capital, such as cows, sheep, and goats, wandered about unheeded in the most crowded thoroughfares; for the common people, instead of living apart from their beasts, as the Greeks did, stabled them in their own houses. Nor was this the only custom which must have seemed strange in the eyes of a newly arrived visitor, for the Egyptians might almost have been said to make a point of doing everything differently from other nations. The baker, seen at the kneading-trough inside his shop, worked the dough with his foot; on the other hand, the mason used no trowel in applying his mortar, and the poorer classes scraped up handfuls of mud mixed with dung when they had occasion to repair the walls of their hovels. In Greece, even the very poorest retired to their houses and ate with closed doors; the Egyptians felt no repugnance at eating and drinking in the open air, declaring that unbecoming and improper acts should be performed in secret, but seemly acts in public. The first blind alley they came to, a recess between two hovels, the doorstep of a house or temple, any of these seemed to them a perfectly natural place to dine in. Their bill of fare was not a sumptuous one. A sort of flat pancake somewhat bitter in taste, and made—not of corn or barley—but of spelt, a little oil, an onion or a leek, with an occasional scrap of meat or poultry, washed down by a jug of beer or wine; there was nothing here to tempt the foreigner, and, besides, it would not have been thought right for him to invite himself. A Greek who lived on the flesh of the cow was looked upon as unclean in the highest degree; no Egyptian would have thought of using the same pot or knife with him, or of kissing him on the mouth by way of greeting. Moreover, Egyptian etiquette did not tolerate the same familiarities as the Greek: two friends on catching sight of one another paused before they met, bowed, then clasped one another round the knees or pretended to do so. Young people gave way to an old man, or, if seated, rose to let him pass. The traveller recalled the fact that the Spartans behaved in the same way, and approved this mark of deference; but nothing in his home-life had prepared him for the sight of respectable women coming and going as they pleased, without escort and unveiled, carrying burdens on their shoulders (whereas the men carried them on their heads), going to market, keeping stalls or shops, while their husbands or fathers stayed comfortably at home, wove cloth, kneaded the potter's clay or turned the wheel, and worked at their trades; no wonder that they were ready to believe that the man was the slave, and the wife the mistress of the family. Some historians traced the origin of these customs back to Osiris, others only as far as Sesostris: Sesostris was the last resource of Greek historians when they got into difficulties. The city was crowded with monuments; there was the temple of the Phœnician Astarte, in which priests of Syrian descent had celebrated the mysteries of the great goddess ever since the days of the XVIIIth dynasty; then there was the temple of Râ, the temple of Amon, the temple of Tumu, the temple of

Bastît, and the temple of Isis.¹ The temple of Phtah, as yet intact, provided the visitor with a spectacle scarcely less admirable than that offered by the temple of the Theban Amon at Karnak. The kings had modified the original plan as each thought best, one adding obelisks or colossal statues, another a pylon, a third a pillared hall. Completed in this way by the labours of a score of dynasties, it formed, as it were, a microcosm of Egyptian history, in which each image, inscription and statue, aroused the attention of the curious. They naturally desired to learn who were the strangely dressed races shown struggling in a battle scene, the name of the king who had conquered them, and the reasons which had led him to construct this or that part of a monument, and there were plenty of busybodies ready to satisfy, as far as they could, the curiosity of visitors. Interpreters were at hand who bartered such information as they possessed, and the modern traveller who has had occasion to employ the services of a dragoman will have no difficulty in estimating the value of intelligence thus hawked about in ancient times. Priests of the lower class, doorkeepers and sacristans were trained to act as *ciceroni*, and knew the main outlines of the history of the temple in which they lived. Menes planned it, Mœris added the northern propylæa, Rhampsinitus those on the west, Psammetichus the south, Asychis those on the east, the most noteworthy

---

¹ This list is taken mainly from one of the mutilated letters found on the back of the *Sallier Papyrus*. The Phœnician Astarte, called a foreign Aphrodite by Herodotus, was regarded by the Egyptians as a counterpart of Bastit, lady of Onkhtoui.

of them all. A native of Memphis, born at the foot of the pyramids, had been familiar with the names of Menes and Cheops from childhood; he was consequently apt to attribute to them everything of importance achieved by the Pharaohs of the old days. Menes had built the temple, Menes had founded the city, Menes had created the soil on which the city stood, and preserved it from floods by his dykes. The thoughtful traveller would assent, for had he not himself observed the action of the mud; a day's journey from the coast one could not let down a plummet without drawing it up covered with a blackish slime, a clear proof that the Nile continued to gain upon the sea. Menes, at all events, had really existed; but as to Asychis, Mœris, Proteus, Pheron, and most of the characters glibly enumerated by Herodotus, it would be labour lost to search for their names among the inscriptions; they are mere puppets of popular romance, some of their names, such as Pirâni or Pruti, being nothing more than epithets employed by the story-tellers to indicate in general terms the heroes of their tales. We can understand how strangers, placed at the mercy of their dragoman, were misled by this, and tempted to transform each title into a man, taking Pruti and Pirâui to be Pharaoh Proteus and Pharaoh Pheron, each of them celebrated for his fabulous exploits. The guides told Herodotus, and Herodotus retails to us, as sober historical facts, the remedy employed by this unhistorical Pheron in order to recover his sight; the adventures of Paris and Helen at the court of Proteus,[1] and the droll tricks played by a thief at the expense of the

[1] Some dragomans identified the Helen of the Homeric legend with the

simple Rhampsinitus. The excursions made by the Greek traveller in the environs of Memphis were very similar to those taken by modern visitors to Cairo: on the opposite bank of the Nile there was Heliopolis with its temple of Râ, then there were the quarries of Turah, which had been

THE STEP PYRAMID SEEN FROM THE GROVE OF PALM TREES TO THE NORTH OF SAQQARAH.[1]

worked from time immemorial, yet never exhausted, and from which the monuments he had been admiring, and the very Pyramids themselves had been taken stone by stone.[2] The Sphinx probably lay hidden beneath the sand, and the

"foreign Aphrodite" who had a temple in the Tyrian quarter at Memphis, and who was really a Semitic divinity.

[1] Drawn by Boudier, from a photograph by Haussoullier.

[2] These are "the quarries in the Arabian Mountain," mentioned by Herodotus without indication of the local name.

nearest Pyramids, those at Saqqarah, were held in small esteem by visitors ;[1] they were told as they passed by that the step Pyramid was the most ancient of all, having been erected by Uenephes, one of the kings of the first dynasty, and they asked no further questions. Their whole curiosity was reserved for the three giants at Gizeh and their inmates, Cheops, Chephren, Mykerinos, and the fair Nitokris with the rosy cheeks. Through all the country round, at Heliopolis, and even in the Fayum itself, they heard the same names that had been dinned into their ears at Memphis; the whole of the monuments were made to fit into a single cycle of popular history, and what they learned at one place completed, or seemed to complete, what they had learned at another.

I cannot tell whether many of them cared to stray much beyond Lake Mœris: the repressive measures of Ochus had, as it would appear, interrupted for a time the regular trade which, ever since the Saite kings of the XXVIth dynasty, had been carried on by the Greeks with the Oases, by way of Abydos. A stranger who ventured as far as the Thebaid would have found himself in the same plight as a European of the last century who undertook to reach the first cataract. Their point of departure—Memphis or Cairo—was very much the same; their destinations—Elephantinê and Assuan—differed but little. They employed the same means of transport, for, excepting the cut of the sails, the modern dahabeah is an exact counterpart of the pleasure and passenger boats

[1] Herodotus does not mention it, nor does any other writer of the Greek period.

shown on the monuments. Lastly, they set out at the same time of year, in November or December, after the floods had subsided. The same length of time was required for the trip; it took a month to reach Assuan from Cairo if the wind were favourable, and if only such stoppages were made as were strictly necessary for taking in fresh provisions. Pococke, having left Cairo on the 6th of December, 1737, about midday, was at Akhmîm by the 17th. He set sail again on the 18th, stayed at Thebes from the 13th of January, 1738, till the 17th, and finally moored at Assuan on the evening of January 20th, making in all forty-five days, fourteen of which were spent at various stopping-places. If the diary of a Greek excursionist or tourist had come down to us, we should probably find in it entries of a very similar kind.[1] The departure from Memphis would take place in November or December; ten or twelve days later the traveller would find himself at Panopolis;[2] from Panopolis to Elephantinê, stopping

[1] Herodotus fixes twenty days for the voyage from Sais to Elephantinê. This period of time must be probably correct, since at the present day dahabeahs constantly run from Cairo to the second cataract and back in two months, including stoppages of ten days to a fortnight for seeing the monuments. The twenty days of Herodotus represent the minimum duration of the voyage, without taking into account the stoppages and accidents which often delay sailing vessels on the Nile. Nine days, which Herodotus gives as the time for reaching Thebes, is not sufficient, if the voyage is undertaken in the usual way, stopping every evening for the night; but it would be possible if the navigation were uninterrupted day and night. This is now rarely done, but it might have been frequent in ancient times, especially in the service of the State.

[2] It would seem clear that Herodotus stopped at Panopolis and had communications with the people of the town. [Panopolis or Khemmis is the present Ekhmîm.—Tr.]

at Coptos and Thebes, would take about a month, allowing time for a stay at Thebes, and returning to Memphis in

LONG STRINGS OF LADEN VESSELS.[1]

February or March. The greater part of the time was employed in getting from one point to another, and the necessity of taking advantage of a favourable wind in going up the river, often obliged the travellers to neglect more than one interesting locality. The Greek was not so keenly alive to the picturesqueness of the scenes through which he passed as the modern visitor, and in the account of his travels he took no note of the long lines of laden boats going up or down stream, nor of the vast sheet of water glowing in the midday sun, nor of the mountains honeycombed with

THE VAST SHEET OF WATER IN THE MIDDAY HEAT.[1]

tombs and quarries, at the foot of which he would be sailing day after day. What interested him above all

[1] Drawn by Boudier, from a photograph by Gautier.

things was information with regard to the sources of the immense river itself, and the reasons for its periodic inundation, and, according to the mental attitude impressed on him by his education, he accepted the mythological solution offered by the natives, or he sought for a more natural one in the physical lore of his own *savants:* thus he was told that the Nile took its rise at Elephantinê, between the two rocks called Krôphi and Môphi, and in showing them to him his informant would add that Psammetichus I. had attempted to sound the depth of the river at this point, but had failed to fathom it. At the few places where the pilot of the barque put in to port, the population showed themselves unfriendly, and refused to hold any communication with the Greeks.

THE MOUNTAINS HONEYCOMBED WITH TOMBS AND QUARRIES.[1]

The interpreters, who were almost all natives of the Delta, were not always familiar with the people and customs of the Saïd, and felt almost as completely foreign at Thebes as did their employers. Their office was confined to translating the information furnished by the inhabitants when the latter were sufficiently civilised to hold communication with the travellers. What most astonished Herodotus at Panopolis was the temple and the games held in honour, so he believed, of Perseus, the son of Danaë. These exercises terminated in an attempt

[1] Drawn by Boudier, from a photograph by Gautier.

to climb a regular " greasy pole " fixed in the ground, and strengthened right and left by three rows of stays attached to the mast at different heights; as for Perseus, he was the ithyphallic god of the locality, Mînu himself, one of whose epithets—Pehresu, the runner—was confounded by the Greek ear with the name of the hero. The dragomans, enlarging on this mistaken identity, imagined that the town was the birthplace of Danaos and Lyncæus; that Perseus, returning from Libya with the head of Medusa, had gone out of his way to visit the cradle of his family, and that he had instituted the games in remembrance of his stay there. Thebes had become the ghost of its former self; the Persian governors had neglected the city, and its princesses and their ministers were so impoverished that they were unable to keep up its temples and palaces. Herodotus scarcely mentions it, and we can hardly wonder at it: he had visited the still flourishing Memphis, where the temples were cared for and were filled with worshippers. What had Thebes to show him in the way of marvels which he had not already seen, and that, too, in a better state of preservation ? His Theban ciceroni also told him the same stories that he had heard in Lower Egypt, and he states that their information agreed in the main with that which he had received at Memphis and Heliopolis, which made it unnecessary to repeat it at length. Two or three things only appeared to him worthy of mention. His admiration was first roused by the 360 statues of the high priests of Amon which had already excited the wonder of his rival Hecatæus; he noted that all these personages were, without exception, represented as mere men, each the son of another man, and he took the opportunity of ridiculing the vanity of his compatriots, who did not hesitate to inscribe the name of a god at the head of their genealogies, removed by some score of generations only from their own. On the other hand, the temple servitors related to him how two Theban priestesses, carried off by the Phœnicians and sold, one in Libya and the other in Greece, had set up the first oracles known in those two countries: Herodotus thereupon remembered the story he had heard in Epirus of two black doves which had flown away from Thebes, one towards the Oasis of Ammon, the other in the direction of Dodona; the latter had alighted on an old beech tree, and in a human voice had requested that a temple consecrated to Zeus should be founded on the spot.[1] Herodotus is quite overcome with joy at the thought that Greek divination could thus be directly traced to that of Egypt, for like most of his contemporaries, he felt that the Hellenic cult was ennobled by the fact of its being derived from the Egyptian. The traveller on the Nile had to turn homewards on reaching Elephantinê, as that was the station of the last Persian garrison. Nubia lay immediately beyond the cataract, and the Ethiopians at times crossed the frontier and carried their raids as far as Thebes. Elephantinê, like Assuan at the present day, was the

---

[1] This indicates a confusion in the minds of the Egyptian dragomans with the two brooding birds of Osiris, Isis and Nephthys, considered as *Zarait*, that is to say, as two birds of a different species, according to the different traditions either vultures, rooks, or doves.

centre of a flourishing trade. Here might be seen Kushites from Napata or Meroë, negroes from the Upper Nile and the Bahr el-Ghazal, and Ammonians, from all of whom the curious visitor might glean information while frequenting the bazaars. The cataract was navigable all the year round, and the natives in its vicinity enjoyed the privilege of piloting freight boats through its difficult channel. It took four days to pass through it, instead of the three, or even two, which suffice at the present day. Above it, the Nile spread out and resembled a lake dotted over with islands, several of which, such as Philæ and Biggeh, contained celebrated temples, which were as much frequented by the Ethiopians as by the Egyptians.

Correctly speaking, it was not Egypt herself that the Greeks saw, but her external artistic aspect and the outward setting of Egyptian civilisation. The vastness of her monuments, the splendour of her tombs, the pomp of her ceremonies, the dignity and variety of her religious formulas, attracted their curiosity and commanded their respect: the wisdom of the Egyptians had passed into a proverb with them, as it had with the Hebrews. But if they had penetrated behind the scenes, they would have been obliged to acknowledge that beneath this attractive exterior there was hopeless decay. As with all creatures when they have passed their prime, Egypt had begun to grow old, and was daily losing her elasticity and energy. Her spirit had sunk into a torpor, she had become unresponsive to her environment, and could no longer adapt herself to the form she had so easily acquired in her youth: it was as much as she could do to occupy fully the narrower limits to which she had been reduced, and to maintain those limits unbroken. The instinct which made her shrink from the intrusion of foreign customs and ideas, or even mere contact with nations of recent growth, was not the mere outcome of vanity. She realised that she maintained her integrity only by relying on the residue of her former solidarity and on the force of custom. The slightest disturbance of the equilibrium established among her members, instead of strengthening her, would have robbed her of the vigour she still possessed, and brought about her dissolution. She owed whatever activity she possessed to impulses imparted to her by the play of her ancient mechanism — a mechanism so stable in its action, and so ingeniously constructed, that it had still a reserve

DARIUS III.[1]

of power within it sufficient to keep the whole in motion for centuries, provided there was no attempt to introduce new wheels among the old. She had never been singularly distinguished for her military qualities; not that she was cowardly, and shrank from facing death, but because she lacked energy and enthusiasm for warlike enterprise. The tactics and armaments by which she had won her victories up to her prime, had at length become fetters which she was no longer inclined to shake off, and even if she was still able to breed a military caste, she was no longer able to produce armies fit to win battles without the aid of mercenaries. In order to be successful in the field, she had to associate with her own troops

[1] Drawn by Faucher-Gudin, from a coin in the *Cabinet des Médailles*.

recruits from other countries—Libyans, Asiatics, and Greeks, who served to turn the scale. The Egyptians themselves formed a compact body in this case, and bearing down upon the enemy already engaged by the mercenaries, broke through his ranks by their sheer weight, or, if they could not accomplish this, they stood their ground bravely, taking to flight only when the vacancies in their ranks showed them that further resistance was impossible. The machinery of government, like the organisation of their armies, had become antiquated and degenerate. The nobility were as turbulent as in former times, and the royal authority was as powerless now as of old to assert itself in the absence of external help, or when treason was afoot among the troops. Religion alone maintained its ascendency, and began to assume to itself

AN ELEPHANT ARMED FOR WAR.[1]

[1] Drawn by Boudier, from a little terra-cotta group from Myrrhina now in the Louvre. This object dates from the time of the kings of Pergamos, and the soldier round whom the elephant winds his trunk in order to dash him to the ground is a Gaul of Asia Minor.

WEAKNESS OF THE PERSIAN EMPIRE

the loyalty once given to the Pharaoh, and the devotion previously consecrated to the fatherland. The fellahîn had never fully realised the degradation involved in serving a stranger, and what they detested in the Persian king was not exactly the fact that he was a Persian. Their national pride, indeed, always prompted them to devise some means of connecting the foreign monarch with their own solar line, and to transform an Achæmenian king into a legitimate Pharaoh. That which was especially odious to them in a Cambyses or an Ochus was the disdain which such sovereigns displayed for their religion, and the persecution to which they subjected the immortals. They accustomed themselves without serious repining to have no longer one of their own race upon the throne, and to behold their cities administered by Asiatics, but they could not understand why the foreigner preferred his own gods, and would not admit Amon, Phtah, Horus, and Râ to the rank of supreme deities. Ochus had, by his treatment of the Apis and the other divine animals, put it out of his power ever to win their good will. His brutality had made an irreconcilable enemy of that state which alone gave signs of vitality among the nations of the decaying East. This was all the more to be regretted, since the Persian empire, in spite of the accession of power which it had just manifested, was far from having regained the energy which had animated it, not perhaps in the time of Darius, but at all events under the first Xerxes. The army and the wealth of the country were doubtless still intact—an army and a revenue which, in spite of all losses, were still the largest in the world—but the valour of the troops was not proportionate to their number. The former prowess of the Persians, Medians, Bactrians, and other tribes of Iran showed no degeneracy: these nations still produced the same race of brave and hardy foot-soldiers, the same active and intrepid horsemen; but for a century past there had not been the improvements either in the armament of the troops or in the tactics of the generals which were necessary to bring them up to the standard of excellence of the Greek army. The Persian king placed great faith in extraordinary military machines. He believed in the efficacy of chariots armed with scythes; besides this, his relations with India had shown him what use his Oriental neighbours made of elephants, and having determined to employ these animals, he had collected a whole corps of them, from which he hoped great things. In spite of the addition of these novel recruits, it was not on the Asiatic contingents that he chiefly relied in the event of war, but on the mercenaries who were hired at great expense, and who formed the chief support of his power. From the time of Artaxerxes II. onwards, it was the Greek hoplites and peltasts who had always decided the issue of the Persian battles. The expeditions both by land and sea had been under the conduct of Athenian or Spartan generals—Conon, Chabrias, Iphicrates, Agesilas, Timotheus, and their pupils; and again also it was to the Greeks—to the Rhodian Mentor and to Memnon—that Ochus had owed his successes. The older nations—Egypt, Syria, Chaldæa, and Elam—had all had their day of supremacy; they had declined in the course of centuries, and Assyria had for a short time united them under her rule. On the downfall of Assyria, the Iranians had succeeded to her heritage, and they had built up a single empire comprising all the states which had preceded them in Western Asia; but decadence had fallen upon them also, and when they had been masters for scarcely two short centuries, they were in their turn threatened with destruction. Their rule continued to be universal, not by reason of its inherent vigour, but on account of the weakness of their subjects and neighbours, and a determined attack on any of the frontiers of the empire would doubtless have resulted in its overthrow.

Greece herself was too demoralised to cause Darius any grave anxiety. Not only had she renounced all intention of attacking the great king in his own domain, as in the days of the Athenian hegemony, when she could impose her own conditions of peace, but her perpetual discords had yielded her an easy prey to Persia, and were likely to do so more and more. The Greek cities chose the great king as the arbiter in their quarrels; they vied with each other in obtaining his good will, his subsidies in men and vessels, and his darics: they armed or disarmed at his command, and the day seemed at hand when they would become a normal dependency of Persia, little short of a regular satrapy like Asiatic Hellas. One chance of escape from such a fate remained to them—if one or other of them, or some neighbouring state, could acquire such an ascendency as to make it possible to unite what forces remained to them under one rule. Macedonia in particular, having hitherto kept aloof from the general stream of politics, had at this juncture begun to shake off its lethargy, and had entered with energy into the Hellenic concert under the auspices of its king, Philip. Bagoas recognised the danger which threatened his people in the person of this ambitious sovereign, and did not hesitate to give substantial support to the adversaries of the Macedonian prince; Chersobleptes of Thrace and the town of Perinthus receiving from him such succour as enabled them to repulse Philip successfully (340). Unfortunately, while Bagoas was endeavouring to avert danger in this quarter, his rivals at court endeavoured to prejudice the mind of the king against him, and their intrigues were so successful that he found himself ere long condemned to the alternative of murdering his sovereign or perishing himself. He therefore poisoned Oohus, to avoid being assassinated or put to the torture, and placed on the throne Arses, the youngest of the king's sons, while he caused the remaining royal children to be put to death (336).[1] Egypt hailed this tragic end as a mark of the vengeance of the gods whom Ochus had outraged. A report was spread that the eunuch was an Egyptian, that he had taken part in the murder of the Apis under fear of death, but that when he was sure of his own safety he had avenged the sacrilege. As soon as the poison had taken effect, it was said he ate a portion of the dead body and threw the remainder to the cats: he then collected the bones and made them into whistles and knife-handles.[2] Oohns had astonished his contemporaries

[1] Plutarch calls the successor of Ochus Oarses, which recalls the name which Dinon gives to Artaxerxes II. Diodorus says that Bagoas destroyed the whole family of Ochus, but he is mistaken. Arrian mentions a son of Ochus about 330, and several other members of the royal Achæmenian race are known to have been living in the time of Alexander.

[2] The body of the enemy thrown to the cats to be devoured is a detail

by the rapidity with which he had re-established the integrity of the empire; they were pleased to compare him with the heroes of his race, with Cyrus, Cambyses, and Darius. But to exalt him to such a level said little for their moral or intellectual perceptions, since in spite of his victories he was merely a despot of the ordinary type; his tenacity degenerated into brutal obstinacy, his severity into cruelty, and if he obtained successes, they were due rather to his generals and his ministers than to his own ability. His son Arses was at first content to be a docile instrument in the hands of Bagoas; but when the desire for independence came to him with the habitual exercise of power, and he began to chafe at his bonds, the eunuch sacrificed him to his own personal safety, and took his life as he had done that of his father in the preceding year (336). So many murders following each other in rapid succession had considerably reduced the Achæmenian family, and Bagoas for a moment was puzzled where to find a king: he at length decided in favour of Codomannos, who according to some was a great-grandson of Darius II., but according to others was not of the royal line, but had in his youth been employed as a courier. He had distinguished himself in the hostilities against the Casduians, and had been nominated satrap of Armenia by Cchns as a reward for his bravery. He assumed at his accession the name of Darius; brave, generous, clement, and possessed with an ardent desire to do right, he was in every way the superior of his immediate predecessors, and he deserved to

added by the popular imagination, which crops up again in the Tale of Satni Khâmois.

have reigned at a time when the empire was less threatened. Bagoas soon perceived that his new *protégé*, whose conduct he had reckoned on directing as he pleased, intended to govern for himself, and he therefore attempted to get rid of him; Bagoas was, however, betrayed by his accomplices, and compelled to drink the poison which he had prepared for Darius. These revolutions had distracted the attention of the court of Susa from the events which were taking place on the shores of the Ægean, and Philip had taken advantage of them to carry into effect the designs against Persia which he had been long meditating. After having been victorious against the Greeks, he had despatched an army of ten thousand men into Asia under the command of Parmenion and Attalus (336). We may ask if it were not he who formed the project of universal conquest which was so soon to be associated with the name of his son Alexander. He was for the moment content to excite revolt among the cities of the Ægean littoral, and restore to them that liberty of which they had been deprived for nearly a century. He himself followed as soon as these lost children of Greece had established themselves firmly in Asia. The story of his assassination on the eve of his departure is well known (336), and of the difficulties which compelled Alexander to suspend the execution of the plans which his father had made. Darius attempted to make use of the respite thus afforded him by fortune; he adopted the usual policy of liberally bribing one part of Greece to take up arms against Macedonia—a method which was at first successful. While Alexander was occupied in the destruction of Thebes, the Rhodian general Memnon, to whom had been entrusted the defence of Asia Minor, forced the invaders to entrench themselves in the Troad. If the Persian fleet had made its appearance in good time, and had kept an active watch over the straits, the advance-guard of the Macedonians would have succumbed to the enemy before the main body of the troops had succeeded in joining them in Asia, and it was easy to foretell what would have been the fate of an enterprise inaugurated by such a disaster. Persia, however, had not yet learnt to seize the crucial moment for action: her vessels were still arming when the enemy made their appearance on the European shore of Hellespont, and Alexander had ample time to embark and disembark the whole of his army without having to draw his sword from the scabbard. He was accompanied by about thirty thousand foot soldiers and four thousand five hundred horse; the finest troops commanded by the best generals of the time—Parmenion, his two sons Nikanor and Philotas, Crater, Clitos, Antigonus, and others whose names are familiar to us all; a larger force than Memnon and his subordinates were able to bring up to oppose him, at all events at the opening of the campaign, during the preliminary operations which determined the success of the enterprise.

The first years of the campaign seem like a review of the countries and nations which in bygone times had played the chief part in Oriental history. An engagement at the fords of the Granicus, only a few days after the crossing of the Hellespont, placed Asia Minor at the mercy of the invader (334). Mysia, Lydia, Caria, and Lycia tendered their submission, Miletus and Halicarnassus being the only towns to offer any resistance. In the spring of 333, Phrygia followed the general movement, in company with Cappadocia and Cilicia; these represented the Hittite and Asianic world, the last representatives of which thus escaped from the influences of the East

THE BATTLE-FIELD OF ISSUS.[1]

and passed under the Hellenic supremacy. At the foot of the Amanus, Alexander came into conflict not only with the generals of Darius, but with the great king himself. The Amanus, and the part of the Taurus which borders on the Euphrates valley, had always constituted the line of demarcation between the domain of the races of the Asianic peninsula and that of the Semitic peoples.

[1] Drawn by Boudier, from a photograph by Lortet.

BAS-RELIEF ON A SIDONIAN SARCOPHAGUS REPRESENTING AN EPISODE IN THE BATTLE OF ISSUS.

Drawn by Boudier, from a photograph.

A second battle near the Issus, at the entrance to the Cilician gates, cleared the ground, and gave the conqueror time to receive the homage of the maritime provinces. Both Northern and Cœle-Syria submitted to him from Samosata to Damascus. The less important towns of

THE ISTHMUS OF TYRE AT THE PRESENT DAY.[1]

Phœnicia, such as Arvad, Byblos, Sidon, and those of Cyprus, followed their example; but Tyre closed its gates, and trusted to its insular position for the preservation of its independence, as it had done of old in the time of Sennacherib and of Nebuchadrezzar. It was not so much a scrupulous feeling of loyalty which emboldened her to take this step, as a keen realisation of what her

[1] Drawn by Boudier, from a sketch by Lortet.

conquest by the Macedonian would entail. It was entirely owing to Persia that she had not succumbed in all parts of the Eastern Mediterranean in that struggle with Greece which had now lasted for centuries: Persia had not only arrested the progress of Hellenic colonisation in Cyprus, but had given a fresh impulse to that of Tyre, and Phœnician influence had regained its ascendency over a considerable part of the island. The surrender of Tyre, therefore, would be equivalent to a Greek victory, and would bring about the decay of the city; hence its inhabitants preferred hostilities, and they were prolonged in desperation over a period of seven months. At the end of that time Alexander succeeded in reducing the place by constructing a dyke or causeway, by means of which he brought his machines of war up to the foot of the ramparts, and filled in the channel which separated the town from the mainland; the island thus became a peninsula, and Tyre henceforth was reduced to the rank of an ordinary town, still able to maintain her commercial activity, but having lost her power as an independent state (332). Phœnicia being thus brought into subjection, Judæa and Samaria yielded to the conqueror without striking a blow, though the fortress of Gaza followed the example set by Tyre, and for the space of two months blocked the way to the Delta. Egypt revolted at the approach of her liberator, and the rising was so unanimous as to dismay the satrap Mazakes, who capitulated at the first summons. Alexander passed the winter on the banks of the Nile. Finding that the ancient capitals of the country—Thebes, Sais, and even

Memphis itself—occupied positions which were no longer suited to the exigencies of the times, he founded opposite to the island of Pharos, in the township of Rakotis, a city to which he gave his own name. The rapid growth of the prosperity of Alexandria showed how happy the founder had been in the choice of its site: in less than half a century from the date of its foundation, it had eclipsed all the other capitals of the Eastern Mediterranean, and had become the centre of African Hellenism. While its construction was in progress, Alexander, having had opportunities of studying the peculiarities and characteristics of the Egyptians, had decided to perform the one act which would conciliate the good feeling of the natives, and secure for him their fidelity during his wars in the East: he selected from among their gods the one who was also revered by the Greeks, Zeus-Ammon, and repaired to the Oasis that he might be adopted by the deity. As a son of the god, he became a legitimate Pharaoh, an Egyptian like themselves, and on returning to Memphis he no longer hesitated to adopt the *pschent* crown with the accompanying ancient rites. He returned to Asia early in the year 331, and crossed the Euphrates. Darius had attempted to wrest Asia Minor from his grasp, but Antigonus, the governor of Phrygia, had dispersed the troops despatched for this purpose in 332, and Alexander was able to push forward fearlessly into those regions beyond the Euphrates, where the Ten Thousand had pursued their victorious march before him. He crossed the Tigris about the 20th of September, and a week later fell in with his rival in the very heart of

Assyria, not far from the village of Gaugamela, where he took up a position which had been previously studied, and was particularly suited for the evolutions of cavalry. At the Granicus and near Issus, the Greek element had played an important part among the forces which contested the field; on this occasion, however, the great king was accompanied by merely two or three thousand mercenaries,

THE BATTLE OF ARBELA, FROM THE MOSAIC OF HERCULANEUM.[1]

while, on the other hand, the whole of Asia seemed to have roused herself for a last effort, and brought forward her most valiant troops to oppose the disciplined ranks of the Macedonians. Persians, Susians, Medes, Armenians, Iranians from Bactriana, Sakæ, and Indians were all in readiness to do their best, and were accompanied by every instrument of military warfare employed in Oriental

[1] Drawn by Boudier, from a photograph.

tactics; chariots armed with scythes, the last descendants of the chariotry which had dominated all the battle-fields from the time of the XVIIIth Theban dynasty down to the latest Sargonids, and, employed side by side with these relics of a bygone day, were Indian elephants, now for the first time brought into use against European battalions. These picked troops sold their lives dearly, but the perfection of the Macedonian arms, and, above all, the superiority of the tactics employed by their generals, carried the day; the evening of the 30th of September found Darius in flight, and the Achæmenian empire crushed by the furious charges of Alexander's squadrons. Babylon fell into their hands a few days later, followed by Susa, and in the spring of 330, Ecbatana; and shortly after Darius met his end on the way to Media, assassinated by the last of his generals.

With his death, Persia sank back into the obscurity from which Cyrus had raised her rather more than two centuries previously. With the exception of the Medes, none of the nations which had exercised the hegemony of the East before her time, not even Assyria, had had at their disposal such a wealth of resources and had left behind them so few traces of their power. A dozen or so of palaces, as many tombs, a few scattered altars and stelæ, remains of epics preserved by the Greeks, fragments of religious books, often remodelled, and issuing in the Avesta — when we have reckoned up all that remains to us of her, what do we find to compare in interest and in extent with the monuments and wealth of writings bequeathed to us by Egypt and Chaldæa? The Iranians received Oriental civilisation at a time when the latter was in its decline, and caught the spirit of decadence in their contact with it. In succeeding to the patrimony of the nations they conquered, they also inherited their weakness; in a few years they had lost all the vigour of their youth, and were barely able to maintain the integrity of the empire they had founded. Moreover, the great peoples to whom they succeeded, although lacking the vigour necessary for the continuance of their independent existence, had not yet sunk so low as to acquiesce in their own decay, and resign themselves to allowing their national life to be absorbed is that of another power: they believed that they would emerge from the crisis, as they had done from so many others, with fresh strength, and, as soon as an occasion presented itself, they renewed the war against their Iranian suzerain. From the first to the latest of the sovereigns bearing the name of Darius, the history of the Achæmenids in an almost uninterrupted series of internal wars and provincial revolts. The Greeks of Ionia, the Egyptians, Chaldæans, Syrians, and the tribes of Asia Minor, all rose one after another, sometimes alone, sometimes in concert; some carrying on hostilities for not more than two or three years; others, like Egypt, maintaining them for more than half a century. They were not discouraged by the reprisals which followed each of these rebellions; they again had recourse to arms as soon as there seemed the least chance of success, and they renewed the struggle till from sheer exhaustion the sword fell from their hand. Persia was worn out by this perpetual warfare, in which at the same time each of

DEATH-THROES OF THE OLD ORIENTAL WORLD

her rivals expended the last relics of their vitality, and when Macedonia entered on the scene, both lords and vassals were reduced ·to such a state of prostration, that it was easy to foretell their approaching end. The old Oriental world was in its death-throes; but before it passed away, the successful audacity of Alexander had summoned Greece to succeed to its inheritance.

INDEX

Egypt, In, 179
  Head of, 159
  Rebels received by, 174
  Scythia invaded by, 201
  Stele of, 219
  Tomb of, 221
Darius II., 275-277
Darius III., Coin of, 367
Darius Codomanos, 373
Datames III., Coin of, 296
Delphi, 62, 63, 118
Delta, The, 122, 347, 350, 353
Dush, Fortress of, 220

E

Ecbatana (Agbatana), 42-44, 66, 171, 180, 258, 352, 383
Ecbatana in Syria, 154
Egypt, Athenian campaign in, 251
  Conquered by Alexander, 379
  Darius in, 178
  Decadence of, 77
  Greek travellers in, 347
  Revolts against Persia, 284
Egyptian alliance with Greece, 291
Egyptian alum, 118
Egyptian dynasties, Last, 312
Egyptian navy, 134
Egyptian stelæ, 219
Elam, 325
Elephants in war, 368
Elephantinê, 363, 365
Eleusis, Map of bay of, 231
Ephesus, Ruins of, 57, 59
Ethiopia, 144, 147
Ethiopian group, 147
Evagoras II., Coin of, 305
Ezekiel (the prophet), 91
Ezra, 343, 345

F

Fayum, Fisheries in, 218

G

Gaza, 136, 380
Granicus, Battle of, 375, 379
Greece, Egyptian alliance, 292
  Persian relations, 195
Greek mercenaries, 331, 370
Greek settlements in Egypt, 122
Greek struggles with Persia, 286, 287
Greek trireme, 227
Greek travellers in Egypt, 347, 361
Gyges, 57

H

Habit, Temple of, 221
Haggai (the prophet), 337

Hakoris, 285-287
Hoplites, Greek, 370
Horses, Iranian sacrifice of, 33

I

Idumæans, 345
India, 189, 320
  Conquest of, 195
Indian coin, 2
Ionia, Revolt of, 203
Iranian altars, 31-35
Iranian architecture, 267
Iranian art, 261
Iranian conquest, The, 3
Iranian genii, 22, 24
Iranian genius, An, 13
Iranian hunting-party, 39
Iranian religion, 3, 11, 26
Iranian sculpture, 265
Issus, 379
  Bas-relief of battle of, 377
  Battlefield of, 376

J

Jeremiah (the prophet), 90
Jerusalem, 336, 339, 344
  Nehemiah at, 340
  Temple of, 338
Jewish captivity, 89, 91, 105
Jewish State, The new, 338
Jews, Return of, to Jerusalem, 107
Judæa, 380

K

Karnak, Gate at, 315
Khabbisha, 221, 222
Khâti, The, 328
Khshatrita, 166-172

L

Lycia submits to Cyprus, 81, 83
Lycian city, 83
Lycian coin, 327
Lycian sarcophagus, 328
Lycian tomb, 326
Lycians, The, 327
Lydia, 48, 63
Lydian coins, 54, 55
Lydian funerary couch, 53
Lydian jewellery, 52
Lydian ornaments, 51

M

Macedonia, 212
Magi, the Persian, 25-38, 334
Marathon, 215
  Battlefield of, 215

INDEX

A

Abydos, 111
Achæmenian empire crushed by Alexander, 383
Achæmenian king, 269, 273
Achæmenian ruins, 258
Achæmenian tombs, 261
Achæmenians, The, 323
Æolians, The, 206
Ahura-mazdâ, 7–14, 34, 36
  Bas-reliefs of, 12, 14, 174
Alexander I. of Macedon, 212, 236
Alexander the Great, 374–380
  Bust in the Louvre, 197
Alexandria, Foundation of, 380
Alum, Egyptian, 118
Alyattes, 48, 49
Alyattes, Tumulus of, 50
Amadaî (Madai). *See* Medes
Amasis, 109, 115, 116, 123, 137
  Adoration of the Apis, 113
  Buildings of, 111
  Favour shown to the Greeks, 117
  Naos of, 114
Amesha-spentas, The, 15–20
Ammon, Oasis of, 145
Amyrtæus, 282, 303
Angrô-mainyus, 19, 22, 35
Apries (Uaphres), 346
Aramæan inscriptions on coins, 325
Aramæan language, 109
Aramæan tribes, 338
Aramæans, The, 323, 326, 335
Aramaic inscription on seal, 337
Aramaic language, 335
Arbela, Battle of, 382
Aristagoras, 206–209
Arpad, 328
Arses, 373
Artaxerxes I., 247–274
Artaxerxes II. (Arsaces), 275, 281, 294, 300, 301, 339
Artaxerxes II. on a coin of Straton I., king of Sidon, 385
Artaxerxes III. *See* Ocbus
Asia Minor, 280, 295, 296, 305, 318, 327
Assyrian states, 329

Astyages (Ishtuvigu), 41
Athenian campaign in Egypt, 251
Athens, 228, 236, 253, 279, 281, 298
Avesta, 9, 11

B

Baal II. (King of Tyre), 45
Babylon, 78, 84, 178, 227, 258, 331, 332, 383
  Capture of, by Cyrus, 101
  Decadence of, 335
  Kings of, 105
  Taken by Darius, 169
Babylonia, 331
Bactriana, 81, 172
Bactrians, The, 80
Bedâwin, The, 340
Behistun, Rocks of, 175
Bel, Chaldæan statuette of, 196
"Bel, Taking the hands of," 104
Bel-marduk, 46, 99
Butô, 351

C

Calah, 329
Cambyses, 130, 131, 140, 145, 151, 153, 352
Carchemish, 328
Caria, 81, 210, 327
Carians, The, 208, 349, 354
Carthage (Qart-hadshat), 144, 177
Chaldæa, 331
Crœsus, 49, 56, 59, 61, 65, 69, 78, 142
Crœsus on his pyre, 75
Cypriot chariot, 209
Cyprus, 68, 208, 284–290, 304
Cyrene, 116, 117, 145, 176, 218
Cyrus, 37–43, 66, 78, 80, 97, 125, 128
  Bas-relief of, 127
  Tomb of, 129
Cyrus, the younger, 279, 302

D

Daphnæ, 218
Darius I., 159, 161, 166, 199, 203, 209
  Army of, 191, 192
  Babylon taken by, 169
  Daric of, 188

INDEX

Map of, 214
Mardonius, 223, 235
Mausolus, Statue of, 327
Mazæos, Coin of the Satrap, 198
Medes, 37, 38, 213, 235
Median Empire, 3
  Fall of, 43
Megabyzos, 251–258
Memphis, 317, 354, 355, 358
  Monuments at, 360
  Taken by Cambyses, 140
  Temples at, 356, 357
Miletus, Site of, 80
Mycale, 237

N

Nabonidus, 44–47, 66, 84, 87
  Unpopularity of, 97
Naophoros, Statue of, 145
Napata, 148
Naucratis, 120–123, 346
  Plan of, 120
Nebuchadrezzar III., 163, 165, 170
Nectanebo I. (Nakht-har-habit), 287, 291, 313, 315
  Head of, 299
  Temple of, 313
Nectanebo II., 299, 310, 312, 315, 316
  Naos of, 314, 316
  Revolt of, 299
Nehemiah, 338
Nehemiah at Jerusalem, 339
Nephorites, 284, 285
Nergal-sharuzur, 46
Nile, View on the, 362
Nineveh, 180, 329

O

Ochus (Artaxerxes III.), 302, 303, 305, 317, 331, 372, 373
  Conquest of Egypt by, 309
Osiris (recumbent), 111

P

Panopolis, Games at, 363
Pelusium, 138
  Battle of, 141
Persepolis, 180, 258
  Necropolis of, 31
  Propylæa of, 267
  Ruins of, 263
  Staircase at, 268
Persia, 63, 281
  Relations with Greece, 195
Persian court etiquette, 269, 271
Persian Empire, Decline of, 369
  Map of the, 321

Reconstruction of, under Ochus, 319
Persian financial system, 187
Persian government, 186
Persian king, 78
Persian main roads, 185
Persian sculpture, 267
Persians, The, 213, 319
Pharnabazus, 291, 292
  Coin of, 291
Philæ, Island of, 110, 312
Philip of Macedon, 372
Philistines, The, 345
Phœnicia, Revolt of, 305
Phœnician fleet, 245
Phœnician galley, 213
Phœnician language, 335
Phœnicians, The, 354
Platæa, 237
  Map of, 238
Polycrates, 195
  Fleet of, 133, 134
Psammetichus II., 346
Psammetichus III., 139
  Head of, 138
Pyramids, The, 358–360

S

Sacæ. *See* Sakæ
Sakæ, The, 78, 80, 213, 235, 320
Salamis, 229–235
Samaria, 380
Sardanapalus, 329
Sardes (Sardis), 50, 58, 204, 235
  Taking of, 207
Satraps, Coins of, 325, 335
Satrapies, The, 183, 185
  Map of the, 181
Scythia, Darius invades, 201
Secudianus (Sogdianus), 274, 275
Shamasherib, 227
Sheshbazzar, 107
Sidon, Destruction of, 307
Smerdis, 130, 131
Smerdis (*pseudo*, Gaumâta), 155, 157
Sparta, 227, 237, 238
Spartans, 236, 286
Susa, 300, 331, 382
  Apadana of, 270
  Capital from, 262
Syria, Conquest of, by Alexander, 379
  Invasion of, under Tachôs, 295
Syrian states, 329
Syrians, The white, 69

T

Tachôs, 295–301, 312
Thebes, 110, 362, 365

INDEX

Thermopylæ, 229
Thracia (*or* Thrace), 211
Tyre, 45, 379

U

Urartu, *or* Kingdom of Van (Armenia), 325

V

Vatican, Lion of the, 317

X

Xerxes I. (Khshayarsha), 225, 226, 247, 271, 332
  Propylæa of, 267
Xerxes II., 274, 275

Z

Zechariah (the prophet), 337
Zion, 336
Zoroaster (Zarathustra), 5-8, 84

www.ingramcontent.com/pod-product-compliance
Lightning Source LLC
Chambersburg PA
CBHW040744020526
44114CB00048B/2903